CW00621840

Inequality, Corruption and the Church

To Jane + Chris
With thanks for your support
and friendship over the
years.
Marti

REGNUM STUDIES IN GLOBAL CHRISTIANITY

Series Preface

In the latter part of the twentieth century the world witnessed significant changes in global Christian dynamics. Take for example the significant growth of Christianity in some of the poorest countries of the world. Not only have numbers increased, but the emphasis of their engagement has expanded to include ministry to a wider socio-cultural context than had previously been the case. The *Regnum Studies in Global Christianity* series explores the issues with which the global church struggles, focusing in particular on ministry rooted in Africa, Asia, Latin America and Eastern Europe.

Not only does the series make available studies that will help the global church learn from past and present, it provides a platform for provocative and prophetic voices to speak to the future of Christianity. The editors and the publisher pray particularly that the series will grow as a public space, where the voices of church leaders from the majority world will contribute out of wisdom drawn from experience and reflection, thus shaping a healthy future for the global church. To this end, the editors invite theological seminaries and universities from around the world to submit relevant scholarly dissertations for possible publication in the series. Through this, it is hoped that the series will provide a forum for South-to-South as well as South-to-North dialogues.

Series Editors

Ruth Padilla DeBorst, President, Latin American Theological Fraternity, Santiago, Chile
Hwa Yung, Bishop, Methodist Church of Malaysia, Petaling Jaya, Malaysia
Wonsuk Ma, Executive Director, Oxford Centre for Mission Studies, Oxford, UK
Damon So, Research Tutor, Oxford Centre for Mission Studies, Oxford, UK
Miroslav Volf, Director, Yale Center for Faith and Culture, New Haven, MA, USA

REGNUM STUDIES IN GLOBAL CHRISTIANITY

Inequality, Corruption and the Church:
Challenges and Opportunities
in the Global Church

Martin Allaby

Copyright © Martin Allaby 2013

First published 2013 by Regnum Books International

Regnum is an imprint of the Oxford Centre for Mission Studies
St. Philip and St. James Church
Woodstock Road
Oxford, OX2 6HR, UK
www.ocms.ac.uk/regnum

09 08 07 06 05 04 03 8 7 6 5 4 3 2 1

The right of Martin Allaby to be identified as the Author of this Work
has been asserted by him in accordance with the Copyright, Designs
and Patents Act 1988.

All rights reserved. No part of this publication may be reproduced, stored in a retrieval system, or transmitted, in any form or by any means, electronic, mechanical, photocopying, recording or otherwise, without the prior permission of the publisher or a license permitting restricted copying. In the UK such licenses are issued by the Copyright Licensing Agency, 90 Tottenham Court Road, London W1P 9HE.

British Library Cataloguing in Publication Data
A catalogue record for this book is available from the British Library

ISBN: 978-1-908355-16-4

Typeset by Words by Design
Cover design by Words by Design
Cover photograph by Nyasha Chingono,
with kind permission for reproduction of the
photograph granted by RelZim.org
Printed and bound in Great Britain
for Regnum Books International by TJI

Contents

Acknowledgments

Many people helped with the research that went into this book. My research supervisors, Deryke Belshaw and Peter Clarke, helped to shape my ideas by critiquing draft chapters and advising on direction at critical points. David Lumsdaine helped me to think more clearly about social science methods and Ben Knighton helped me improve my analysis and interpretation of my interview material. Students and staff at the Oxford Centre for Mission Studies, and friends and colleagues in Kathmandu, helped me develop my ideas through their comments during various research seminars. Gabriele Price gave valuable advice on the multiple regression analysis.

All my key informants were generous in sharing their experiences and opinions. I could not have met some of them without the help of several people who arranged introductions for me: Joy Famador, Vylma Ovalles and Niels and Amyjay Riconalla in the Philippines; Reginald Nalugala for Kenya; Joshua Banda and Lawrence Temfwe in Zambia; and Graham Gordon in Peru. Anna Porter was generous with her time in helping me to find my way around Lima, and she translated most of the interviews there. My daughters Elaine and Lydia transcribed most of the interviews. Melba Maggay, Ben Knighton, Irene Mutalima and Graham Gordon reviewed the draft chapters on the Philippines, Kenya, Zambia and Peru, respectively. All the deficiencies that remain are mine.

I am grateful to all the individuals and churches that supported this work financially through their donations to Interserve, which was my employer during most of this research. My wife, Sue, was a constant source of encouragement and she kept our family intact in Kathmandu while I was away in Oxford or the case-study countries, not least during Nepal's revolution in April 2006.

Figures

Tables

List of Acronyms

ACDA	Alliance of Christian Development Agencies
ACK	Anglican Church of Kenya
AIC	African Inland Church
CBCP	Catholic Bishops Conference of the Philippines
CCZ	Christian Council of Zambia
CFJS	Christians for a Just Society
CONEP	National Evangelical Council of Peru
CRWRC	Christian Reformed World Relief Committee
DFID	Department for International Development
EAK	Evangelical Alliance of Kenya
EFZ	Evangelical Fellowship of Zambia
FOCIG	Fellowship of Christians in Government
FOCUS	Fellowship of Christian Unions
GDP	Gross Domestic Product
GNI	Gross National Income
IEP	Peruvian Evangelical Church
INGO	International Non-Government Organization
ISACC	Institute for the Study of Asian Church and Culture
JIL	Jesus Is Lord
KACC	Kenya Anti-Corruption Commission
KANU	Kenya African National Union
MMDA	Metro-Manila Development Authority
MRTA	Tupac Amaru Revolutionary Movement
NCCK	National Council of Churches of Kenya
NCCP	National Council of Churches in the Philippines
NGO	Non-Government Organization
PCEC	Philippine Council of Evangelical Churches
PDL	Purpose-Driven Life
TAN	Transparency and Accountability Network
TI	Transparency International
UCCP	United Church of Christ in the Philippines
ZAFES	Zambian Fellowship of Evangelical Students
ZEC	Zambian Episcopal Conference

Introduction

Two Big Questions

Everyone should be concerned about extreme economic equality, because it affects a country's chances of eradicating extreme poverty. It does this in two ways. First, extreme inequality of incomes and of land ownership retards economic growth[1] (though there is some evidence that moderate inequality in richer countries is associated with economic growth there).[2] Second, for a given level of economic growth, countries with less equal distribution of incomes tend to experience a smaller reduction in poverty.[3] So countries with extreme inequality tend to stay poor as a whole, and their poorest citizens are especially unlikely to escape poverty.

Before going any further I need to address a possible misunderstanding about inequality. Inequality is not necessarily a result of unfairness (though it may be). In some situations inequality reflects fair rewards for natural talent and hard work. Some people with right-of-centre politics were initially wary when I discussed this research with them, because they assumed I must be a socialist if I was concerned about inequality. However, as you will see by the end of Chapter 2, this book is not about whether governments are left-wing or right-wing, but about whether they are accountable or corrupt. So please do not stop reading if you disapprove of socialism. There is something important here for everyone, whatever their politics.[4]

This book addresses two big questions. Why is economic inequality greatest in Christian, and especially Protestant, developing countries? And can the church reduce those economic inequalities? Before reading anything about my answers to those questions you probably want to know a little about me and the

---

[1] William Easterly, 'Inequality Does Cause Underdevelopment: Insights from a new instrument' *Journal of Development Economics* 84/2 (2007), 755-76.

[2] Robert Barro, 'Inequality and Growth in a Panel of Countries' *Journal of Economic Growth* 5 (2000), 5-32.

[3] World Bank, *Attacking Poverty: World Development Report 2000/2001* (Oxford: Oxford University Press 2001), 55.

[4] As Chapter 2 will demonstrate, governments tend to redistribute resources from rich to poor in countries where they are relatively accountable to their citizens (by and large the high income countries of the world). Unfortunately the opposite is true in most of the rest of the world: governments tend to redistribute resources from the poor to the rich, because they have very limited accountability to their citizens. So a concern to reduce economic inequality implies a belief in the importance of the accountability of governments to their citizens, but not in the size of those governments.

perspective from which I approached them. I am a Protestant Christian and most of my close relatives are Anglican clergy. I am male, middle aged, and married with three children. I am a British GP and public health specialist, and I have worked in India and Nepal as a GP and public health specialist for ten years. My interest in this subject developed as I tried to understand poverty while working in Asia, and most of the research presented in this book was done while my home was in Kathmandu.

You would be right to ask whether my answers to the two big questions are biased by my own Christian faith. My reply is that I tried to let my opinions be guided by the evidence rather than vice versa and the verdict of the external examiner at my PhD viva, who is not a Christian but was a professor of economics at the University of Oxford, is reassuring on that point. Regarding the statistical material in Chapter 2 he wrote that 'care is taken to evaluate the evidence using appropriate criteria', and his assessment of my handling of all the interview material was that 'it is interpreted carefully and without any obvious bias'. In Chapter 4 I have described how I designed and conducted the four country case studies, so that you can decide for yourself whether you think they provide a valid account of the situation in those countries.

My Initial Research Journey

When I first considered taking this on as a research project in 2001 I was two years into a nine year period working in Nepal, a poor country that until 2006 was officially a Hindu state. Throughout that period I was employed by Interserve, a Protestant missionary society. Implicitly or explicitly, many of my colleagues took the view that a Christian worldview helps to reduce poverty. An example of this view is given by Darrow Miller:[5]

> Many have noticed, perhaps for the first time, that the lands with the least access to the gospel are also the neediest ... Physical poverty doesn't just happen. It is the logical result of the way people look at themselves and the world, the stories they tell to make sense of their world. Physical poverty is rooted in a mindset of poverty, a set of ideas held corporately that produce certain behaviours. These behaviours can be institutionalised into the laws and structures of society. The consequence of these behaviours and structures is poverty.

However, some surprising evidence was emerging that Christianity is associated with extreme economic inequality, particularly in countries where democracy is weak;[6] and since extreme economic inequality tends to keep the

---

[5] Darrow Miller, *Discipling Nations: The power of truth to transform cultures* (Seattle: YWAM Publishing 2001), 65, 67.
[6] M Gradstein, B Milanovic and Y Ying: 'Democracy, Ideology and Income Inequality: An empirical analysis' *World Bank Policy Research Working Paper* (2001) No. 2561 Washington DC.

poorest people poor, this is bad news for anyone who thinks a Christian worldview might help to reduce poverty. My own introduction to the surprising connection between Christianity and extreme economic inequality came during a medical lecture in Kathmandu in 2001. The speaker was describing the well-known observation that egalitarian societies tend to enjoy relatively good health, even if they are quite poor overall. He cited the example of the state of Kerala in southwest India, which is poor but has low levels of inequality, good child survival and long life expectancy. At various points over the previous 20 years I had read about Kerala in books by Christian authors, all of whom attributed these characteristics to Kerala's long history of Christianity (the Mar Thoma church there believes that Saint Thomas founded a church in Kerala in the first century AD).

Imagine my surprise when the speaker (who is not a Christian, as far as I know) concluded his description of Kerala by attributing the egalitarian nature of its society to its long history of socialist and communist governments. Keen to demonstrate that his interpretation of the data must be flawed and that Christian heritage should take the credit, I set about compiling some published statistics on Christianity and economic inequality in different parts of the world.

The Statistical Association between Christianity and Economic Inequality

I ended up with a map similar to Figure 1.1. The map shows how the Gini coefficient for the distribution of consumption varied between countries in, or close to, the year AD 2000.[7] As you can see, the most unequal countries are in Latin America (which is mainly Catholic), sub-Saharan Africa (which is largely a mixture of Protestant and Catholic), plus the Philippines (Catholic), Papua New Guinea (Protestant), Iran (Islamic) and China.[8] The most economically egalitarian countries are in northern Europe (historically Protestant).

Although many Islamic countries do not report any data, nearly all of those that do appear to be quite egalitarian economically: Senegal, Guinea, Mali, Mauritania, Morocco, Algeria, Tunisia, Egypt, Jordan, Turkey, Pakistan, Bangladesh, Malaysia and Indonesia. The only notably unequal Islamic countries are Niger and Iran.

A World Bank Policy Research Working Paper was the first publication formally to demonstrate that economic inequality is greatest in Christian, and

---

[7] The Gini coefficient is probably the most widely used indicator of inequality. The way in which it is calculated is described in more detail later in this chapter, but at this point it is sufficient to note that a higher value of the Gini coefficient indicates greater inequality.

[8] Economic inequality in China has risen steeply since the early 1980s, when reported Gini coefficients were below 0.3. Such a rapid change is very unusual by historical standards.

especially Protestant, developing countries.[9] Although I disagree with them, the authors interpreted this as evidence that religion may be an important determinant of inequality - in other words, that Christianity causes inequality, at least in countries where democracy is weak.

To me as a Christian, the observation that economic inequality tends to be greatest in Christian developing countries was shocking. Extreme economic inequality seems incompatible with Jesus' command to 'love your neighbour as yourself'.

Figure 1.1 Gini coefficient of income distribution c. AD 2000

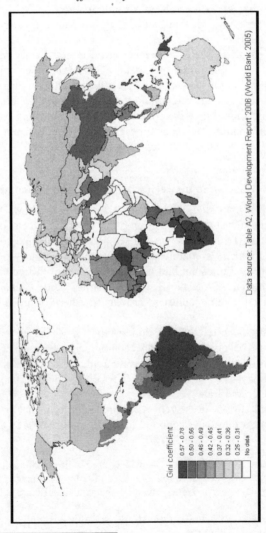

---

[9] Gradstein, Milanovic and Ying: 'Democracy, Ideology and Income Inequality'.

An early practical application of Jesus' teaching can be found in Saint Paul's second letter to the church at Corinth, where Paul was clearly sympathetic to the plight of a community that had fallen on hard times (II Corinthians 8:13-15):

> Our desire is not that others might be relieved while you are hard pressed, but that there might be equality. At the present time your plenty will supply what they need, so that in turn their plenty will supply what you need. The goal is equality, as it is written: 'The one who gathered much did not have too much, and the one who gathered little did not have too little.'

The map presented in Figure 1.1 shows that Jesus' teaching has had little effect in countries where most people describe themselves as his followers. Worse than this, the gap between those who 'gather little' and those who 'gather much' is actually greatest in countries where a majority of people are Christians. Whatever Christian charitable activities may be going in those countries (and there have always been plenty of them in every country I have visited), they are failing to address the gap between rich and poor. Could it even be, I asked myself, that, by propagating a Christian worldview, the activities of Christian missionaries are unwittingly contributing to greater economic inequality, and hence greater poverty?

Reasons for Doubting that Christianity Causes Economic Inequality

For the first couple of years after starting this research project I was unsure whether the association between Christianity and economic inequality represents cause and effect, but eventually two observations made this seem unlikely.

First, it is very difficult to attribute the apparent economic equality of Nepal and India (see Figure 1.1) to their prevailing Hindu religion. I spent nine years living in the Hindu kingdom of Nepal, where I experienced on a daily basis the importance of recognizing social hierarchy by using the correct form (high, middle or low) every time you address other people, and I saw at firsthand how the Hindu caste system reinforces a strong social hierarchy where everyone has their expected position and role. Our upper caste landlord was appalled when he saw me watering the garden: 'It is not right for a doctor to do this. You must hire a gardener'.

A Hindu author has written that Hinduism 'believes in the innate inequality of all men ... The first step towards a reconstruction of the Hindu philosophy of morals would be to challenge the organisation of society on the basis of hereditary castes and the practice of untouchability.'[10] The Hindu view of innate inequality is reflected in data on the relationship between religious adherence and contemporary attitudes towards economic inequality. Data from

---

[10] Saral Jhingran *Aspects of Hindu Morality* (Delhi: Motilal Banarsidass1989), x, 217.

the World Values Survey show that Hindus are more likely than any other religious group (Protestant, Catholic, Buddhist, Muslim or Jew) to support incentives for effort over equality of incomes.[11] So it is implausible that the relatively egalitarian economies of India and Nepal can be attributed to their Hindu religion; and if religion is not a strong determinant of economic inequality in India and Nepal, it seems unlikely that it is a strong determinant of economic inequality anywhere else.

My second reason for doubting that the association between Christianity and economic inequality is causal was an alternative explanation that emerged as I was reading some research that has nothing to say about religion at all, but deals instead with land abundance as an underlying cause of economic inequality.[12] Brief inspection of the list of countries included in those authors' dataset revealed that land abundant countries tend to be Christian, while land scarce countries typically are not. This suggested that religion might be associated with the true causes of economic inequality, but not be a cause of inequality itself. Chapter 2 presents the evidence that this is indeed the case.

When you have read that chapter you will see why I tightened up my second question from the rather general 'Can the church reduce economic inequalities?' to focus on the church and corruption. The analysis in Chapter 2 shows that reductions in corruption in any country should reduce economic inequality by ensuring that a greater proportion of government revenue is used to benefit the majority of the population rather than ruling elites. The opportunity for reducing inequality by reducing corruption is particularly great in Protestant developing countries, because they have relatively large governments. Not only is the impact on economic inequality of controlling corruption likely to be greater in Protestant developing countries, but there is also some evidence that Protestantism is associated with less corruption, though this effect is weaker in low- and middle-income than in high income countries, and the mechanism that explains the association between Protestantism and less corruption is unclear. If Protestants in low- and middle-income countries could strengthen whatever it is that they do to help control corruption, the benefits for those countries would be enormous. But before getting into the meat of the argument it is essential to define a few key concepts.

---

[11] L Guiso, P Sapienza and L Zingales 'People's Opium? Religion and economic attitudes' *Journal of Monetary Economics* 50/1 (2003), 225-82.
[12] E Leamer, H Maul, S Rodriguez and P Schott: 'Does Natural Resource Abundance Increase Latin American Income Inequality?' *Journal of Development Economics* 59 (1999), 3-42.

Definitions of Key Concepts

Economic inequality

The indicator of economic inequality that I use throughout this book is the Gini coefficient of the distribution of consumption (or the Gini coefficient of the distribution of income, for countries where data on consumption are not available).[13] Other indicators of inequality are available, but the Gini coefficient is widely used, easy to grasp, and as valid as any of the alternatives. To calculate the Gini coefficient for a country, researchers conduct a detailed questionnaire survey across a large, representative sample of households. They collect information about the income and / or consumption of each member of the household, then (for consumption data) convert it into monetary values. Imagine that the households are then arranged from left to right in order of increasing consumption or income (cumulative population), and that the consumption or income of each successive household is added to the total for all the preceding households (cumulative consumption or income). This will produce something like the curved line in Figure 1.2, and the Gini coefficient measures the deviation of this curved line from a straight, 45 degree reference line, which is what would be plotted if all households had the same consumption or income. It is defined as the area of the curved segment (area A in Figure 1.2) divided by the area of the triangle (area A plus area B).

The highest possible value of the coefficient is one (if a single household has all the income or consumption) and the lowest is zero (if there is total equality among all the households). In practice, the range of observed values of the Gini coefficient covers almost half of what is mathematically possible, ranging from 0.71 in Namibia (consumption-based) to 0.25 in Sweden (income-based).

Figure 1.2 The Gini coefficient

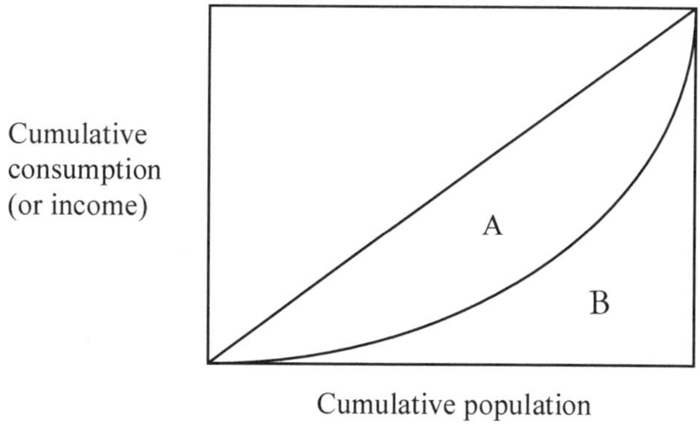

Cumulative consumption (or income)

A

B

Cumulative population

---

[13] High income countries and most countries in Latin America usually measure income distribution. Most other countries report consumption distribution. The implications of this for making comparisons between countries are discussed in Chapter 2.

Prevailing religion

For the purposes of this study I labelled a country as having a prevailing religion if at least 50 per cent of the population describe themselves as following that religion, and no more than 20 per cent describe themselves as following any other religion, according to data published in the World Christian Encyclopaedia.[14] It is important to acknowledge that people who describe themselves as following a particular religion do not necessarily have beliefs and practices that would be considered orthodox by the religion's leaders, and their religion may be more of a nominal affiliation than a matter of personal conviction.

I described religions that have spread across a wide geographic area (Buddhism, Christianity, Hinduism, Islam and Judaism) as 'major religions', and those that have remained more confined geographically as 'local religions'. I classified countries without a single prevailing religion as 'multi-faith'. I labelled 'Christian' countries as Catholic if there are at least 50 per cent more Catholics than other Christians, and vice versa for being labelled Protestant; I labelled those with a closer balance of Catholics and other Christians as 'mixed Christian'. I further subdivided Protestant, Catholic and mixed Christian countries into those that are 'old' (all of them in Europe), those that are 'extensions' of the old (Australia, New Zealand, Canada and the United States), and those that are 'new' (in Latin America, Africa and Asia). The value of distinguishing between the 'old' and 'new' Christian countries becomes apparent in Chapter 2 when examining the typical values of the proposed determinants of economic inequality in each of those groups.

Protestantism, Evangelicalism and Pentecostalism

Protestantism originated in the 16th-century Reformation, and its basic doctrines, in addition to those of the ancient Christian creeds, are justification by grace alone through faith, the priesthood of all believers, and the supremacy of Holy Scripture in matters of faith and order. A great variety of doctrinal views and polities exist among Protestants.[15]

Evangelicals are Protestants who, according to the sociologist David Bebbington, have four constant characteristics: conversionism (emphasis on the need for change of life), activism (emphasis on evangelistic and missionary efforts), biblicism (a special importance attributed to the Bible, though not necessarily the fundamentalist concept of "inerrancy") and crucicentrism (emphasis on the centrality of Christ's sacrifice on the cross).[16] Pentecostals are

---

[14] D Barrett, G Kurian, T Johnson eds *World Christian Encyclopedia* 2nd edn (Oxford: Oxford University Press 2001)

[15] Encyclopædia Britannica 'The Protestant Heritage' *Encyclopædia Britannica Online Library Edition* Available at http://library.eb.co.uk/eb/article-9109446 Accessed on 21.4.10

[16] David Bebbington *Evangelicalism in Modern Britain: A history from the 1730s to the 1980s* (London: Unwin Hyman 1989).

Christians who emphasize baptism in the Holy Spirit, evidenced by speaking in tongues, prophecy, healing, and exorcism.[17]

At the start of this research I used the term 'Protestant', because it is widely used by other authors who have written about the relationships between religion, economic inequality and corruption. However, when I was designing the country case studies that form the bulk of this book I switched to the term 'Evangelical', because most Protestants in developing countries are Evangelicals and the term 'Evangelical' is more widely used in those contexts than the term 'Protestant'.

Following the practice of the various local authors who contributed country case-study chapters to the series 'Evangelical Christianity and Democracy in the Global South', I treated Pentecostals as part of the Evangelical sector.[18] After completing my country case studies the sociologist Paul Gifford published a book that questions the extent to which Pentecostals in Kenya and Zambia fit Bebbington's definition of Evangelicals. Gifford wrote:

> This Pentecostal Christianity centres primarily on success/victory/wealth. That is why it is misleading to describe this Christianity as evangelical, for even basic ideas of evangelicalism have been transformed out of all recognition, even if the words are preserved. The cross is not frequently mentioned, but when it is, it is more in the following vein: 'Through Jesus Christ, all curses were destroyed at the cross of Calvary. This implies that every believer is a success in every sphere of life.'[19]

By the end of this study I could see that Gifford was making a fair point, so I went back over the interview material I had gathered to see whether excluding Pentecostals from the definition of Evangelicals would alter the main findings. I found that it made little difference.

Corruption

A widely used contemporary definition of corruption is 'the abuse of public office for private gain'. A World Bank definition of corruption starts with this short phrase then elaborates on specific ways in which, in its view, public office may be abused:

> Public office is abused when an official accepts, solicits, or extorts a bribe. It is also abused when private agents give or offer bribes to circumvent public policies and processes for competitive advantage and profit. Public office can also be abused for personal benefit even if no bribery occurs, through patronage and

---

[17] Oxford Dictionaries Pro Available at http://english.oxforddictionaries.com/definition/Pentecostal?region=us Accessed on 20.8.12

[18] Terence Ranger *Evangelical Christianity and Democracy in Africa* (Oxford: Oxford University Press 2009).

[19] Paul Gifford *Christianity, Politics and Public Life in Kenya* (London: Hurst and Co 2009), 150.

nepotism, the theft of state assets, or the diversion of state revenues. Corruption can also take place among private sector parties, yet interface with and affect public sector performance: for example, collusion among bidders to a public procurement with the intent to defraud the state can seriously distort procurement outcomes. [20]

The question remains of how the boundary between proper and corrupt use of public office should be defined. Suggested answers include 'the legal rules provided by statute books and court decisions', 'the best opinion and morality of the time' (in other words, the judgements of the elite), or public opinion more broadly.[21] An important consequence of these considerations is that the definition of corruption may change over time and from one society to another. A particular problem may arise when, within the same society, public opinion and legal standards regarding acceptable behaviour are at odds with each other. This is most likely in non-western countries where public opinion may consider patrimonial authority to be appropriate but where legal standards, imported relatively recently from the West, do not.

I dealt with this problem in two different ways. For the quantitative analysis in Chapter 2 I accepted the World Bank's definition of corruption, by virtue of using the World Bank's indicator for 'control of corruption'.[22] I think this was reasonable given that the purpose of the analysis in Chapter 2 was simply to confirm that there is a relationship between this indicator (or a compound variable that includes this indicator) and economic inequality, regardless of legal or public opinion in any of the countries involved regarding the meaning of the indicator.

I needed a different approach for the key informant interviews in the country case studies, because each informant might have their own interpretation of 'corruption'. Understanding all those different interpretations would be a research project in its own right, so I needed some way of trying to

---

[20] World Bank 'Strengthening Bank Group Engagement on Governance and Anticorruption' Available at http://siteresources.worldbank.org/DEVCOMMINT/ Documentation/21046515/DC2006-0017(E)-Governance.pdf, accessed 24.3.07.

[21] A Heidenheimer and M Johnston eds *Political Corruption: Concepts and contexts* 3rd edn (London: Transaction Publishers 2002), 140.

[22] It is more politically acceptable for the World Bank to describe this as an indicator of 'control of corruption', but it is actually just a measure of corruption. It is based on two different types of source information. The first is the responses of individuals or domestic firms with first-hand knowledge of the situation in each country to survey questions such as 'On average, what percent of total annual sales do firms pay in unofficial payments to public officials?' Since each of these surveys usually covers a limited number of countries, the scores from the survey data are calibrated onto a global scale using data from global networks of correspondents of commercial business information providers such as the Economist Intelligence Unit (Kaufmann D, Kraay A and Mastruzzi M 2004: 'Governance Matters III: Governance indicators for 1996-2002' *World Bank Economic Review* 18/2:253-87).

ensure that the informants and I were all talking about the same thing. I briefly considered asking informants to use the 'misuse of public office' definition of corruption that underpins the World Bank indicator, but was concerned that this would get the interviews off to a bad start since the World Bank has few supporters in poor countries. This definition also retains the problem that different cultures may have different views about what constitutes misuse of public office. So I chose instead to start each interview by saying that I was interested in informants' opinions based on the following definition of corruption:

> Corruption determines the extent to which public resources result in material benefit for elites rather than the majority

The advantage of this definition is that it operates independently of legal standards or public opinion. It is simply concerned with who gains and who loses, in terms of material wellbeing, from particular actions. By defining corruption in terms of its consequences, rather than on the basis of public opinion or legal standards regarding the processes involved, the definition is transferable across different cultures. And when I started doing the interviews this definition seemed to make sense to my informants and to be acceptable to them.

Having defined these key concepts, the next chapter addresses the first big question: why is economic inequality greatest in Christian, and especially Protestant, developing countries?

Why Extreme Inequality and Christianity Co-Exist

In this chapter I will show that non-religious variables account for much of the international variation in levels of economic inequality. I will then explore how this result helps us to understand the initial puzzle of the statistical association between Christianity and economic inequality. To guide my thinking in this area I spent several months reviewing what other researchers have written about the causes of economic inequality. To cut a fairly long story short, they have found that the variables that most plausibly explain the differences in economic inequality across countries are:

- What a country exports (with economic inequality being greater in countries where exports from mining and large plantations or farms form a large proportion of total exports)[1]
- The redistributive effect of government (with economic inequality being greater in countries with governments that are both large and corrupt)
- Access to finance (with economic inequality being greater in countries with limited access to credit).

A huge amount has also been written about a hypothesis proposed by Simon Kuznets in 1955.[2] He conceptualized economies as having two main sectors, agricultural and industrial, with average incomes being higher in the industrial than in the agricultural sector. On that basis, economic inequality would be greatest in moderately developed societies, where the proportions of people engaged in agriculture and in industry are similar (so that many are poor and many are rich). There would be less inequality in 'undeveloped', mainly agricultural societies (because most people are poor) and in highly 'developed', mainly industrial societies (because most people are rich).

---

[1] Perhaps surprisingly, exports of oil and other fuels are not significantly related to economic inequality. A possible explanation of this is that mining and large plantation or farm exports became economically important before fuel exports did – typically while the exporting countries were under colonial rule. Fuel exports have become economically more important since the exporting countries became independent of colonial rule, and hence there may have been greater pressure for national rulers to spread the proceeds from fuel exports more broadly than was the case when mines and large plantations or farms were established at a time of colonial rule.

[2] Simon Kuznets 'Economic Growth and Income Inequality' *American Economic Review* 45 (1955), 1-28

Although some researchers build the Kuznets hypothesis into their analyses, I decided against this for two reasons. First, it has not stood up very well when it is tested by actual data. Second, it has potentially damaging consequences. It could easily undermine concern about economic inequality on the grounds that it is just a phase that developing countries need to go through on their way to becoming rich. It also provides no useful clues as to what might be done to reduce economic inequality. The only choice presented to poor countries by the Kuznets hypothesis is 'stay poor, or accept widening inequalities until you become rich'.

Having put Kuznets' hypothesis to one side, I set about assembling all the available data for an analysis that would test whether, after adjusting for the effects of what a country exports, the redistributive effect of government, and access to finance, Christianity is significantly correlated with the distribution of consumption.

My analyses were limited to countries that have never had Communist governments, for both theoretical and practical reasons. The theoretical reason is that the inequality-inducing effect of exports from mining and large plantations or farms depends on private ownership of the means of production. It would therefore be very surprising if the model worked equally well in countries that have experienced a period of state ownership of the means of production, and this meant that ever-Communist and never-Communist countries would have to be analyzed in separate groups. When I attempted to conduct a separate analysis of data from countries that have had a Communist government, I encountered the practical problem that there were only nine ever-Communist countries (Albania, Czech Republic, Estonia, Ethiopia, Latvia, Nicaragua, Poland, Slovenia, and Serbia and Montenegro) for which a full set of data for the necessary indicators was available, which was too few to permit a multiple regression analysis.

Indicators for a Model of Economic Inequality

At this point I need to provide a few details about the indicators I used to represent what a country exports, the redistributive effect of government, and access to finance.

An indicator of exports from mining and large plantations and farms

The definition of mineral exports is relatively straightforward: it comprises crude fertilizers and minerals, metal ores and scrap, gems, non-ferrous metals, and gold. Measuring exports from large-scale plantations or farms is less straightforward, because the available data combine the exports of small- and large-scale producers. The indicator I used is defined as:

Exports of food and agricultural raw materials as a percentage of total exports, multiplied by the Gini coefficient of land ownership.

This indicator will be high for countries where a large proportion of exports are accounted for by food or agricultural raw materials grown on large plantations or farms, and it can be calculated for a wide range of countries. By adding this indicator to the proportion of total exports accounted for by minerals, I arrived at a summary indicator of the extent to which mining or large-scale plantations or farms dominate production (hereafter referred to as 'mining and large plantations or farms').[3]

An indicator of the redistributive effect of government revenue

I used the following indicator (hereafter referred to as 'government revenue multiplied by corruption control') to reflect the net effect of government revenue:

Government revenue as a percentage of GDP, multiplied by the World Bank's index of control of corruption for that country.

Two sets of comparisons serve to illustrate how this indicator operates. First, Zimbabwe and Germany have very similar levels of government revenue (expressed as a percentage of GDP): 29 per cent v. 30 per cent. However, Zimbabwe has a much worse score for control of corruption (-0.87) than Germany (+1.74). Under these circumstances it is unlikely that government involvement in the economy has the same effect on the distribution of consumption in Zimbabwe as it does in Germany. Recently reported Gini coefficients for these countries were 0.57 for Zimbabwe and 0.28 for Germany. The second comparison is between Pakistan and Zimbabwe. Pakistan's score for control of corruption (-0.80) is similar to Zimbabwe's. However, government revenue represents a much smaller proportion of the economy in Pakistan (only 14 per cent of GDP), so the government has much less opportunity to contribute to inequality through misusing public funds. The recently reported Gini coefficient for Pakistan is just 0.27.[4]

This indicator captures two important concepts. First, since the index of control of corruption can be either positive or negative, the direction in which government revenue affects economic inequality depends on whether

---

[3] At this point I must apologise in advance for a necessary but unwieldy bit of mathematics concerning this indicator. There are rules concerning the variables used in multiple regression modelling, which is the method I used to examine the possible causes of inequality. One of those rules is that all the variables must have an approximately normal distribution, with data clustered around the mean value and tailing off symmetrically towards higher and lower values. As is often the case in these situations, the simplest way of achieving this was to calculate the logarithm of each value for this indicator before putting it into the model. The disadvantage of this is that the process becomes unintelligible to anyone unfamiliar with logarithms. But I hope the text, the maps, and most of the graphs will still be clear.

[4] World Bank *Equity and Development: World Development Report 2006* (Oxford: Oxford University Press 2005), Table A2.

corruption is above or below a certain critical tipping point. If the government is sufficiently accountable to its citizens (above the tipping point), then allowing government to grow and control a larger share of the economy will tend to reduce the gap between rich and poor, as government will tend to tax the rich and redistribute resources to those in greater need. Conversely, if the government is corrupt and unaccountable to its citizens (below the tipping point), then allowing government to grow and control a larger share of the economy will tend to increase the gap between rich and poor, as ruling elites and their cronies raid the public coffers to enrich themselves at the expense of their citizens.

To find the tipping point between governments that redistribute resources from rich to poor, and those that redistribute resources from poor to rich, I tried setting the tipping point at different levels on the 'control of corruption' scale and picked the level that gives the best overall fit for all the data in the multiple regression model.[5] It turns out that surprisingly few countries are on the healthy side of the tipping point. Both Italy and Greece, for example, have 'control of corruption' scores that fall on the wrong side of the tipping point, implying that their governments tend to redistribute resources from poor to rich.[6]

The second important concept captured by the indicator 'government revenue multiplied by corruption control' is that the extent to which government revenue affects economic inequality, whether increasing it or decreasing it, depends on the size of government revenue relative to GDP: big governments can have big effects on economic inequality (as in Germany and Zimbabwe, for example), but small governments can only ever have small effects on economic inequality (as in Pakistan).

The indicator 'government revenue multiplied by corruption control' does not distinguish between grand corruption and petty corruption, but since both forms of corruption are likely to increase inequality this is not a major problem. When a small ruling elite steals a substantial proportion of government revenue, it is easy to imagine how national economic inequality will increase. But similar effects might also be expected when a larger pool of lower level officials all take a smaller cut.

An indicator of access to credit

I used the indicator 'domestic credit provided by the banking sector' as a measure of access to credit. This indicator suffers from the same skewed distribution as the indicator 'mining and large plantations or farms', so I had to use logarithms for this one as well.

---

[5] The tipping point that gave the best fit corresponds to +1.00 on the World Bank's scale for measuring control of corruption (D Kaufmann, A Kraay and M Mastruzzi M 'Governance Matters III: Governance indicators for 1996-2002' *World Bank Economic Review* 18/2 (2004), 253-87).

[6] Jumping ahead a little, Figure 2.4 shows the data for 'government revenue multiplied by corruption control' and the Gini coefficient, and the position of the tipping point.

Criteria for including countries in the analysis

I included all the never-Communist countries for which it was possible to obtain a full set of data for the indicators 'mining and large plantations or farms', 'government revenue multiplied by corruption control', 'access to credit', and the Gini coefficient for the distribution of consumption or income. This yielded 77 never-Communist countries for analysis. Two areas of the world are particularly under-represented: the necessary data were available for only 17 out of 34 never-Communist countries in sub-Saharan Africa, and only 8 out of 17 in the Middle Eastern Crescent.

Results of the Model of Economic Inequality

Table 2.1 presents the main result of the multiple regression analysis. For each explanatory variable, the standardized Beta coefficient and its associated p value indicate how well that particular variable explains economic inequality. The further the value of the standardised Beta coefficient from zero (whether in a positive or negative direction) the better the variable in question has performed in explaining economic inequality; p values below 0.05 are conventionally regarded as indicating that a correlation is statistically significant.

Table 2.1 Results of multiple regression model (outcome variable: Gini coefficient of consumption c. AD 2000)

Explanatory variables	Standardized Beta coefficients (p value)
'Mining & large plantations or farms'[7]	0.321 (<0.0005)
'Government revenue x corruption control'	-0.521 (<0.0005)
'Domestic credit provided by the banking sector'	-0.169 (0.07)
Protestant or mixed Christian	0.175 (0.09)
Catholic	0.099 (0.30)

The results in Table 2.1 support the following conclusions:

---

[7] The distributions of the indicators 'Mining and large plantations or farms' and 'Domestic credit provided by the banking sector' are both skewed towards zero. For the interest of any statistically minded readers, I used a logarithmic transformation to give them the normal distribution that is required for any data that are used in a multiple regression model.

- The nature of what a country exports, as reflected in the indicator 'mining and large plantations or farms', is a powerful influence on economic inequality (standardized Beta coefficient = 0.321). Figure 2.1 shows how this indicator varies around the world.
- The redistributive effect of government, as reflected in the indicator 'government revenue x corruption control', is an even more powerful influence on economic inequality (standardized Beta coefficient = -0.521). Figure 2.2 shows how this indicator varies around the world.
- Access to credit is less important (standardized Beta coefficient = -0.169) and is not statistically significant (p = 0.07).
- After taking account of indicators representing those three explanatory variables, neither Protestantism nor Catholicism is significantly associated with inequality in the distribution of consumption. When compared with a reference group comprising 'all other religions', there is a tendency towards greater economic inequality in the Protestant or mixed Christian group, but it is not statistically significant (p = 0.09); it arises largely because that group of countries includes South Africa and Namibia, which are the only two countries to have enacted apartheid law. There is also a smaller tendency towards greater economic inequality in the Catholic group, but again it is not statistically significant (p = 0.30).

Implications of the Results

The bottom line of the preceding analysis is that the powerful influences on economic inequality are the redistributive effect of government, and what a country exports, but not its prevailing religion. The idea that Christianity itself is a powerful influence on economic inequality does not stand up to scrutiny. The World Bank paper which suggested that religion may be an important determinant of inequality[8] got this wrong because the authors failed to take into account these other, non-religious, influences on economic inequality.

However, even if Christianity is not a cause of economic inequality, Christians are left with some challenging questions. Why do Christianity and economic inequality exist side by side in so many countries, in apparent denial of Jesus' command that Christians should love their neighbours as themselves? And what should Christians do if they want to reduce the extreme economic inequalities that keep people in poverty?

---

[8] Gradstein, Milanovic and Ying: 'Democracy, Ideology and Income Inequality'.

Figure 2.1 Exports from mining and large plantations or farms, as a percentage of total exports in AD 2000

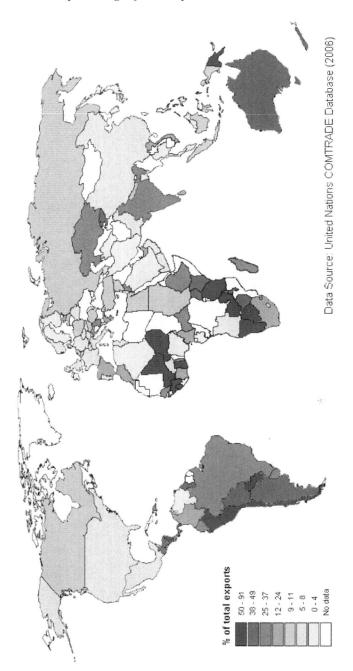

Data Source: United Nations COMTRADE Database (2006)

% of total exports

50 - 91
38 - 49
25 - 37
12 - 24
9 - 11
5 - 8
0 - 4
No data

Figure 2.2 'Government revenue x corruption control' in AD 2000

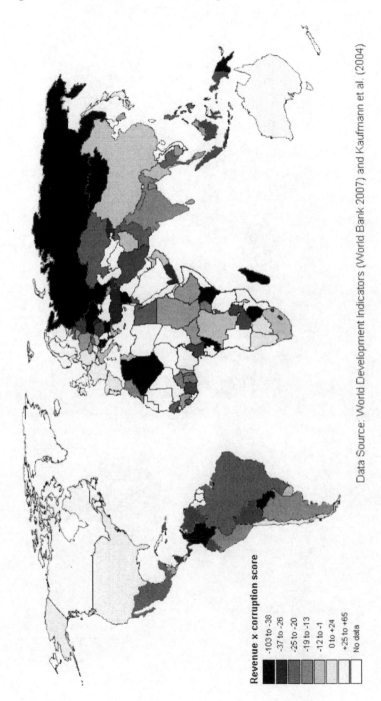

Crude Relationships Between the Causes of
Economic Inequality and Prevailing Religion

To understand why Christianity and economic inequality exist side by side in so many countries I examined carefully the relationships between the indicators 'mining and large plantations or farms', 'government revenue multiplied by corruption control' and prevailing religion. It turns out that there are clear relationships between them (Table 2.2, Figures 2.3 and 2.4).

Figure 2.3 plots economic inequality (the Gini coefficient) against the logarithm version of the indicator 'mining and large plantations or farms'. In this figure, and in Figures 2.4, 2.6 and 2.7, each square, triangle, cross, and diamond represents one country. Countries with few exports from mining and large plantations or farms tend to have egalitarian economies, so they appear in the bottom left quadrant of Figure 2.3. Countries with major exports from mining and large plantations or farms tend to have unequal economies, so they appear in the top right quadrant of Figure 2.3.

Figure 2.4 plots economic inequality (the Gini coefficient) against the indicator 'government revenue x corruption control'. The vertical dashed line in Figure 2.4 represents the tipping point on the scale of corruption. Countries that are more corrupt than this tipping point all have a negative value of the indicator 'government revenue x corruption control'; they tend to have very unequal economies, so they appear in the top left quadrant of Figure 2.4. Countries that are less corrupt than the tipping point all have a positive value of the indicator 'government revenue x corruption control'; they tend to have egalitarian economies, so they appear in the bottom right quadrant of Figure 2.4.

From Table 2.2 and Figures 2.3 and 2.4 one can draw the following conclusions as to why Christianity is associated with economic inequality. 'New Protestant or mixed Christian' countries are economically unequal because their economies are dominated by mining or large plantations or farms,[31] and because they have large and corrupt governments.[32] 'New Catholic countries' have the same problems, but to a lesser extent.

The 'old Protestant or mixed Christian' and 'old Catholic' countries are similar to one another in terms of economic equality, but for somewhat different reasons: the inequality that would be expected in 'old Protestant or mixed Christian' countries with moderate mining and large plantation or farm activities (exemplified by New Zealand and Australia in Figure 2.1) is countered by the redistributive effect of government revenue managed by 'clean' governments (in Figure 2.2 both New Zealand and Australia have a

---

[31] So they tend to appear in the top right quadrant of Figure 2.3, and in Table 2.2 they have the highest mean value (1.54) of the indicator Log[1 + 'mining & large plantations or farms'].

[32] So they tend to appear in the top left quadrant of Figure 2.4, and in Table 2.2 they have a strongly negative mean value (-26) of the indicator 'Government revenue x corruption control'.

score in the range +25 to +65 for the indicator 'government revenue x corruption control', indicating that their governments are having a major effect in redistributing resources from rich to poor).

Table 2.2 Mean values of indicators representing the causes of economic inequality, by prevailing religion

Prevailing religion (number of countries)	Log[1 + 'mining & large plantations or farms']	'Government revenue x corruption control'	Government revenue as % of GDP	Corruption control	Log [Domestic credit provided by the banking sector]	Gini coefficient
New Protestant / mixed Christian (14)	1.54	-26	26	-1.19	1.74	0.53
New Catholic (17)	1.48	-21	19	-1.17	1.85	0.46
Multi-faith, excluding Madagascar [33] (7)	1.15	-13	18	-0.99	1.71	0.42
Hindu-Buddhist, excluding Japan [34] (4)	1.18	-19	15	-1.30	1.71	0.37
Islamic (11)	1.01	-28	23	-1.29	1.80	0.36
Jewish (1)	0.66	12	43	0.27	1.87	0.35
Old Protestant / mixed Christian (13)	1.10	38	34	1.11	1.62	0.25
Old Catholic (8)	0.96	21	38	0.56	1.78	0.25
Hindu-Buddhist (Japan)	0.36	8	21	0.39	1.50	0.18

---

[33] Madagascar, a 'multi-faith' country is excluded from the table because it is an extreme outlier, with government revenue equal to 59% of GDP.

[34] Japan is shown separately from the other 'Hindu-Buddhist' countries because it has very different data values from the rest.

Figure 2.3 Relationship between mining and large plantations or farms and economic inequality

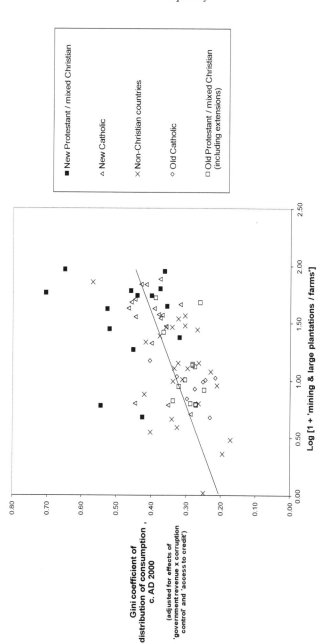

Figure 2.4 Relationship between 'government revenue multiplied by index of control of corruption' and economic inequality

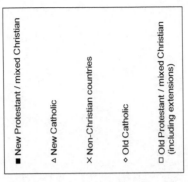

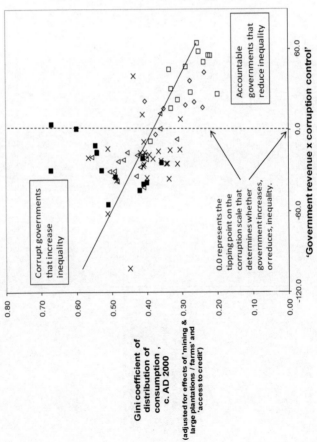

When compared with the 'old Protestant or mixed Christian' countries, the 'old Catholic' countries have more corrupt governments,[35] and hence less economic redistribution through government,[36] but their economies are still quite egalitarian (Gini coefficient = 0.25) because they are less dominated by mining or large plantations or farms.[37]

Hindu-Buddhist and Islamic countries have the highest levels of corruption on average,[38] so their governments increase economic inequality through the revenue they control.[39] However, their economies have fairly low levels of mining and large plantations or farms, so their overall level of economic inequality is only moderate.[40]

Christianity and 'Mining and Large Plantations or Farms'

Why on earth do the 'new Protestant or mixed Christian' and 'new Catholic' countries tend to have exports based on mining and large plantations or farms? It is hard to imagine that there is anything in their Christianity that makes them more enthusiastic about mining and plantations than about other economic activities, such as manufacturing, services, or subsistence farming, so one suspects there is some other explanation – and there is.

In this section I will present evidence that the high levels of exports based on mining and large plantations or farms observed today among 'new Protestant or mixed Christian' and 'new Catholic' countries has nothing to do with religion. Rather, this phenomenon is the result of diverse effects of indigenous conditions in soon-to-be-colonized areas, before European colonialists arrived. The next three paragraphs outline how this came about, then the rest of this section describes the supporting evidence for this.

Change of religion and the emergence of an economy dominated by mining and large plantations or farms are distinct processes, but they have both tended to occur in parts of the world that were sparsely populated in AD 1500. Only sparsely populated societies have become majority Christian since AD 1500, and only sparsely populated societies have developed economies that are dominated by mining or large plantations or farms (with climate being an additional factor in the case of plantations and farms).

---

[35] In Table 2.2 the mean index of corruption control for the 'old Catholic' countries is only +0.56, compared with +1.11 for the 'old Protestant or mixed Christian' countries.

[36] In Table 2.2 the mean value of the indicator 'government revenue x corruption control' for the 'old Catholic' countries is only +21, compared with the more favourable value of +38 for the 'old Protestant or mixed Christian' countries.

[37] In Table 2.2 the mean value of the indicator Log[1 + 'mining & large plantations or farms'] for the 'old Catholic' countries is 0.96, compared with the more inequality-inducing value of 1.10 for the 'old Protestant or mixed Christian' countries.

[38] In Table 2.2 the mean index of corruption control for the Hindu-Buddhist countries (excluding Japan) is – 1.30, and for Islamic countries it is – 1.29.

[39] So they tend to appear in the top left quadrant of Figure 2.4.

[40] So they tend to appear in the bottom left quadrant of Figure 2.3.

As Jared Diamond has elegantly argued,[41] sparsely populated societies are easily dominated by a colonizing culture because they typically lack superior technology, sophisticated political organization and a written script. One aspect of this susceptibility to cultural domination is that a colonized society is more likely to adopt the religion of its colonizers. In the period since AD 1500 that religion happens to have been Christianity. To illustrate this with an example, when the British colonized Africa they left behind lots of Christians, because sparsely populated African societies lacked a sophisticated major religion and were therefore susceptible to conversion; but when the British colonized India they left behind lots of Hindus, not Christians, because densely populated Indian societies already had a sophisticated major religion and they were unlikely to convert from it.

Sparsely populated societies also produced very little in the way of manufactured items that European colonialists wanted to buy. Instead, they offered vast areas of minimally occupied land that the Europeans could use for mining or plantations. Sticking with examples from British colonial history, when the British colonized sparsely populated Africa they started by buying slaves and ivory. But there was little else they wanted to buy, and land was fairly easy to take, so they moved on to establishing mines and large plantations. Conversely, when the British colonized densely populated India there was more that they wanted to buy, such as silks and spices, and there was less land for the taking, so they established fewer mines and large plantations. The rest of this section describes the evidence that supports the account I have just given.

Estimates of population density in AD 1500

The argument here requires estimates of population density in different parts of the world in the year AD 1500. Population census figures began to be available for America, considerable parts of Europe, and Australia from around 1800 and, for much of the rest of the world, only in the twentieth century. Since there are no accurate census counts from AD 1500, one has to rely on estimates. The source I used contains estimates of population numbers for 90 areas of the world going as far back as 400 BC.[42] Figure 2.5 shows how population density in AD 1500 was much greater in Europe and Asia than in the rest of the world.

Experts in this have pointed out that modern estimates for the Aboriginal population of Australia before modern immigration began in 1788 vary by an order of five; that pre-1492 estimates of Amerindian populations vary by at least the same multiple; and that estimates of the population of Africa at the beginning of the modern era range from 16.5 million to around 50 million

---

[41] Jared Diamond *Guns, Germs and Steel* (London: Random House 1997).
[42] C McEvedy and R Jones *Atlas of World Population History* (New York: Penguin 1978).

(three fold variation).[43] My justification for using these estimates, despite their limitations, is twofold. First, provided the errors in the estimates are random they may obscure a correlation between variables but are unlikely to produce correlations where none truly exist. Second, the likely errors in the estimates are probably small or moderate in relation to the range of values observed, which range from about one person per 100 square kilometres in New Zealand and Uruguay to about 8000 people per 100 square kilometres in the Indian sub-continent. There is noise in these data, but there are strong signals as well.

Population density, economic inequality and 'mining and large plantations or farms'

There is a strong relationship between population density in AD 1500 and economic inequality in AD 2000 and, to a lesser extent, between population density in AD 1500 and 'mining and large plantations or farms' in AD 2000. Figure 2.6 shows the relationship between population density in AD 1500 and economic inequality c. AD 2000 for the 77 countries incorporated in the regression analysis above. The countries are arranged in six groups. The 'old Catholic' and 'old Protestant or mixed Christian' group are all European countries (the three rather sparsely populated countries are Finland, Sweden and Norway). The group labelled 'extensions of old Protestant or mixed Christian' comprises four of the five most sparsely populated countries (New Zealand, Australia, Canada and the United States). They are relatively egalitarian (and Christian).

The 'new Catholic' and the 'new Protestant or mixed Christian' groups were both less densely populated in AD 1500 than the countries that remain non-Christian today; they are also more unequal than the non-Christian countries. Taking the 'new Catholic', 'new Protestant or mixed Christian' and 'non-Christian' groups together, there is a strong negative correlation between population density in AD 1500 and the Gini coefficient c. AD 2000: densely populated countries tend to be egalitarian (R square = 0.47, p < 0.0001). This tendency is also apparent within each of these three categories of country; in other words, it happens irrespective of prevailing religion.

Figure 2.7 repeats the analysis, but this time with 'mining and large plantations or farms' as the outcome variable; taking the 'new Catholic', 'new Protestant or mixed Christian' and 'non-Christian' countries there is a moderate negative correlation between population density in AD 1500 and 'mining and large plantations or farms' in AD 2000 (R square = 0.17, p < 0.002).

---

[43] J Caldwell and T Schindlmayr 'Historical Population Estimates: Unravelling the consensus' *Population and Development Review* 28/2 (2002),183-204.

Figure 2.5 Estimated population density in AD 1500

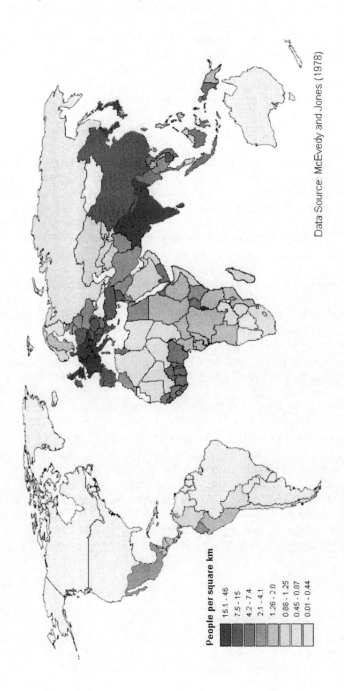

Figure 2.6 Relationship between population density in AD 1500 and economic inequality c. AD 2000

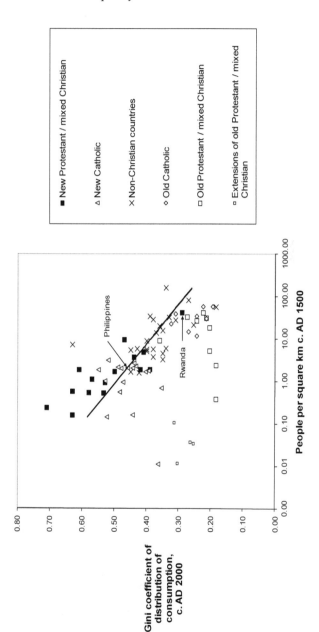

Figure 2.7 Relationship between population density in AD 1500 and mining
and large plantation or farm exports c. AD 2000

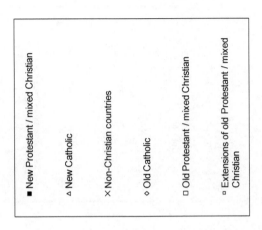

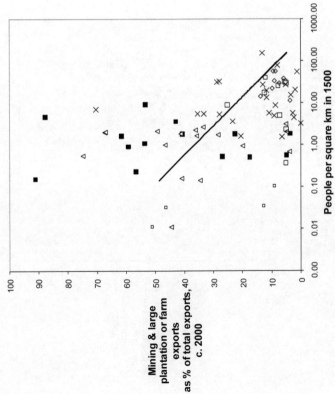

*The relationship between low population density
and large plantations or farms*

The tendency for sparsely populated colonies to be used for large-scale plantations or farms has been described by a number of authors.[44] Percy Courtenay offered the following explanation of the relationship between population density and the use to which colonies were put. He classified colonial 'hinterlands' as hinterlands of settlement, hinterlands of conquest, and hinterlands of exploitation, with the role adopted by a colony depending both on its indigenous population density and on its climate (Table 2.3). He described these three types of hinterland as follows:

> Hinterlands of settlement, or farm colonies, were those overseas territories, essentially 'temperate', whither the European migrated, and where he settled, farmed, or otherwise earned his living in a way familiar in Europe ...

> The hinterlands of conquest were best exemplified by the Portuguese and Dutch colonies in south and south-east Asia. In regions of dense indigenous occupance and unfamiliar environmental conditions, the interest of the metropolitan powers was, initially at least, less in land as a productive asset than in the organization of the indigenous population to produce wealth for the benefit of the intruding European traders ...

> Hinterlands of exploitation: In areas of unfamiliar environmental conditions but of sparse and generally culturally less advanced indigenous population, the European 'entrepreneur' or chartered trading company evolved a different production system. In these situations there was usually the opportunity, provided by the ready availability of land, for the cultivation, by European initiative, of crops that were either new to Europe or which in the past had been obtainable only sporadically or at great expense from distant Asian suppliers ... It was in the colonized lands of sparse indigenous population, where the metropolitan powers were interested in the production of tropical and sub-tropical commodities under mercantilist policies to Europe, that Best (1968) recognized the development of the 'pure plantation economy'. [45]

The establishment of plantation economies (in the sparsely populated hinterlands of exploitation) had much more far-reaching effects within those colonies than the establishment of trading settlements in the densely populated hinterlands of conquest. Using Java as an example of a densely populated colony, Courtenay pointed out that, although the Javanese were required to reserve one fifth of the land of each village for the compulsory cultivation of

---

[44] Lloyd Best 'Outlines of a Model of Pure Plantation Economy' *Social and Economic Studies* 17(1968), 283-328; Percy Courtenay *Plantation Agriculture* (London: Bell and Hyman 1980); Leamer, Maul, Rodriguez and Schott: 'Does Natural Resource Abundance Increase Latin American Income Inequality?'
[45] Courtenay *Plantation Agriculture*, 20-23.

crops for export, this system left them primarily still as subsistence cultivators, as indigenous people working their own land for themselves.[46] There was much more radical disruption to the indigenous economy in the plantation colonies that emerged in sparsely populated colonies such as the West Indies and Brazil, because the scarcity of labour meant that plantation owners resorted to slave labour.

Table 2.3 Relationship between population density and use of colonial hinterlands

		Indigenous population density and cultural development	
		Dense population, culturally advanced	Sparse population, culturally less advanced
Extent of environmental familiarity	Familiar (cool or warm temperature)	Fringe impact only e.g. China Japan	Hinterlands of settlement (farm colonies) e.g. North Atlantic states of North America
	Unfamiliar (tropical or sub-tropical)	Hinterlands of conquest (trading settlements) e.g. Java	Hinterlands of exploitation (plantation colonies) e.g. West Indies, Brazil

I have not found a comparable analysis of the relationship between population density and the emergence of economies dominated by mining, but it remains the case that such economies are heavily concentrated in parts of the world that were sparsely populated in AD 1500. Among the 77 countries included in the regression analysis, ten countries (Australia, Bolivia, Botswana, Central African Republic, Chile, Namibia, Papua New Guinea, Peru, Sierra Leone and Zambia) had mineral exports that accounted for more than 20 per cent of total exports in AD 2000. Only one of these countries (Sierra Leone) is estimated to have had a population density of more than two persons per square kilometre in AD1500, which puts them at the sparsely populated end of the global scale at that time (Figures 2.5 and 2.7).

The relationship between low population density and Christianization
There are also strong relationships between population density in AD 1500 and change of religion between AD 1500 and AD 2000 (Table 2.4 and Figures 2.8 and 2.9). Among the 77 countries included in the multiple regression analysis, only countries that followed a local, not a major, religion in AD 1500 have

---

[46] Courtenay *Plantation Agriculture*, 22.

become majority 'Christian' since then (the 17 'new Catholic' countries, 14 'new Protestant or mixed Christian' countries and four 'extensions of old Protestant or mixed Christian' countries). These countries were, on average, an order of magnitude less densely populated in AD 1500 than those that followed a major non-Christian religion at that point. None of the latter had become predominantly Christian by AD 2000.

Table 2.4 Relationships between population density and religion

Mean population / sq. km c. AD 1500 (range)	Religion in AD 1500 (number of countries)	Religion in AD 2000 (number of countries)
3 (0.01 – 20)	Local religions (43)	New Catholic (17) New Protestant or mixed Christian (14) Extensions of old Protestant or mixed Christian (4) Multi-faith (6) Hindu-Buddhist (1) Islamic (1)
24 (0.4 – 55)	Catholic (17)	Old Catholic (8) Old Protestant or mixed Christian (9)
27 (2 – 150)	Any other major religion (17)	Islamic (10) Hindu-Buddhist (4) Multi-faith (2) Jewish (1)

The sparsely populated countries that followed local religions in AD 1500 correspond broadly to Courtenay's hinterlands of settlement and hinterlands of exploitation, but not his hinterlands of conquest (which were densely populated). In religious terms, the hinterlands of settlement are 'extensions of old Protestant / mixed Christian' (Canada, the US, Australia and New Zealand), while many of the hinterlands of exploitation are 'new Catholic' or 'new Protestant or mixed Christian' (much of Latin America, the Philippines and Papua New Guinea). The densely populated countries that followed a non-Christian major religion in AD 1500 correspond broadly to Courtenay's hinterlands of conquest (south and south-east Asia) and areas of fringe impact (east Asia).

Why have the sparsely populated hinterlands of settlement and hinterlands of exploitation become majority Christian (as 'extensions of old Protestant or mixed Christian', or 'New Protestant or mixed Christian' or 'New Catholic', respectively) while the densely populated hinterlands of conquest have not?

Figure 2.8 Prevailing religion in AD 1500

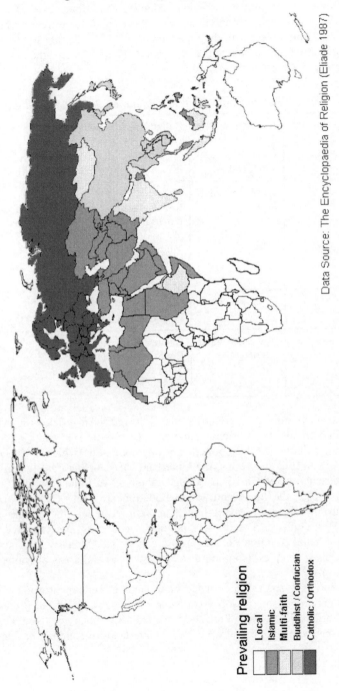

Figure 2.9 Prevailing religion in AD 2000

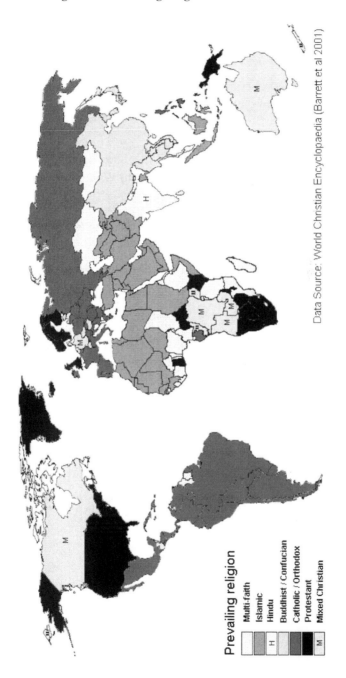

The switch of the countries categorized as 'extensions of old Protestant or mixed Christian' from the 'local religions' category is simply explained: indigenous people are now outnumbered by the descendants of Christian immigrants from Europe. But in the case of all the 'new Protestant or mixed Christian' and the 'new Catholic' countries, large numbers of indigenous people have apparently converted to Christianity. 'Conversion' can mean a change in religious affiliation, a change in religious conviction, or both.[47] What we are dealing with here is a change in religious affiliation, which may or may not have been accompanied by a change in religious conviction. There are broadly four explanations of why some societies have changed their religious affiliation in large numbers, while others have not, and all of them can be related to population density. The four explanations involve, in turn, the role of force in coercing or preventing conversion; the extent to which pride in one's own culture outweighs the appeal of any alternative culture; the disrupting effect of modernization on traditional African societies; and a similar disrupting effect of modernization on the microcosmic worldview of local religions.

The role of force is evident both in the Christianization of Latin America and in the resistance to Christian conversion of China, Japan and Islamic societies. On the Christianization of Latin America, John Chasteen writes that 'most Spanish and Portuguese people who came to the Americas in the 1500s believed that spreading the "true religion", even by force, was a good thing'.[48] David Burnett writes that 'the military superiority of the Spaniards was so pronounced that small armies numbering a few hundreds were able to vanquish well-organized Aztec armies of thousands ... They razed the temples and replaced them with Christian churches.'[49] Conversely, Christian mission has sometimes been heavily constrained in societies that were strong enough to use force to control conversion (and these were typically densely-populated societies that followed a non-Christian major religion). For example, Burnett notes that in Islamic societies 'when a Muslim becomes a Christian he may have to face the penalty of being rejected by the community, his wife may be taken from him, or he may have to face the ultimate penalty of death'.[50] Likewise, the historian Kenneth Latourette writes that 'in the eighteenth century persecution contributed to the slow recession of Christianity in China.

---

[47] Emefie Ikenga-Metuh, 'The Shattered Microcosm: A critical survey of explanations of conversion in Africa' in K Petersen (ed.) *Religion, Development, and African Identity* (Uppsala: Scandinavian Institute of African Studies, 1987).

[48] John Chasteen *Born in Blood and Fire: A concise history of Latin America* (London: WW Norton 2001), 58.

[49] David Burnett *Clash of Worlds* 2nd edn (London: Monarch Books 2002), 132.

[50] Burnett *Clash of Worlds*, 130.

It drove Christianity underground in Japan from early in the seventeenth until the third quarter of the nineteenth century.'[51]

Regarding the role of cultural pride, Burnett writes that 'when a society is strong and proud of its culture, it is not as easy for an individual to convert to another culture. The sense of group identity tends to weld the community together as a coherent whole.'[52] He attributes the resistance of Islamic societies to Christian conversion in part to their sense of wounded pride at being colonized for a period by the Christian nations of Europe: 'this was only to produce additional hatred and resentment from the Muslim peoples – it was an offence to their honour, and a reproach to their religion'.[53] Conversely, Latourette argued that many communities in Africa may have converted to Christianity, despite resentment at being colonized, because some perceived the culture of the colonizers as offering many advantages over their own: 'Christianity came in association with what appeared to be a higher culture and was accepted along with other aspects of that civilization'.[54] Likewise, the historian Adrian Hastings writes that:

> All the conquerors claimed to be Christian, and at the end of the nineteenth century it would have seemed overwhelmingly obvious that power, riches, and knowledge belonged to the Christian nations. It would have been very strange if Africans did not, in the situation of conquest, seek to share in the beliefs of their conquerors.[55]

As for the disrupting effect of modernization on traditional African societies, John Trimingham attributed the move from African traditional religions to Christianity and Islam to the collapse of the structures of traditional African societies and African worldviews. This happened when secular processes of modernization, such as improvements in transport and communications, exposed them to circumstances beyond the 'shattered microcosm' of their previous lives:

> Village religion is serviceable only within the circumscribed bounds of village life. When horizons are widened, its limitations are felt, and this led many to adopt either Islam or Christianity parallel to those aspects of the old religions which are still serviceable.[56]

---

[51] Kenneth Latourette *A History of the Expansion of Christianity* (London: Eyre and Spottiswoode 1939-47), VII, 486.

[52] Burnett *Clash of Worlds*, 130.

[53] Burnett *Clash of Worlds*, 115.

[54] Latourette *A History of the Expansion of Christianity* VII, 485.

[55] Adrian Hastings *The Church in Africa, 1450-1950* (Oxford: Clarendon Press 1994), 405.

[56] John Trimingham *Islam in West Africa* (Oxford: Clarendon Press 1959), 21.

Robin Horton gave a very similar explanation, but with the additional point that the drift into the mission churches was not simply a passive exercise.[57] It involved a measure of rethinking and adaptation of traditional beliefs to the realities of the structural changes in society. He argued that the important spiritual beings in the African microcosm are the lesser spirits, which offer explanation, prediction and control of the affairs of the local community and its environment. Ideas about a supreme being, who is concerned with the world as a whole, tend to be vague, with poorly developed techniques for approaching him. People interpret modernization's disruption of their microcosm as a retreat of the lesser spirits and an indication that the supreme being is taking direct control of the everyday world. This prepares them to accept the supreme being presented to them by Christian or Islamic missionaries, but they do so on their terms; the supreme being should offer explanation, prediction and control of everyday events, even though these aspects of the religion may not be important to the missionaries. Although Horton does not elaborate on this, a corollary of his model is that people whose religion already includes a supreme being (Hinduism Islam and Judaism) or a comprehensive philosophy of life (Buddhism) should be less ready to accept the Christian missionaries' offer of a supreme being.

Recalling that densely populated societies tend to have superior technology, more sophisticated political organization, a written script, and greater resistance to germs,[58] each of the preceding explanations of change in religious affiliation can be related to population density. Since sparsely populated societies lacked sophisticated political organization and had limited technology, they were more susceptible to forced 'conversion', and more likely to perceive the culture of the colonizers as offering advantages over their own. The social structures and worldviews of these sparsely populated societies were 'microcosmic', and hence severely challenged by their encounter with modernity when they were colonized.

None of this is to deny that specifically religious factors have contributed to 'conversion' when this has involved a change in conviction, rather than merely a change in affiliation. Ikenga-Metuh argues that 'the extent and depth of missionary influence has generally not been appreciated ... No fair assessment of conversions in Africa can be made without listing Muslim and Christian enterprise as a major contributory factor.'[59] Lamin Sanneh has stressed the importance of mother tongue translation of the Bible, which 'encouraged local people to embrace the new religion while also embracing their own cultures'.[60] However, Christians have dedicated themselves to Bible translation and other

---

[57] Robin Horton: 'African Conversion' *Africa: Journal of the International African Institute* 41/2 (1971), 85-108.
[58] Diamond, *Guns, Germs and Steel.*
[59] Ikenga-Metuh 'The Shattered Microcosm', 23-4.
[60] Lamin Sanneh *Encountering the West, Christianity and the Global Cultural Process: The African Dimension* (Maryknoll: Orbis 1993), 16.

missionary enterprises for many years in densely populated Asian societies, without comparable large-scale changes in religious affiliation, so it seems that these factors can play only a limited role in explaining large-scale changes in religious affiliation in Africa.

Rwanda and the Philippines as test cases

Two countries have histories that qualify them as useful cases for further testing the argument that conversion to Christianity and economic exploitation by other countries (typically through mining or large-scale plantations or farms) are distinct processes, both of which have been more likely in sparsely populated societies. In AD 1500 Rwanda was, by a considerable margin, the most densely populated part of Africa, with a density comparable to Asian countries (Figures 2.5 and 2.6). Unlike Asia, however, it has converted to Christianity and was a 'mixed Christian' country in AD 2000. It therefore provides a unique opportunity to assess whether it is low population density, or Christianity, that predisposes a society to the emergence of an economy dominated by mining or large scale plantations, and the economic inequality that accompanies it. Although detailed export data are not available, Rwanda is not a mining or large plantation economy: 'The Rwandan economy is based on the largely rain-fed agricultural production of small, semi-subsistence, and increasingly fragmented farms. It has few natural resources to exploit'.[61] The result is that Rwanda has a more egalitarian economy than any other 'new Protestant or mixed Christian' or 'new Catholic' country (Figure 2.6). Christianity has not produced economic inequality in a densely populated country, and this observation supports the argument that it is not Christianity per se that has produced economic inequality anywhere else.

The second useful test case is the Philippines. Its economic and religious history has many similarities with Latin America: it was ruled by Spain for three hundred years, Catholicized, developed a sugar export economy and has a rather unequal economy today (Figure 2.6). A very obvious difference is its proximity to China, and the people who were most successful in exploiting economic opportunities in the Philippines were not the Spanish, but first the Chinese mestizos (particularly during the period AD 1850 to 1898), and later the pure Chinese.[62] An American government mission to the Philippines in 1921 reported that 'most of the retail stores, the import and export business, financial institutions and corporations are in the hands of Americans and foreigners, especially Chinese'.[63] So it is clear that although the Spanish succeeded in Catholicizing the Philippines, they were not the ones who

---

[61] US State Department, 'Background Note: Rwanda' Available at http://www.state.gov/r/pa/ei/bgn/2861.htm#econ, Accessed 7.10.09

[62] Edgar Wickberg 'The Chinese Mestizo in Philippine History' *Journal of Southeast Asian History* 5/1 (1964), 62-99.

[63] Onofre Corpuz *An Economic History of the Philippines* (Quezon City: University of the Philippines Press 1997), 248.

exploited it economically. The Philippines was amenable to conversion by the Spanish and it was also susceptible to economic exploitation by the Chinese – but these were distinct processes.

In summary, conversion to Christianity and economic exploitation by other countries (typically through mining or large-scale plantations or farms) are, in principle, distinct processes, both of which have been more likely in sparsely populated societies. This is not to deny that, in practice, Christian mission and commercial interest have often been closely related. It can be argued that Christianity (in both its Catholic and, later, Protestant forms) played a part in European motivation to acquire colonies, so that the colonizers of the countries that were destined to become raw product exporters were Christians, rather than followers of any other religion. David Bosch writes that, for Catholic Spain and Portugal, 'colonialism and mission, as a matter of course, were interdependent; the right to have colonies carried with it the duty to Christianize the colonized'.[64] The economic historian David Landes also identifies a degree of religious motivation in the Spanish expansion, which was 'seen as an extension of divinely blessed and papally sanctioned crusade'.[65] Of colonialism and mission by Protestant nations, Bosch observes that, from the nineteenth century, 'colonial expansion would once again acquire religious overtones and also be intimately linked with mission'.[66] A well known example is the conviction of the Victorian missionary explorer David Livingstone that, to fulfil God's purpose for the world, it was necessary that 'those two pioneers of civilization - Christianity and commerce - should ever be inseparable'.[67]

However, it seems likely that the European nations would have sought to acquire colonies even without the motive of Christian mission. Landes writes that, following Christopher Columbus' initial contact with the Americas, 'for a quarter of a century, the Spanish sailed about the Caribbean, touching the continents to south and north, always disappointed not to find the treasures that presumably lay beyond the next landfall ... always they asked after gold'.[68] Their primary motive was financial gain, not religious conversion. Likewise, for the expansion of the Protestant nations, Bosch observes that their initial motivation, prior to the nineteenth century, was 'thoroughly secular'.[69] Thus, for both Catholic and Protestant nations, mission is more plausibly seen as a legitimizing factor, rather than a primary motive for colonial expansion.

This distinction, in principle if not always in practice, between the processes of religious change and of economic exploitation is supported by Robert

---

[64] David Bosch *Transforming Mission: Paradigm shifts in theology of mission* (New York: Orbis Books, Mary Knoll 1991), 227.
[65] David Landes *The Wealth and Poverty of Nations: Why some are so rich and some so poor* (London: Abacus 1998), 99.
[66] Bosch *Transforming Mission*, 303.
[67] William Monk, ed. *Dr. Livingstone's Cambridge lectures* (Cambridge 1858), 19.
[68] Landes *The Wealth and Poverty of Nations*, 101.
[69] Bosch *Transforming Mission*, 303.

Woodberry's analysis of the distinct interests of different Western groups, including business elites and missionaries, in colonial contexts:

> Four major Western groups competed to maximize their interests: businesspeople, colonial governments, settlers, and missionaries ... Business elites primarily wanted to make money and make it quickly. Life expectancies of Europeans in the colonies were often dismally low. Thus, business people often wanted to make money and get home before they died - especially in areas with high death-rates.
>
> Colonial administrations wanted stability, taxes, prestige, and political support back home. They wanted to prevent uprisings that threatened their lives and the lives of settlers and were sometimes willing to use extreme violence in order to squelch rebellion. Home governments pressured them to make sure expenditures did not exceed revenues.
>
> Settlers wanted to maintain control of land and resources, preserve their privileged status vis-a-vis indigenous peoples, and sustain their privileged access to senior colonial positions. They also wanted to prevent uprisings that threatened their lives and property.
>
> Missionaries primarily wanted to convert people. Sometimes this led them to intervene on behalf of those they were trying to convert. During the colonial period, missionaries were also often in a unique bridging position between the colonized and the colonizing state.[70]

The Relationship Between Government Revenue and Religion

Moving on to the relationship between government revenue and religion, rich countries tend to have larger governments than poor countries, but once this is taken into account the 'new Protestant or mixed Christian' countries have higher levels of government revenue than predicted from GNI per capita, and the 'new Catholic' countries have lower levels than predicted (their data points fall, respectively, above and below the regression line in Figure 2.10). However, among the 'old' Christian countries, exactly the opposite is true: Catholic countries have higher than predicted levels of government revenue, and the levels in Protestant or mixed Christian countries are lower than predicted. It is most unlikely that Protestantism and Catholicism would have opposite influences on the size of government in different parts of the world, so a better explanation is needed for the existence of large governments in 'new Protestant or mixed Christian' countries.

Although the explanation I am about to give needs further work to substantiate it, I think the reason most of these 'new Protestant or mixed

---

[70] Robert Woodberry 'The Shadow of Empire: Christian missions, colonial policy, and democracy in postcolonial societies' (PhD thesis, University of North Carolina at Chapel Hill 2004), 79-80.

Christian' countries have large governments is that they were ruled as British colonies for a significant period after 1945. During this period Britain was establishing the welfare state at home, and set about encouraging its remaining colonies to do the same. British intent to benefit its colonies through government finance was expressed through the Colonial Development and Welfare Act 1940. Under this Act the basis on which the UK gave financial assistance to its colonies changed from commercial self-interest to 'any purpose likely to promote the development of the resources of any colony or the welfare of its people'.[71] Financial assistance was allocated mainly to roads, education, natural resources, health, water supplies and sanitation. This assessment is consistent with the view of the historian Roland Oliver, who wrote that:

> Perhaps the greatest misfortune of modern African nations was that their approach to independence coincided with a period when it was generally believed that the way to a better future lay through more and longer term state planning, with its implementation led by a large and ever-expanding public sector.[72]

The architects of British post-1940 colonial policy might be disappointed by the results: it seems that British influence, far from 'promoting the welfare of the people' as intended, contributed to the establishment of large governments in former colonies which, because they are corrupt, promote the welfare of ruling elites.

The Relationship Between 'Control of Corruption' and Religion

The extent to which a country controls corruption depends largely on how rich it is and, although Protestantism has arguably reduced corruption in developed countries, any similar impact in developing countries is quite modest. Figure 2.11 repeats the exercise performed in Figure 2.10, but with 'control of corruption' rather than 'government revenue' as the outcome variable. It shows that 'control of corruption' is strongly related to GNI per capita, but after allowing for this the 'old Protestant' countries do better than expected at controlling corruption (they lie above the regression line in Figure 2.11). 'Old Catholic' countries do slightly worse, and 'new Catholic' countries do much worse, than expected.

Figure 2.12 repeats the exercise performed in Figure 2.11, but splits the 'new Protestant' and 'new mixed Christian' countries into separate groups, and

---

[71] Foreign and Commonwealth Office 'Colonial Development and Welfare Acts 1929-70: A brief review' (London: HMSO 1971), 7.

[72] Roland Oliver *The African Experience* (London: Weidenfeld & Nicolson 1991), 241.

splits the 'non-Christian' group into 'Islamic', Hindu-Buddhist' and 'multi-faith' countries.[73]

Figure 2.10 Relationship between Gross National Income per capita and government revenue as a percentage of GDP c. AD 2000

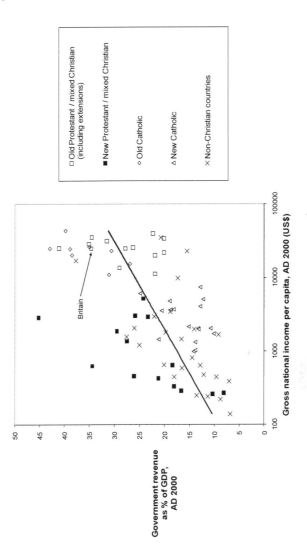

---

[73] Twenty three countries (12 of them Islamic) that lacked sufficient data to be included in the multiple regression modelling, do have data on GNI per capita and control of corruption, so I have added them to Figure 2.12.

After controlling for GNI per capita 'new Protestant' and 'new mixed Christian' countries are, on average, slightly less corrupt than Islamic and multi-faith countries, but not Hindu-Buddhist countries (Figure 2.12). However, all these differences are too small to be statistically significant. Although Protestantism may help restrain corruption, any such influence is weak relative to the strong association between poverty and corruption. Protestant developing countries are poor, and their perceived level of corruption reflects their poverty rather than their Protestantism.

Figure 2.11 Relationship between Gross National Income per capita and index of control of corruption c. AD 2000

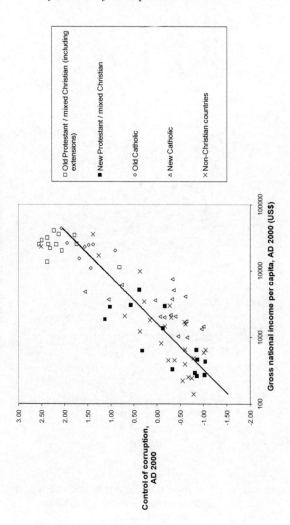

Figure 2.12 Relationship between Gross National Income per capita and index of control of corruption among all low- and middle-income countries with any data c. AD 2000

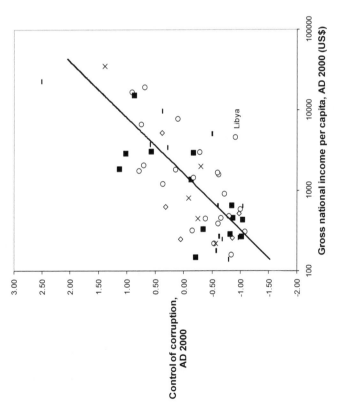

What about the Protestant Work Ethic?

A number of people have asked me whether Max Weber's thesis about the Protestant work ethic helps to explain the association between Christianity and economic inequality. They were probably thinking along the following lines: Protestantism facilitated the widespread adoption of behaviours that were conducive to business success,[74] and business success tends to increase economic inequality. So that explains the association between Christianity and economic inequality.

Although I think there is probably some truth in Weber's thesis about the Protestant work ethic, I do not think it helps to explain the association between Christianity and extreme economic inequality, for the following reasons. Protestant developing countries are not unequal because they are Protestant, but because they tend to have economies based on export of raw products and governments that are both large and corrupt. Neither of these influences on economic inequality is connected with notions of a Protestant work ethic, and some of them have no obvious connection with Protestantism at all.

The emergence of raw-product-exporting economies cannot be attributed to Protestantism, since the same phenomenon is seen in predominantly Catholic developing countries (Table 2.2 and Figure 2.3). Likewise, the relatively large size of government in former British colonies cannot plausibly be attributed to Protestant influence in Britain because 'old Catholic' countries tend to have bigger governments than 'old Protestant or mixed Christian' ones (Table 2.2 and Figure 2.10). Of the variables that influence economic inequality, Protestantism has played an active role in only one (control of corruption) and this is unrelated to Weber's ideas about the Protestant work ethic.

There is, however, a different Weberian concept that is relevant to the relationship between religions and economic inequality: 'rational bureaucratization'. According to Weber, the ideal-type rational bureaucrat conducts official business in strict accordance to impersonal rules; he is responsible only for the impartial execution of assigned tasks and must sacrifice his personal judgment if it runs counter to his official duties.[75] To a large extent, Protestant developing countries are economically unequal because they have large governments that bend the rules to favour their friends. If the large governments that are found in Protestant developing countries applied rules impartially, economic inequality in those countries would be reduced, regardless of which religion prevailed.

---

[74] Max Weber *The Protestant Ethic and the Spirit of Capitalism* (London: Allen & Unwin 1930).
[75] Max Weber *From Max Weber: Essays in sociology* (London: Routledge & Kegan Paul 1948).

Summary

Indicators representing the explanatory variables identified by previous researchers (what a country exports, the redistributive effect of government, and access to finance) account for much of the between-country variation in economic inequality among never-Communist countries. After these explanatory variables have been taken into account, there is no significant association between prevailing religion and the Gini coefficient for the distribution of consumption.

The 'new Protestant or mixed Christian' and 'new Catholic' countries of sub-Saharan Africa, Latin America and the Caribbean are economically unequal because they tend to have economies that are dominated by mining or large farms or plantations. They fit the description of 'hinterlands of exploitation' (sparsely populated tropical or sub-tropical countries where unoccupied land was available for the taking, but labour was scarce). By comparison with the densely populated 'hinterlands of conquest' in south and south-east Asia, their pre-colonial culture was relatively unsophisticated in terms of technology, political organisation and religion, so they were much more likely to convert to the Christian religion of their European colonizers, whether as a result of force, a sense that the culture of the Europeans offered greater benefits than their own, or the collapse or adaptation of their traditional worldviews in response to secular processes of modernization.

The 'new Protestant or mixed Christian' countries (in sub-Saharan Africa and the Caribbean, plus Papua New Guinea) also tend to have governments that are larger than expected given their GNI per capita. Although they are slightly less corrupt than expected given their GNI per capita, they do not control corruption well enough to prevent government revenue being used to benefit ruling elites rather than the majority of the population. This misuse of government resources contributes substantially to the high levels of economic inequality seen in 'New Protestant' countries.

Having developed this answer to the puzzle of why economic inequality is greatest in Christian, and especially Protestant, developing countries, I wanted to understand better the relationship between Christians and corruption in countries where there are lots of Christians, lots of corruption, and high levels of economic inequality. But first I needed to return to the library to discover what has been written about various aspects of corruption.

Thinking About Corruption

Why Fighting Corruption is Important

In the previous chapter I highlighted one cogent reason why fighting corruption is important: it should help ensure that public resources are used for public benefit rather than as a source of enrichment for elites. More broadly, the World Bank regards corruption as

> among the greatest obstacles to economic and social development. It undermines development by distorting the rule of law and weakening the institutional foundation on which economic growth depends. The harmful effects of corruption are especially severe on the poor, who are hardest hit by economic decline, are most reliant on the provision of public services, and are least capable of paying the extra costs associated with bribery, fraud, and the misappropriation of economic privileges. Corruption sabotages policies and programs that aim to reduce poverty, so attacking corruption is critical to the achievement of the Bank's overarching mission of poverty reduction.[1]

Why Corruption is a Recent Topic

The current widely held view that corruption is harmful to economic and social development is very different from a point of view that was widely held at one time: that corruption stimulates economic development by breaking through bureaucratic bottlenecks, serving as an informal price system, making rigid official development policies more flexible and humane, and by putting public resources and favourable decisions up for bids, channelling them to people and groups able to use them efficiently.[2] This rosy assessment of the effects of corruption has lost credibility more recently, as it has become clear that such claims of economic benefits from corruption often rest on accounts of particular transactions in isolation, while ignoring the strongly negative systemic and longer-term effects of corruption.[3] The old view that corruption actually stimulates economic development may help to explain why the World

---

[1] World Bank 'Overview of Anticorruption' Available at http://web.worldbank.org/WBSITE/EXTERNAL/TOPICS/EXTPUBLICSECTORAND GOVERNANCE/EXTANTICORRUPTION/0,,contentMDK:21540659~menuPK:3844 61~pagePK:148956~piPK:216618~theSitePK:384455,00.html Accessed 17.7.10.

[2] Nathaniel Leff: 'Economic Development through Bureaucratic Corruption' *American Behavioral Scientist* 8/3(1964), 8-14.

[3] Heidenheimer and Johnston *Political Corruption*, 305.

Bank, which now has Governance and Anti-Corruption as a major theme, was virtually silent on the matter until 1996. In the Bank's own words:

> For much of the history of the World Bank Group, corruption was considered nearly a taboo subject — something that many were aware of but did not speak of or address. President Wolfensohn changed that attitude in 1996, when he publicly committed the institution to fighting the 'cancer of corruption'. In September 1997, the Board endorsed the World Bank's first anticorruption strategy, and in parallel, the 1997 World Development Report deepened global understanding that an effective state is crucial for development. In 2000 the Board endorsed a Public Sector Governance Strategy that recognized corruption as an outcome of a poorly functioning governance system.[4]

A cynic might ask whether, by making corruption 'nearly a taboo subject' for half a century, the World Bank has actually perpetuated poverty – but better a late conversion than none at all.

Causes of Corruption – the Logic of Limited Access Orders

Before reviewing potential approaches to fighting corruption it is important to consider why corruption is so prevalent. Douglass North and colleagues offer a 'framework for interpreting recorded human history' that proposes some answers to this question. They observe the obvious fact that 'the upper-income, advanced industrial countries of the world today all have market economies with open competition, competitive multi-party democratic political systems, and a secure government monopoly over violence' and note that 'these societies use competition and institutions to make it in the interests of political officials to observe constitutional rules, including consolidated political control over all organizations with the potential for major violence'.[5] They describe such societies as 'Open Access Orders'.

They argue that these societies have an equilibrium that is fundamentally different from that of all middle and low-income developing countries today, and all countries before about AD 1800. The norm in all these societies, which they call 'Limited Access Orders', is that political elites divide up control of the economy, each getting some share of the spoils, or rents.[6] In explaining

---

[4] World Bank 'Strengthening Bank Group Engagement on Governance and Anticorruption', 38.
[5] D North, J Wallis and B Weingast 'A Conceptual Framework for Interpreting Recorded Human History' National Bureau for Economic Research Working Paper (2006) 12795, Cambridge MA, 4.
[6] In this context 'rent' does not have its commonplace meaning of 'income from hiring out land or other durable goods'. Rather, it refers to 'economic rent', which is defined as 'a payment for the services of an economic resource above what is necessary for it to remain in its current use' (Black et al. 2009). Examples of 'rent-seeking' include firms

how such Limited Access Orders arise and persist, their starting point is that 'the anthropological literature on primitive societies suggests that most primitive societies were extremely violent' and that hence 'the benefits of even moderate limits on violence are large enough to gain support from most non-elites as well as elites'.[7] Such limits on violence are obtained 'when a dominant coalition emerges that provides powerful individuals and groups with incentives to refrain from violence'. The interests of the dominant coalition are served as it creates rents for itself by limiting the access of others to political and economic opportunities. 'Since outbreaks of violence reduce the rents, the elite factions have incentives to be peaceable most of the time. Adequate stability of the rents and thus of the social order requires limiting access and competition.'[8] According to this analysis, it is not only the elites that have an interest in maintaining limited access. Even the majority who are being exploited economically may hesitate to push for reform because they fear the disorder and violence that may follow if the established order is destabilized.

Not only do the majority benefit through better control of violence and increased personal security, but as a result overall economic productivity is also enhanced. This range of benefits for all leads them to describe limited access orders as the 'natural state' of society:

> Limited Access Orders have been the default option for human societies over the last ten thousand years. We have termed the political and economic structure of the limited access order the natural state for a reason: it is the natural form of human society. The implications for development policy are enormous. Natural states are not failed states, they are typically not produced by evil men with evil intentions, and they are not the result of pathologies in the structure of these societies. Nothing is unnatural about natural states. And because natural states are not sick, policy medicine will not cure them.[9]

It is hard to disagree with these authors that Limited Access Orders are the most common form of human society, though many would struggle to agree that there is nothing evil or pathological about them. If any 'policy medicine' exists, they would be keen to find it.

What Has Helped Some Countries to Reduce Corruption

Robert Neild observes that the institutions required to keep corruption in check are well known – well paid military, police and civil services selected by merit; an independent judiciary; laws and regulations that inhibit corruption, good

---

forming a cartel to raise prices and governments requiring producers to pay for licences without providing any useful service.

[7] North, Wallis and Weingast 'A Conceptual Framework', 10.

[8] North, Wallis and Weingast 'A Conceptual Framework', 4.

[9] North, Wallis and Weingast 'A Conceptual Framework', 70-71.

audit systems; a free press. But he poses the key question 'What has sometimes given rulers the will and the ability to introduce these institutions which, in their very nature, constrain the degree to which they, the rulers, can pursue power and wealth?'[10] Perhaps because the development literature did not regard corruption as a serious problem until the 1990s, systematic attempts to answer this question are quite recent. A notable contribution is from the political scientist Daniel Treisman, who analysed which of various plausible determinants are statistically related to various indexes of corruption. He found support for six arguments:

> Countries with Protestant traditions, histories of British rule, more developed economies, and (probably) those with high exposure to imports were rated less 'corrupt'. Federal states were more 'corrupt' than unitary ones. While the current degree of democracy was not significant, long exposure to democracy was associated with lower corruption ... The six most robustly significant variables — British heritage, Protestant tradition, log per capita GDP, federal structure, uninterrupted democracy, and openness to imports — do an impressive job of explaining countries' corruption ratings. Together these variables can account for more than 89% of the variation in each of the Transparency International indexes.[11]

A major limitation in Treisman's analysis is that the single variable 'log per capita GDP' is far more powerful than any of the other explanatory variables: it alone accounted for 73 per cent of the variation in the corruption in his model. This means that the answer to the question 'What is the most effective way of reducing corruption?' is largely the answer to the question 'What is the most effective way of increasing per capita GDP?' But what Treisman's analysis does offer is some clues about which variables may influence corruption after other variables, especially per capita GDP, have been taken into account. The results are described below in a little more detail, with the variables presented in order of diminishing influence on corruption.

Colonial history

After per capita GDP, countries' colonial histories were the next most significant variable in predicting current levels of corruption. Perhaps surprisingly, there was no clear evidence that countries that have never been colonized are less corrupt today. Britain and her former colonies have a substantial advantage: 'a British heritage by itself reduces perceived corruption by more than one point — and possibly by more than two — on the 10-point

---

[10] Robert Neild Public *Corruption: The dark side of social evolution* (London: Anthem Press 2002), 201.

[11] Daniel Treisman 'The Causes of Corruption: A cross-national study' *Journal of Public Economics* 76/3(2000), 436.

corruption scale'.[12] Treisman examined two, mutually compatible, explanations for this finding.

> First, this might reflect the fact that most former British colonies inherited a common law tradition from their previous colonizers. In common law systems, law is made by judges on the basis of precedent, rather than on the basis of codes drawn up by scholars and promulgated by central governments. Second, I hypothesized that colonial heritage might influence countries' degree of corruption not just via the type of legal system — based on judicial precedent or on codes — but also via the traditional ways in which justice had come to be administered. In former British colonies, I suggested, the colonizers left behind not just a particular accumulation of precedents and case law but also a particular 'legal culture' that emphasized procedural justice over substantive issues far more than in countries colonized by other powers.

He concluded that there is slightly stronger evidence for the 'legal culture' than the 'common law' explanation for the corruption-reducing legacy of British rule. He describes the British 'legal culture' as 'an almost obsessive focus on the procedural aspects of law' and adds the following quote from Eckstein: 'The British ... behave like ideologists in regard to rules and like pragmatists in regard to policies. Procedures, to them, are not merely procedures, but sacred rituals'.[13] 'This willingness of judges to follow procedures even when the results threaten hierarchy ... clearly increases the chance that official corruption will be exposed'.[14]

Democracy, the structure of the state, and imports

Treisman notes that 'the most notable thing about the estimates of the impact of democracy is how small they are. The highest estimate of the impact of 45 years of uninterrupted democracy was that it would reduce the corruption score by about 1.5 points on a 10-point scale.' The apparent effect of state structure was even smaller: 'depending on the model, a state that was federal tended to rank from about half a point to more than one point higher on the corruption scale than a similar state that was unitary'.[15]

As for the relationship between corruption and low imports, Treisman was unable to establish clearly the direction of causation; 'but whichever way causation runs, the effect is surprisingly small ... an increase in the share of imports in GNP from 0 to 10% would yield somewhere from a 0.1 to a 0.2 point decrease in the corruption score'.[16]

---

[12] Treisman 'The Causes of Corruption', 418.
[13] Harry Eckstein 'Case Study and Theory in Political Science' in Gomm, Hammersley and Foster eds *Case Study Method: Key issues, key texts* (London: Sage 2000), 119-64.
[14] Treisman 'The Causes of Corruption', 403.
[15] Treisman 'The Causes of Corruption', 430, 433.
[16] Treisman 'The Causes of Corruption', 435.

Douglass North and colleagues offer an interesting explanation for the novel appearance since AD 1800 of a number of rich, democratic and relatively uncorrupt countries. In their analysis, combating corruption requires a society to change from being a Limited Access Order to an Open Access Order. Two crucial components of the transition are that it is not intended by the ruling elite, and the necessary institutional changes persist 'only when they are compatible with the incentives and constraints of those in power':

> The tipping point comes when open access in one dimension – economic or political – commands sufficient power to press successfully for open access to the commanding heights in the other dimension... When the tipping point is reached, the dominant coalition finds that its internal arrangements are better served by supporting intra-elite competition, rather than intra-elite cooperation to perpetuate existing mechanisms of rent-creation. That is, it makes sense for the elites to define themselves impersonally as citizens, rather than as kings, dukes, earls, etc.[17]

They note that such transitions do not happen frequently in history, but when they do they occur 'in a period of time that is quite short by historical standards, something of the order of fifty years or less'.

Although not starting with the same theoretical framework, Michael Johnston offers a similar account of the ways in which corruption came to be reduced in societies which now enjoy relatively low levels of corruption:

> Historically, many societies reduced corruption in the course of contending over other, more basic issues of power and justice. Checks against various abuses were not so much schemes for good governance as political settlements – rules that contending interests could live with and could enforce by political means, allowing them to pursue their own interests while protecting themselves against predation by others. The institutions and norms of low-corruption countries ... were created and continue to work not just because they are 'good ideas', but because they engage and protect lasting interests in society ... The matter at hand might have been land, taxes, religion, or language, but the deeper issue was who had power, how they got it, and what could and what could not be done with it ... Magna Carta, for example, was not a ringing declaration of the rights of humanity or a scheme for good government, but rather a set of limits laid down by members of the aristocracy weary of royal abuses. Critical notions of accountability of government in England emerged out of a blood feud between crown and parliament over taxation, religion, and the accountability of royal ministers – not as reforms but as clubs to swing in a political brawl. Similarly, election reform in nineteenth-century Britain – the secret ballot, limits on expenditure, and the long struggle over rotten boroughs – was in part aimed at checking the 'old

---

[17] D North, J Wallis, S Webb and B Weingast 'Limited Access Orders in the Developing World: A new approach to the problems of development' *World Bank Policy Research Working Papers* (2007) No. 4359, Washington DC, 23-24.

corruption', but also helped party leaders impose order on, and control the costs of, the growing nationwide competition for votes.[18]

These perspectives on how corruption was reduced and democracy became established underpin one of the possible strategies for reducing corruption that I will outline at the end of this chapter.

Protestantism

Treisman found that countries with a larger proportion of Protestants in 1980 have lower levels of perceived corruption; the proportion that were Muslim, Catholic or Anglican had no significant effect. The apparent effect of Protestantism is quite small: 'an additional 5–10% of the population that was Protestant, would reduce a country's corruption rating by one-tenth of a point'.[19] Treisman's analysis does not examine whether the relationship between Protestantism and control of corruption varies according to GDP per capita, but the analysis already presented in Figures 2.11 and 2.12 suggests that the effect may be stronger in high income countries (which have a long Protestant history) than in low or middle income countries (where Protestantism is more recent).[20] Treisman outlines four possible interpretations of the effect of Protestantism:

> One interpretation of this is that a greater tolerance for challenges to authority and for individual dissent, even when threatening to social hierarchies, renders Protestant societies more likely to discover and punish official abuses. An alternative view is that Protestant cultures are less understanding toward lapses from grace and press more urgently to institutionalize virtue and cast out the wicked. 'Protestants, particularly sectarians, believe that individuals are personally responsible for avoiding sin, while other Christian denominations, particularly the Catholic church, place more emphasis on the inherent weakness of human beings, their inability to escape sin and error, and the need for the church to be forgiving and protecting' (Lipset and Lenz 2000:120). A third possibility is that a focus on the family rather than the individual in many traditions other than Protestantism leads to 'amoral familism' [21] and nepotism. A fourth view is that Protestant traditions — in which the separation of church and

---

[18] Michael Johnston *Syndromes of Corruption: Wealth, power and democracy* (Cambridge: Cambridge University Press 2005), 217-8.

[19] Treisman 'The Causes of Corruption', 427.

[20] The association between Protestantism and control of corruption in high-income countries does not necessarily reflect a high level of Protestant faith commitment today. As Bryan Wilson has argued, 'a net of rational bureaucratic regulation can supplant the moral densities, the conscientious sensitivities and the commitments once generated by communities of faith' ('The Functions of Religion: a Reappraisal' *Religion* 18 (1988), 199-216).

[21] The Oxford English Dictionary defines familism as 'the feeling existing between members of a family'.

state is more pronounced than in, say, Catholicism or Islam — lead to a more vibrant, autonomous civil society that monitors the state more effectively. In this view, the impact of religion is not so much cultural as institutional.[22]

The first and the last of these interpretations imply that Protestantism constrains corruption by fostering an active civil society that holds rulers to account. The middle two interpretations assume that it constrains corruption by fostering honest behaviour in individuals. Each interpretation has different implications for Protestant churches that seek to use past evidence of a Protestant advantage as a guide to reducing corruption today. Should they concentrate on building up the personal holiness of their followers, or on fostering a vibrant civil society? Unfortunately, Treisman concludes that he lacks any data to distinguish clearly between these competing interpretations.

Current Strategies for Reducing Corruption

In this section I will outline four broad strategies for reducing corruption that can be found in the current literature. The first has been described as the 'consensus package' and is promoted particularly strongly by the World Bank.[23] It comprises efforts to bring about in low- and middle-income countries the following characteristics of high income countries: an effective and accountable state, strong civil society and greater competition in politics and the economy. As noted in the previous sections, these characteristics of today's high income (and low-corruption) countries emerged over decades or even centuries. Since this timescale is too slow and uncertain for a modern development agenda, the essential added ingredient, to accelerate the process to an acceptable pace, is the second strategy: 'leadership by country-level reformers', who are the key to ensuring that the 'consensus package' falls into place. These first two approaches are integrated in the World Bank's 2007 strategy for 'Strengthening Engagement on Governance and Anticorruption'.

The third strategy arises out of the kind of assessments described by Douglass North and Michael Johnston: elites in corrupt societies are so well entrenched that reforms to institutions there will only survive if they are compatible with the short-term interests of the elites. Rather than confront corrupt elites directly, it is better to pursue responses to corruption that both keep the elites satisfied and help the country they rule to move forward a little. The fourth strategy is 'promote honest behaviour through Protestant preaching'. This strategy needs to be considered for at least two reasons. First, 'institutionalising virtue and casting out the wicked' was proposed by Daniel Treisman as one of the mechanisms that may explain the correlation between Protestantism and reduced corruption. Second, it is probably the easiest and

---

[22] Treisman 'The Causes of Corruption', 427-8.
[23] Johnston *Syndromes of Corruption*, 16-23.

most widely adopted response of churches to corruption. Each of these strategies will now be described in a little more detail and critiqued.

The World Bank 'consensus package'

The World Bank package comprises reforms that are intended to:
- Improve the capacity, transparency, and accountability of state institutions, in areas such as financial management, public service delivery and the legal system.
- Create a competitive and responsible private sector.
- Increase opportunities for participation and oversight by civil society, the media, and communities.[24]

Recognising that many powerful players in corrupt countries may not share the Bank's enthusiasm for these reforms, the Strategy acknowledges that:

> A critical aspect is to align the incentives of state officials with these goals, through an appropriate combination of rules, restraints, and rewards; competitive pressures; and voice and partnership. The incentives of non-state actors, too, need to be aligned with these goals, especially those of businesses and other nongovernmental entities that often play a pivotal role in undermining governance.[25]

Phrases such as the 'incentives of state officials' resonate with the language used by Douglass North in describing the process through which they believe Limited Access Orders have sometimes transitioned into Open Access Orders: 'institutional changes persist only when they are compatible with the incentives and constraints of those in power'.[26]

Unfortunately for the many countries that are Limited Access Orders, many leading writers on corruption see little prospect for success of the World Bank's strategy: 'transiting from one order to another (in either direction) is not easy and it does not happen frequently in history'.[27] Neild identifies several huge obstacles to the success of the World Bank strategy:

> It is hard to see how the international economic agencies and their member governments can introduce incentives that would cause corrupt rulers to say to themselves 'if I do not attack corruption I may be punished so severely that I shall lose power, whereas if I attack it I shall be rewarded so generously that my hold on power will be maintained or enhanced.' Not only are the rich countries and their agencies in this respect impotent, they commonly have been and are

---

[24] World Bank 'Strengthening Bank Group Engagement on Governance and Anticorruption', 47.

[25] World Bank 'Strengthening Bank Group Engagement on Governance and Anticorruption', 47.

[26] North, Wallis, Webb and Weingast 'Limited Access Orders in the Developing World', 5.

[27] North, Wallis and Weingast 'A Conceptual Framework', 26.

accomplices in corruption abroad, encouraging it by their actions rather than impeding it. First, there was the uninhibited use by both sides in the Cold War of corruption and covert operations, including 'destabilization' by arming dissidents, assassination, election rigging and the like, to topple regimes and obstruct the legitimate access to power of political parties perceived to belong to the other side. Secondly, firms from the rich countries have been in the habit of paying bribes to rulers and officials in order to gain export contracts, notably for arms and construction projects... Thirdly, there is the problem of the corruption-inducing effects of the purchase, by the rich countries and their international corporations, of concessions in Third World countries to exploit natural deposits of oil, copper, diamonds and the like.[28]

Johnston expresses doubts about whether this 'consensus package' could be effective in reducing corruption in low- and middle-income countries, even if there was the broad-based international will and credibility to do so, because it seeks to bypass the prolonged process of political struggle through which today's high income countries acquired the institutions represented by the package:

> Checks and balances, accountable leaders, liberal markets, competitive elections and administrative transparency do much to control corruption in countries where it is the exception rather than the rule, and where they enjoy broad-based legitimacy. It does not follow, however, that the absence of such factors is what explains corruption where it is extensive, nor that putting them in place will control the problem ... The state and politics are, often as not, seen as parts of the problem, rather than as essential elements of development and reform. Governing is reduced to public management functions while complex questions of democracy and justice are to be addressed through technically sound 'good governance' rather than politics ...[29]

Neild contrasts the very different forces that have influenced the evolution of state institutions in high-, compared with low- and middle-income, countries:

> I see no grounds for expecting standards of public conduct in Third World countries now to be anything like those that have evolved in northwestern Europe. The evolution of their societies has been quite different. Military competition, except perhaps in one or two temporary instances, has not helped to induce cleaner government. The main popular demand for reform that shaped these nations has been the demand for independent government, something quite different from the demand for better government that welled up in Europe. The constitutions and legal codes with which the ex-colonies emerged at independence typically contained rules which, rather than having evolved locally,

---

[28] Neild *Public Corruption*, 208-9.
[29] Johnston *Syndromes of Corruption*, 19,22.

had been imposed by colonial rulers from Europe and were then adopted, with modifications, at the time of independence. These rules were not deeply rooted. The institutions required to keep corruption in check were young and frail. Typically only a small minority of the population was Western-educated and versed in the adopted rules. In these conditions it would have been astonishing if the new rules had not come to be widely broken as people saw, and competed for, the power and wealth that were newly open to them.[30]

North and colleagues go so far as to describe the sort of efforts described in the official World Bank Strategy as 'futile':

> Most development policy today is based on models of the developed world and attempts to make developing countries look more like developed ones. However, the social dynamics of developed countries fundamentally differ from those of developing countries. Development practitioners therefore face a mismatch between the development problems they seek to address and the available tools. They aim to implement social, economic, and political institutions characteristic of the developed West in societies that often cannot even secure basic physical order. To improve state capacity they might, for example, administer donor funds conditional on improving government transparency through better financial auditing of public funds. But they do so in countries where potential leadership groups compete for control through violence, intimidation, and occasionally the ballot box, and where new groups replace old groups at regular intervals. Development practitioners face the futility of trying to solve a problem without knowing its cause and to build state capacity in societies that regularly dismember their governments. Development tools based on industrial country experiences are ill-suited to the development goals in developing countries.[31]

Perhaps the greatest strength of the World Bank Strategy is its candour about the enormous difficulty of combating corruption: 'global trends in governance and corruption indicate that, while some progress may have been made in strengthening state capacity and accountability worldwide, there is little evidence that this has had a significant aggregate impact on reducing corruption overall'.[32] In other words, the enormous task of combating corruption is to be undertaken with a high level of uncertainty as to whether the proposed strategy will work. The specific successes identified in the Strategy are at the level of 'combating certain types of administrative corruption, such as petty bribes to utility officials, tax collectors, licensing officials, and inspectors'. But it goes on to acknowledge that:

---

[30] Neild *Public Corruption*, 206-7.
[31] North, Wallis, Webb and Weingast 'Limited Access Orders in the Developing World', 2.
[32] World Bank 'Strengthening Bank Group Engagement on Governance and Anticorruption', 41-42.

In many states, however, forms of corruption with deep political roots—such as state capture and procurement corruption—have been more difficult to address. Political and business interests, including multinational corporations from developed countries, often collude to obstruct progress in combating corruption; unravelling these networks is extremely difficult.

Following on immediately from the preceding quote is the conclusion that 'Thus, it is clear that effective leadership from both arenas is essential to tackling the problem', which brings us to the second broad strategy for combating corruption, on which the World Bank strategy rests.

Support country-level leaders who are committed to reform

The theme of leadership recurs throughout the World Bank Strategy. Great hopes are pinned on 'the key role of country-level reformers in moving forward the governance reform agenda'. One of the three key lessons the Bank says it has learned over the past decade is that 'institutional reforms can succeed, especially when there is committed country leadership and coalition of reformers, so Bank programs must work closely with reform leaders in government'.[33]

While agreeing that leadership by country-level reformers can be very important, two critical points can be made. The first is that this strategy has been most successful in small states such as Singapore, and it is unclear whether this success can be extrapolated to larger states.

Second, the World Bank's Strategy pays too little attention to the risks faced by country-level reformers. In his assessment of the task faced by country-level reformers in the most corrupt countries the economist Paul Collier wrote:

> Within the societies of the bottom billion there is an intense struggle between brave people who are trying to achieve change and powerful groups who oppose them. The politics of the bottom billion is not the bland and sedate process of the rich democracies but rather a dangerous contest between moral extremes... Although the reformers have truth on their side, truth is just another special interest, and not a particularly powerful one. The villains willing to lie in order to defeat change have an advantage over those constrained by honesty. Reformers do not have it easy.[34]

If such people are the key to reform, we need to understand as well as possible what motivates them to accept high personal risks for the sake of reform, and what may help or hinder them personally as they do so.

---

[33] World Bank 'Strengthening Bank Group Engagement on Governance and Anticorruption', 8.

[34] Paul Collier *The Bottom Billion: Why the poorest countries are failing and what can be done about it* (Oxford: Oxford University Press 2007), 180, 192.

Promote honest behaviour through Protestant preaching

In the anti-corruption strategies reviewed here there is almost no mention of anything that might be categorised as 'preaching'. This reluctance to consider the role of Protestant preaching is surprising, given the frailty of the alternative strategies and the evidence that it may possibly be effective.[35]

Tailor the strategy to elite self-interest

Both Michael Johnston and Douglass North are sceptical that the 'consensus package' of reforms can work, though Johnston expresses greater optimism about the prospects for this where there are powerful leaders committed to reform. In place of the 'consensus package', these authors argue that effective strategies for combating corruption need to start by looking at the interests of the current ruling elites, and then pursue only those reforms that are compatible with elite interests. This turns the World Bank Strategy (which can be summed up as 'present the goals of the consensus package then seek to align the incentives of state officials and non-state actors with these goals') on its head.

The Protestant Contribution to Strategies for Reducing Corruption

Given Daniel Treisman's evidence that Protestantism seems to protect against corruption, it is pertinent to ask which of these anti-corruption strategies may represent mechanisms through which Protestantism exerts this effect. Treisman himself suggests that Protestantism may help foster a vibrant civil society (which is an important component of the 'consensus package') and also that it may promote honest behaviour through its emphasis on personal responsibility for avoiding sin. He does not consider the possibility that Protestant countries may have Protestant leaders who are particularly committed to reform, but this nonetheless seems a possible mechanism that deserves consideration. Only the fourth strategy (tailoring the anti-corruption strategy to elite self-interest) seems unlikely as a mechanism whereby Protestantism protects against corruption. On this basis, there are three broad anti-corruption strategies that may account for Protestantism's protective effect against corruption:

- Promoting honest behaviour through Protestant preaching
- Reforming government by having Protestants inside government
- Promoting civic oversight of government

In the rest of this book I will describe what I heard from key informants in four case study countries about the extent to which contemporary Protestantism actually contributes to fighting corruption through any of these strategies. The case study countries were the Philippines, Kenya, Zambia and Peru, each of which has lots of Christians, lots of corruption, and high levels of economic inequality. The key informants described plenty of challenges regarding the

---

[35] Treisman 'The Causes of Corruption', 427.

relationship between Christians and corruption, but also some inspiring ways in which some Christians are making a difference.

Designing the Country Case Studies

I vividly remember having lunch with an African Evangelical leader in 2006, as I was about to design my country case studies looking at ways in which Protestants might be helping to reduce corruption. He warned me that I might be disappointed if I came to Africa, telling me that in his country the churches were high on the government's list of institutions that should be investigated for corruption. When I checked out what others had written about this, I found conflicting opinions. For example, the sociologist David Martin has characterized Evangelicals in positive terms, as people who exert a political impact through 'the adoption of economic and work disciplines' and 'a concern for broad moral principles'.[1] Conversely, the sociologist Paul Gifford describes the role of churches, including Evangelical churches, in sub-Saharan Africa in very different, and negative, terms. For example, he has written that:

> A church's legal decisions cannot command much respect, since committees are often thought to be stacked beforehand, or patronage dispensed to predetermine the decision. Thus there seems little significant difference between the exercise of leadership in the churches and in national life generally; indeed, in some places it may sometimes be more autocratic and self-seeking.[2]

Given these sharply contrasting perspectives on the role that Evangelicals might play in relation to corruption (whether as part of the problem or as part of the solution) I wanted to avoid making any initial assumptions on this point. This led me to frame the broad questions that I wanted to address through the country case studies as follows:

- To what extent do Evangelicals in each country have a reputation for honest behaviour?
- Where corruption within the Evangelical sector is perceived to be a problem, what do Evangelical leaders see as the causes?
- To what extent do Evangelical leaders in each country think that Evangelicals are effective in opposing corruption through each of the three anti-corruption strategies listed in the previous chapter (promoting

---

[1] David Martin 'The Evangelical Upsurge and Its Political Implications' in Peter Berger (ed) *The Desecularization of the World: Resurgent religion and world politics* (Grand Rapids Michigan: Eerdmans 1999), 39.

[2] Paul Gifford *African Christianity: Its public role* (London: Hurst and Co 1998), 343-5.

honest behaviour through Evangelical preaching, reforming government by having Evangelicals inside government, and promoting civic oversight of government)?

Selecting suitable countries to study

I selected countries according to two theoretical and three pragmatic criteria. The first theoretical criterion was that they should be typical of countries that are economically very unequal (which means that they should have low or middle per capita incomes, large and corrupt governments, and economies that are dominated by mining or large plantations or farms), so that any conclusions from the case studies could be generalized to other very unequal countries. My second theoretical criterion was that they should include a mix of African and non-African countries, in view of the possible contrast between the reputation of Evangelicals in Africa and their reputation in other southern continents.

My pragmatic criteria were that each country should be easily accessible from either the UK or Nepal (which were the two bases from which I planned to make my visits), be willing to grant a visa for a short visit, and be safe enough to ask questions about corruption.

Zimbabwe appeared to be a good fit with most of the criteria, but my chances of getting a visa looked very slim, so I had to rule it out. Columbia and Papua New Guinea were both a good fit with all the criteria apart from personal safety: kidnapping of foreigners was commonplace in Columbia at the time (2007 – 2008), and a lawyer with recent experience of working in Papua New Guinea told me to expect death threats if I started asking too many questions there. Having excluded these three countries, the four countries that provided the best overall fit with the above criteria were the Philippines, Kenya, Zambia and Peru.

Selecting suitable informants to interview

I tried to get interviews with five types of informants:

- Leaders of Evangelical churches, denominations and umbrella bodies, as listed in the relevant country sections of the World Christian Encyclopedia.[3]
- Evangelicals who hold leadership positions as professionals, in business or in Evangelical NGOs that focus on socio-economic justice.
- Representatives of secular anti-corruption NGOs. In each country this included the national office of Transparency International.
- Senior staff in government agencies that have a role in opposing corruption, such as Anti-Corruption Commissions and Auditor-General's offices.

---

[3] Barrett, Kurian, Johnson eds *World Christian Encyclopedia.*

- Representatives of major non-Evangelical churches, particularly the Catholic Church.

I chose the first two groups to obtain a broad spectrum of the views of Evangelical opinion leaders in each country, and the other three groups to provide an independent assessment of the views of the Evangelicals. To the extent that the views of the Evangelical leaders were supported by non-Evangelicals they could be regarded as reflecting more than just the personal or denominational interests of the Evangelicals.

I managed to interview a total of 101 key informants, of whom 81 are Evangelicals. Tables 4.1 and 4.2 give an overview of the numbers and occupations of the key informants in each country, according to whether or not they are Evangelicals.[4] Leadership positions in the case-study countries tend to be occupied by men, so I ended up interviewing many more men than women. Women were better represented in Zambia (7 out of 23 informants) and the Philippines (7 out of 25) than in Peru (only one woman) or Kenya (no women at all).

Tables C.1 to C.4 in Appendix C give the occupation, religious affiliation, age group and gender of each informant, and the date and location of the interview. For many informants I did not succeed in getting consent to identify them by name, so in the chapters that follow I identified them using alphanumeric codes which link to Appendix C.

My Approach to the Interviews

The interviews were semi-structured, which meant that I had a shopping list of topics to cover, but had considerable freedom in the sequencing of questions, their exact wording, and the amount of time and attention given to different topics. At the start of each interview I gave a very brief synopsis of Chapter 2, for several reasons. First, it explained why I had asked for the interview. Second, it acknowledged the western colonial role in establishing economies based on mining or large farms and plantations, and the contribution this makes to economic inequality today; I think this helped to address any concerns that my research was limited to western criticism of corruption in low- and middle-income countries. Finally, it clarified the definition of corruption I wanted us both to use during the interview: that corruption determines the extent to which public resources result in material benefit for elites rather than the majority.

After I had completed all the interviews I looked at all the examples my informants had used when talking about corruption, to see whether they fitted this definition. There were a few exceptions, such as the Filipino informant (Ph5) who mentioned pastors who demand a particular rate for officiating at a

---

[4] Some of the representatives of secular anti-corruption organisations and some of the senior staff in government agencies that have a role in opposing corruption turned out to be Evangelicals, so they are included in Table 4.1.

wedding, rather than being willing to accept the normal token of appreciation; and two informants in Zambia (Z15 and Z18), who both described poor women who make ends meet by brewing illicit alcohol at home. But I found that the vast majority of informants' comments were consistent with the definition of corruption I had asked them to use. My first question in each interview was always:

- How do you see the relationship between the churches and corruption in your country?

At an appropriate point in the interview I asked:

- How do you think Evangelicals can best contribute to opposing corruption?

Table 4.1 Evangelical informants

Occupation	Philippines	Kenya	Zambia	Peru
Leaders of Evangelical churches, denominations or umbrella bodies	2	8	9	12
Professionals, businesspeople and leaders of Evangelical NGOs	13	5	5	12
Working for secular anti-corruption NGOs	2	1	1	1
In government leadership positions	5	2	3	0
Total	22	16	18	25

Table 4.2 Non-Evangelical informants

Occupation	Philippines	Kenya	Zambia	Peru
Leaders of non-Evangelical churches, denominations or umbrella bodies	3	1	2	0
Professionals, businesspeople and leaders of Catholic NGOs	0	0	1	2
Working for secular anti-corruption NGOs	1	2	1	2
In government leadership positions	0	0	1	4
Total	4	3	5	8

Unless the topic had already come up in response to my initial, open-ended questions I looked for an opportunity to ask about these specifics:

- Do you think there is any difference between Evangelicals and Catholics as regards their reputation for honest behaviour?
- How do you see the role of Evangelical preaching in opposing corruption?
- What about the potential for opposing corruption by having Evangelicals working within government? (In Kenya and Zambia I also asked informants specifically how they interpreted the actions of former Presidents Moi and Chiluba, respectively.)
- What about the potential for Evangelicals to oppose corruption by promoting oversight by civil society and communities?

At the end of each interview I asked whether there were any other important aspects of opposing corruption that we had not talked about.

Turning the Interviews into Country Case Studies

The advantage of using a semi-structured approach to interviewing people is that the conversation can flow fairly freely. The downside is that turning 20 to 30 free-flowing conversations into a coherent story about a country, while remaining faithful to the opinions of each individual, takes a lot of work. To ensure that I been fair to my informants I sent the relevant draft chapter to each of them in the Philippines, Kenya and Zambia, asking them whether I had represented their views fairly. I heard back from 16 of them; none of them thought I had misrepresented them, and given this positive feedback I decided not to send the draft chapter to informants in Peru, as this would have required translating the draft chapter into Spanish.

For a final check I sent each draft country case-study chapter to a reviewer with substantial experience of the country concerned, asking them to point out any errors of fact and to advise whether the conclusions of the chapter seemed balanced. The four chapters that follow are the final versions of that process.

The four country case study chapters contain numerous acronyms, mostly of the names of church denominations and Christian non-government organizations. The names are given in full when they first appear in the text, but thereafter acronyms are used. A full list of all the acronyms appears at the front of the book.

Philippines Country Case Study

Introduction

The Philippine islands were first seen by a European in AD 1521, when the Portuguese navigator Ferdinand Magellan reached them during his attempted circumnavigation of the globe in the service of Spain. Miguel López de Legazpi led the first Spanish expedition to achieve lasting results, in AD 1564, and he was immediately followed by representatives of various Roman Catholic religious orders. They soon accomplished the nominal conversion to Roman Catholicism of all the local people under Spanish administration, though the Muslims in the south were never completely subdued by Spain.

Manila dominated the islands as both political and commercial centre. The exchange of Chinese silks for Mexican silver from Acapulco not only kept those Spanish who were seeking quick profit, but also attracted a large Chinese community. Although they were the victims of periodic massacres at the hands of suspicious Spanish, the Chinese persisted and soon established a dominance of commerce that survived through the centuries. Manila was also the ecclesiastical capital of the Philippines. The governor-general was civil head of the church in the islands, but the archbishop vied with him for political supremacy. In the late seventeenth and eighteenth centuries the archbishop, who also had the legal status of lieutenant governor, frequently won. Augmenting their political power, religious orders and bishops acquired great wealth, mostly in land.

The growth of commercial agriculture in the nineteenth century resulted in the appearance of a new class. Alongside the landholdings of the church and the rice estates of the pre-Spanish nobility there arose haciendas of coffee, hemp, and sugar, often the property of enterprising Chinese-Filipino mestizos. Some of the families that gained prominence in the nineteenth century have continued to play an important role in Philippine economics and politics.

Between 1892 and 1898 several Philippine independence movements challenged Spanish rule, but the Philippines emerged from Spanish control as a colony of the United States. The Americans gave a high priority to education. Literacy doubled to nearly half in the 1930s, and by 1939 about a quarter of the population could speak English, a larger proportion than for any of the native dialects. American attempts to create equality of economic opportunity were more modest and less successful. The trend toward greater concentration of ownership, which began in the 19th century, continued during the American period, despite some legal barriers.

The Republic of the Philippines was formally proclaimed in July 1946. The Republic's longest-serving President to date is Ferdinand Marcos, who ruled from 1965 to 1986. Rapid development of the economy brought prosperity during Marcos's first term but his second term was troubled by civil unrest, which he cited as the reason for declaring martial law in 1972. Under Marcos, economic inequality increased greatly and many people experienced an absolute decline in their standard of living.[1] Reports that Marcos had won the 1986 election through fraud stirred a revolt, the first EDSA 'revolution', in which elements in the armed forces combined with 'People Power' to bring Marcos down. He fled the country, allegedly taking with him large amounts of illegally gained wealth. According to one author, 'the amount of graft that occurred under Marcos was truly staggering. Whether the estimates are $5 billion or $20 billion, the Marcos regime perfected the art of corruption.'[2]

Economically, the Philippines is among the most unequal third of countries included in the quantitative analysis in Chapter 2, and the sociologist Randy David has characterized Philippine society as 'a thin layer of rich and successful people floating in an ocean of absolute poverty'.[3] The Philippines also has unfavourable values for most of the indicators of the proposed determinants of economic inequality, though not for 'mining and large plantation or farm exports'. According to the model of economic inequality developed in Chapter 2, this suggests that economic inequality in the Philippines is more a consequence of corrupt government than of what the country produces.[4] Table 5.1 shows the Philippines' position in respect of some selected indicators, including those relevant to the analysis of economic inequality in Chapter 2.

The author of the Philippines chapter in the 'Evangelicalism and Democracy' series includes Pentecostals within the Evangelical fold:

> By the mid-1990's 'Evangelicalism' became a technical term for individuals, churches, and organizations which belonged to the Philippine Council of Evangelical Churches (PCEC) and the Philippines for Jesus Movement (PJM) or were sympathetic ... The PCEC comprises major 'conservative Evangelical' denominations ... along with 'classic Pentecostal' denominations ... PJM comprises major indigenous Pentecostals, or 'charismatic Evangelical' churches

---

[1] James Boyce *The Philippines: The political economy of growth and impoverishment in the Marcos era* (London: Macmillan 1993), xiii.

[2] David Kang *Crony Capitalism: Corruption and development in South Korea and the Philippines* (Cambridge: Cambridge University Press 2002), 148.

[3] Randy David *Reflections on Sociology and Philippine Society* (Quezon City: University of the Philippines Press 2001), 237.

[4] This is consistent with Alfred McCoy's observation that 'Under the Republic (1946-72) ... the Philippine political system was not based so much on the extraction of "surplus" from the production of new wealth but on a redistribution of existing resources and the artificial creation of rents – in effect, rewarding favored families by manipulating regulations to effect a reallocation of existing wealth' (*An Anarchy of Families: State and family in the Philippines* (Quezon City: Ateneo De Manila University Press1994), 12).

... 'Evangelical' sometimes includes evangelistically inclined and less politically left-leaning Protestant churches in the National Council of Churches in the Philippines (NCCP).[5]

Table 5.1 Philippines values for selected indicators

Indicator (year)	Value	Rank, among the 77 countries included in the quantitative analysis
GNI per capita (2003)	$1,100	56 (Rank 1 = greatest GNP per capita)
Percentage of the population living on less than $1.25 a day at 2005 international prices (2005)	23%	62 (Rank 1= lowest percentage on <$1.25)
Gini coefficient of consumption (2000)	0.46	57 (Rank 1= lowest Gini coefficient)
Mining and large plantation or farm exports, as percentage of total exports (2000)	5%	15 (Rank 1= lowest percentage)
Control of corruption (pessimistic view) (2000)	-1.46	55 (Rank 1= greatest positive value)
Government revenue x corruption control (2000)	-22	50 (Rank 1= greatest positive value)

Table 5.2 Percentage of Filipinos estimated to belong to various Christian categories

Estimated percentage of the population in each group in AD 2000	Barrett et al. (2001)	Johnstone et al. (2001)
Christians	89.7	93.2
Roman Catholics	82.4	67.1
Evangelicals	2.4	16.7
Pentecostals / charismatics	26.4	14.1
Evangelicals plus Pentecostals / charismatics	28.8	30.8

As for the proportions of the population in the major Christian categories, different sources agree that the Philippines remains predominantly Roman

---

[5] David Lim 'Consolidating Democracy: Filipino Evangelicals in between "People Power" events, 1986-2001' in Lumsdaine David (ed) *Evangelical Christianity and Democracy in Asia* (Oxford: Oxford University Press 2009), 235-84.

Catholic, but have widely differing estimates for the proportion that are Evangelicals (Table 5.2). The text of the Philippines entry in Johnstone's 'Operation World' states that 'Evangelicals ... have increased to about 10 per cent of the population'[6] and this is close to the estimate of eight or nine per cent given to me by staff of the PCEC. Despite these confusing statistics it seems safe to conclude that the majority of Filipinos are Roman Catholics, and Evangelicals are a minority.

The material in this chapter regarding the relationship between Evangelicals and corruption in the Philippines is based on my interviews with 26 key informants in February - March 2007 and July 2008. Table C.1 in Appendix C gives brief details of the occupation, age, gender and religious affiliation of the key informants, and the dates and locations of the interviews.

The Reputation of Evangelicals for Honest Behaviour

A number of informants thought that Evangelicals in the Philippines have a better reputation for honest behaviour than either Catholics or liberal Protestants. One might expect Evangelical leaders to give themselves a good report in this respect, and some of them did. For example, Ph14, an Evangelical bishop, said that:

> Evangelical faith helps people economically, because when you become a believer you become a better steward, you become an excellent worker. The problem with the Catholic Church is you earn salvation by merits. So in a sense you are actually bribing God, and if you can bribe God, it's easy to bribe other people.

Ph9, an Evangelical who works for the Alliance of Christian Development Agencies, compared liberal Protestants unfavourably to Evangelicals: 'NCCP uses the scriptures, but it does not actually translate into the lives and approaches of the people who work at NCCP.' Both these perspectives could just represent prejudice against the religious competition. However, a positive view about Evangelical character was also clearly expressed by leaders of secular anti-corruption organisations. Dolores Español, Chairperson of Transparency International in the Philippines, said:

> I am not a Catholic follower any more, but I am more of a born-again Christian. Catholicism does not discourage – or they do not regard greed as – sin. Whereas if you are a true believer of Christ, then greed is certainly sin. When I embraced the faith of a born-again Christian then I found peace, I found enjoyment, I found satisfaction. And I shunned worldly lusts - lust of the eyes, lust of the flesh…so I am happier now!

---

[6] Johnstone, Mandryk, Johnstone *Operation World,* 521.

Ph24, Director of a secular anti-corruption NGO, saw similar differences between Evangelicals and Catholics:

As a non-Evangelical, I would say that in the Philippines the Evangelicals would tend to be the people you would trust more than the non-Evangelicals. Several years ago I was driving in Metro Manila, and a traffic officer pulled me over for a violation. So I gave him my license, as is the standard procedure, and he was angling for a bribe. He handed me back my license and said, 'Well, maybe we can fix this - you can just give me some money for coffee.' And then I gave him back my license and I said to him, 'Just give me the ticket.' And he looks at me and goes, 'Are you Christian?' And I said, 'No, I'm not a Christian. Why?' He said, 'Because only Christians would turn their licenses back to me'... If I were to meet an Evangelical in government, my bias would be to tend to believe that these people have their integrity intact. The Catholics, I would doubt. I'm a Catholic myself but my experience with a lot of Catholics has not been good ... If I meet someone who is an Evangelical in government, my tendency would be to believe that they are morally upright, someone I would trust more ... there are good Catholics of integrity, but I wish that I'd seen more Catholics being a little more trustworthy.

Evangelical behaviour may not always match their good reputation

Several Evangelical leaders thought that Evangelicals sometimes fail to live up to their reputation for honest behaviour. Ph5, a member of staff of a Christian anti-corruption NGO, described three examples of 'corruption' within Evangelical churches that had come up in a recent workshop on governance. The first two seem relatively trivial: one concerned a pastor demanding a particular rate for officiating at a wedding, rather than being willing to accept the normal token of appreciation, and the other concerned pastors who use their position to promote certain products as a way of supplementing their income. The third example, concerning church fund-raising for relief operations following a calamity, seems potentially more serious since the sums of money involved could be larger. Ph5 said: 'To whom are you going to distribute the funds first? Is it a member of the congregation that you are giving favour to? It may not go to the right beneficiaries'. She thought that many churches lack a culture of financial transparency, or systems to support it:

Because you give high respect to the minister, when it comes to financial accountability, some people are embarrassed or shy about saying, 'How did you spend the money?' Nobody would do that outright, upfront. Not all churches have systems where the pastor does not hold the money, where there's an external auditor - so they had trouble, because somebody got tempted.

Ph7, an Evangelical theologian, commented that 'Almost every person I know has no second thoughts about bribing a policeman when you're caught in a traffic violation, or paying a government clerk some bribe to speed up the movement of your paper'. Ph3, also an Evangelical theologian, thought that,

On the whole, Evangelicals pay attention to their own personal morality. But whether they avoid doing acts that could be construed as corruption in dealing with government offices, I really do not know, because I know some who would compromise. They are conservative Christians, but if they are caught in a traffic violation they will easily give a bribe to avoid a long hassle. Or they would give a bribe to get their licence, a passport or a visa. We still have to learn biblical ethics, to be consistent in what we say and in what we do.

Although he was the only informant to express this view, BJ Sebastian, an Evangelical businessman, thought there is no difference, on average, between Evangelicals and Catholics:

To be honest, and I'm quite disappointed with this, in terms of being reform-minded it does not really matter whether people are Catholic or Evangelical, but if they are reform-minded they are usually devout Catholic or committed Evangelical. Unfortunately, most Evangelicals are a different kind of person on Sunday from the other six days. They give the excuse that 'This is the secular world. If I don't do this everybody else is going to. And anyway this is secular, this is nothing to do with God'.

Preaching about Corruption

The FOCIG approach – reform national government through preaching

Despite these acknowledged shortcomings, the reputation of Evangelicals in the Philippines is sufficiently good that a number of informants expressed confidence in the strategy of the Fellowship of Christians in Government (FOCIG), an Evangelical NGO that is trying to reform government through preaching. This strategy will be described at some length, because it is being attempted on a substantial scale in the Philippines, but not in any of the other case-study countries. The essence of the strategy is to use the power of the Catholic state to provide opportunities to commend Evangelical faith to senior government staff, then teach them that God expects them to provide excellent, honest public service.

FOCIG was founded by Niels and Amyjay Riconalla, a husband and wife team. Niels started his career as an economist working for the government's National Economic Development Authority. He described the evolution of his thinking and methods as follows:

I concluded that the reason the Philippines was not progressing as we should, given all the resources and the level of education that we have, was moral in nature. We did not use our resources wisely and equitably; a few rich people were controlling the fruits of development. So in 1989 the Lord gave me the burden: 'Why don't you form an organisation and do something about it?' The verse that really spoke to me was Matthew 5:13-16: 'You are the salt of the earth, the light of the world.' So we formed FOCIG in 1989. If you want to solve a lot of problems in this country, notably corruption, then we as Christians in the government should play a key role. We're on the inside and we can do something about it. One of our focuses now in terms of prevention of corruption is bringing the word of God to the people. In partnership with the church, we said the best way to solve the problem of corruption in the Philippines is to solve the root cause, which is a corrupt, greedy heart that can only be solved through the Word of God. Our target since two years ago is to hit the top people in government. So we partner with the church and we are accredited with the Office of the Presidential Council on Values Formation under the Office of the President. In 2005 the Secretary of National Defence approved our proposal to conduct moral values training for the top brass of the Armed Forces of the Philippines. We use Rick Warren's 'Purpose-Driven Life' (PDL) because it's not only a best-seller but has also been recommended by the Catholic Church. We have seen amazing results in the Army. Now we are arranging a schedule of PDL seminars for our Chief Justice, who has requested us to help him reform the entire judiciary. We are also focusing on the Bureau of Internal Revenue (BIR). After nine years of trying to get into the BIR, they now welcome our partnership. And the Presidential Council on Values Formation has endorsed us to the Chief of Police, General Calderon, to conduct the PDL seminars among the police.

Two generals who were converted to Evangelical faith through FOCIG's PDL seminars described their experiences to other army officers in the following words.
Ph10's account

In 2005, I was designated as Chief of the newly created Office of the Internal Auditor of the Armed Forces of the Philippines, one of the tools of the Chief of Staff to enhance the efficiency and effectiveness of the organization. In July 2005, I received a directive from the Chief of Staff, instructing me and other generals to attend the Purpose Driven Life seminar for 6 consecutive Thursdays beginning August. I was not too happy about this because I had a lot of things to do. With a heavy heart, I attended the seminar. But as it went on I began to understand the purpose of my life. I became interested to learn more about the teachings of Christ as found in the Bible. I felt a hunger deep within me to know more about Him and His principles and apply them daily in my life. I have accepted Christ into my life as my Lord and Saviour ... After the PDL graduation, I requested FOCIG to conduct PDL seminars among my staff in order for them to acquire the attitude necessary in the performance of their duty. After their graduation, I requested a Bible study every Friday afternoon. I have noticed significant changes of behaviour of our personnel.

Being promoted to Commanding General of the 2nd Infantry Division, whose mission is to create an environment conducive to economic development for the people in our area of responsibility (Region IV), I found out that God is the answer. We have to bring Jesus to the hearts of everyone. This was confirmed when I met and had a lengthy discussion with Ka Bernie and Ka Masong, former rebels who have surrendered to the law and to Jesus Christ, whom they renounced when they joined the Communist New People's Army. They have come to realize that the solution to our country's problems is not by armed revolution but a spiritual revolution. If we will only follow the commandments of loving God above all and our fellowmen, then 37 years of insurgency will end. This will bring peace, progress and development for our people. My conviction is to facilitate the conduct of the PDL Seminar, Bible study, and establish livelihood programs in support of this spiritual revolution to finally solve the insurgency in our country.

Niels Riconalla of FOCIG felt that conversion had changed the General's strategy from a 'warrior type' in which officers 'really want to kill those who rebel against the government, they're very confrontational' to a 'developmental approach. He has been requested by the Chief of the Army to lecture on this model, so I hope that it will affect the entire army.' Another perceived benefit of the General's conversion was a stricter enforcement of rules:

The General requested us to conduct the PDL seminar among his staff of 50 internal auditors. So the majority of these people now have professed to receive Christ into their lives and now there's an ongoing Bible study in his office. As a result of that they discovered one General who was retiring and who hid one million litres of gasoline for his retirement. The one who replaced him is a Christian and he told me they were able to recover it and save the Armed Forces 35 million pesos.

Ph26's account
Ph26 was also 'invited' to attend the Purpose Driven Life seminar, though he notes that 'the invitation was sent to me in the form of an instruction: "You are required to go to GHQ"'. His account to a group of army officers was as follows:

After I accepted Jesus I started thinking how I could serve my purpose as a Presidential Security Group (PSG) Commander. During the May elections, I told our men, 'We will fulfil our job description, and that's that.' I proved it to them when I was at PSG. I was able to draw the line between politics and our duty to protect the President and not project the President. So people saw no PSG vehicles with 'Vote Gloria' stickers. I would not allow it because I knew that it was prohibited. If her campaign managers wanted to bring her in a car with posters then it had to be a private vehicle.

In conversation, Ph26 also described how his conversion had changed his response to being offered a large bribe:

A businessman came to me offering military equipment for the PSG to buy. There were only the two of us talking at that time. He said 'General, if you will buy from me this equipment I will give you 60 per cent commission.' I asked 'How is that possible?' and he said: 'I have overpriced my equipment by 100 per cent.' I said: 'Don't proceed with your presentation. You have insulted me and you have insulted this institution. There is no more corruption here.' If I had decided to buy all the equipment I would have got 30 million pesos.

Niels Riconalla of FOCIG interpreted this as 'a clear result of God's word working in the heart of a person, for him to say "No" to corruption'. Despite these encouragements, Niels was sober about the scale of the challenge: 'I have been with this government for the last 22 years and it's very frustrating to see very little progress.' He described how he draws inspiration from his hero William Wilberforce: 'How long did it take him to fight for the abolition of slavery? Forty-two years. This kind of fight is a long term effort, and in the short term it's hard to measure – but our hope is God alone, Jesus Christ.'

Praise for FOCIG

Several Evangelical informants expressed unreserved praise for what FOCIG is doing. Ph16, a leader of the Christian Reformed World Relief Committee, said 'FOCIG are the champions, I very much admire their work'. BJ Sebastian, an Evangelical businessman, described their strategy as 'the best contribution of the Evangelical community to eradicating corruption: getting more principled men and women there, particularly in the Armed Forces. More of the Evangelical community should support FOCIG, because they're doing the right thing.' He went on to say:

> There is a growing class of people who are beginning to be interested in, if not already practicing, a very faith-based work lifestyle. There's been an explosion of this in the marketplace in the Philippines over the last five to ten years, mainly because of the influence of churches like Greenhills Christian Fellowship, Christ's Commission Fellowship, Victory Christian Fellowship, organisations like the Fellowship of Christians in Government (FOCIG) and very small businessmen's fellowships ... We don't know how far can you get with what FOCIG is doing, attacking the heart with the gospel. When Jonah preached to Nineveh the entire city repented, so maybe we can get the entire city. But only the Lord can do that.

Ph17, an Evangelical professor of history, also saw individual conversion as the Evangelical niche for fighting corruption:

> If the Evangelical churches can find more Christians who are in charge of procurement they can make a difference. The Catholics can do things with the World Bank, the Evangelicals can focus on individual conversions. They will certainly have an organisational impact somewhere. Collectively, you accumulate and aggregate the conversions.

These sentiments were echoed by Ph11, an Evangelical lecturer in politics: 'The church can do a lot, I think. The greatest potential to do a lot would be the moral tenacity, I think, of people in the faith-based sector.' Referring to his ambition to renew the capital city, Robert Nacianceno, the General Manager of Metro-Manila Development Authority (MMDA), said 'Before I can do anything in Metro Manila there should be a spiritual renewal.' Dolores Español felt that:

The most promising approach for addressing corruption is internalising moral values, ethical standards and practices. The individual should be converted, because corruption is a behavioural problem. Before the change to internalising moral values, TIs main approach was changing systems. But we believe that it will not work, because corrupt people can easily mislead those who are introducing systemic changes. They are two or three steps ahead of the people who would want to introduce systemic change... If the people manning the system are corrupt, there is no way you can change the system to make it clean.

Even Ph24, a Catholic, said:

In my experience with FOCIG it does seem that the Evangelicals within government are trying to make sure that there are circles of integrity. I'm not aware of any Catholic groups out there doing similar things to FOCIG, banding together and saying: 'As government workers we've got to apply our Catholic duties to our jobs'.

Reservations about FOCIG

However, a number of Evangelical leaders expressed reservations about FOCIG's likely impact on corruption. Ph13, a senior Evangelical church leader, saw two limitations of the FOCIG approach: failing to address government structures that in his view need to change (see the section below headed 'PCEC's approach to advocacy'), and confusion about people's concept of Christ:

If you look at the PDL approach it's basically spiritual right now. You can hardly transform a nation by making everyone goody two shoes. You have to redeem structures that have been used for evil purposes - government fund management, for instance - and Evangelicalism hardly addresses those issues. The Evangelicals of this nation have not tried to even articulate the Christology of change and transformation. So when you ask a government official to accept Christ you might be thinking 'He's going to accept Christ as his Lord and Saviour', but the guy will be thinking, 'Which Christ do I accept now? Is it the baby Christ, is it the dead Christ?' Christ has been part of our society for 300 years. But we've got the wrong Christ.

Ph6, an Evangelical mission mobiliser, praised FOCIG but warned of the risk of them being co-opted:

The FOCIG approach is very noble, it's the best from Evangelical theology, it's one of the best ways to transform the political evils. The weakness of it is that sooner or later they will have to grapple with the issue of eliminating corruption, and that needs systemic change. Religious people normally are conservative, so there's a danger for FOCIG of being co-opted by the religious right. So I'm watching out for the curriculum of their discussion groups, because my prediction is it will turn more and more towards religious stuff rather than social issues. I'm glad they're connected to Christian Convergence for Good Governance, so we can keep them accountable.

Ph19, an Evangelical who works for a secular anti-corruption NGO, while noting that 'evangelism and discipleship are the strengths of Evangelicals - they can change people', nonetheless said that 'the FOCIG approach is overly spiritual. The premise is that when people in government are converted, that a Christian government worker will automatically extend his or her Christianity in the workplace; but I think that's a very sweeping assumption.' Her advice was that 'you have to extend the FOCIG approach, and not just talk about salvation and eternal life and all these spiritual things'. She had differed with FOCIG over whether to support prosecutions for corruption:

> FOCIG started to stop the legal aid that we provide for some of the victims of corruption, because they say 'It's antagonistic of the gospel'. So they're saying we cannot preach the love of Christ if we are fighting against someone in the court. But I think the love of God and His justice are inseparable, and the moment we said that we want to fight corruption, that means we will have enemies in the future.

Jovita Salonga, former President of the Senate, wondered how far many Evangelicals would be willing to act: 'The FOCIG approach has an impact on people. The trouble is that Evangelicals take pride in being honest, but that's not enough. You have to do something about it – that is moral integrity.' Ph15, an Evangelical attorney who works for COMELEC (the Commission on Elections), said 'I believe in the FOCIG way, but these good people may be used as a legitimizing factor, instead of becoming a catalyst for change.'

While considering the risks of co-option, it is interesting to note that Ph24, Director of a secular anti-corruption NGO, sees as particularly promising an approach that combines support for reform-minded leaders, such as those that FOCIG aims to produce, with surveillance to keep them accountable:

> What generally works is partnering with like-minded government officials, those that are already oriented towards reform, towards greater transparency, and that's what we've generally done in department of Education, Health. We have started up a new partnership with the Department of Public Works and Highways where we have road users, road service providers, good governance advocates, government representatives, academic representatives – and the whole point there is to look over the shoulder of the government, to make sure they're doing their jobs correctly. The reforms that we've tried out to date have always depended on the political will of the person dealing with it. What we want to do is to identify second tier leaders, the Under-Secretaries, and help them stay the course and not give up, because I can imagine to be in that position as a reformer, to be ostracised and persecuted because of what you're trying to do, is a tough thing to experience alone. And while one of the things we do in TAN is criticise government where we see fit, we also realise the flipside of that coin is to identify the areas of good, and support that.

To those from a western liberal tradition, it may seem surprising that only one informant expressed any hint of concern about the way in which FOCIG accesses its audiences, which is by using the authority of the state to oblige government employees to attend seminars with a religious content. The sole expression of concern came from Ph24 (a Catholic), though even he wondered whether the poor functioning of liberal democratic ideas in the Philippines might justify FOCIG's approach:

> If people volunteer their time to attend these seminars then that's one thing, but to use their resources and require them is… But then, do you accept Western liberal democracy lock, stock and barrel? The way I see it right now it's just not functioning. With a weird party system, with an electorate that's largely uneducated, it's hard to expect good political outcomes. So you may get to a point where you say the ends may justify the means.

Reforming Government by Having Evangelicals Inside Government

Evangelical informants described two different approaches to reform through Evangelical involvement in government: an Evangelical seeking election as President, and Evangelical attempts to influence local government.

An Evangelical seeking election as President

In 2004 Brother Eddie Villanueva, a prominent Evangelical and leader of the Jesus Is Lord Church (JIL), ran unsuccessfully for President. Most Evangelical informants who mentioned his attempt assessed it negatively. Ph14, an Evangelical bishop, said he thought that 'Brother Eddie was so naïve about his involvement - he was swallowed by the politicians'. Two Evangelical informants mentioned that they had tried to dissuade him from running. Ph7, an Evangelical theologian, recalled that:

> We wrote Brother Eddie a six-point letter to dissuade him. There was no point in him standing. People in the far-off places hadn't even heard of him. And he lacked time to put up a programme that will be attractive beyond the Evangelical community. He would spend millions of pesos and divide the Evangelical community.

BJ Sebastian, an Evangelical businessman whose advice Brother Eddie had sought out, said he had given him the following advice:

> If God called you to be President, He would have prepared you to do that. What kind of equipping have you had for running the government? You've never run a government agency. You've never won an elected post. You've never run a local government. You've not even been a legislator. If you really think that God is calling you to a political career, then you allow Him to equip you. Maybe you should run first as you local Congressman, and represent your District in Congress. If God prospers you there, perhaps you should run as a national

Senator. And if God prospers you there, then you are prepared for the highest office in the land.

When Brother Eddie lost the election he disputed the result in a way that Sebastian considered 'objectionable – looking like a poor loser, just like any other Filipino politician. His participation in the political sphere has been a disaster. And now many people even suspect that his main motivation for growing the JIL church was political.' Other negative assessments were offered by Ph4, an Evangelical author, who said that she did not vote for him because 'he had no experience in governance and he lacked the competence to rule this country' and by Ph11, an Evangelical lecturer in politics, who felt that 'the Evangelical community has been more divided since Brother Eddie ran for President'.

Only two informants gave positive assessments of Brother Eddie's decision to campaign for the Presidency. Ph19, an Evangelical who works for a secular anti-corruption NGO, thought that 'Brother Eddie running in the 2004 Presidential election helped raise awareness among Evangelicals about engaging in politics or getting involved in good governance.' Finally Ph24, a Catholic who heads the same NGO, said:

> Our only Protestant President has been Ramos, all the rest have been very public about their Catholicism. They're seen with their spiritual advisors and praying on a rosary. There is such a disconnection between their public display of Catholicism and their actions. It's especially frustrating to see Sunday Catholics – so pious sitting in communion on Sunday - run this country into the ground on Monday morning ... I identified Brother Eddie as perhaps the guy I wanted to see win. He seemed to represent a different way of looking at things, solving problems; and again, I believe Evangelicals to be people of integrity.

Evangelical reformers within local government

A different suggested strategy whereby Evangelicals might try to reform government from the inside is to regard national government as a lost cause and aim instead to improve local government. This view was articulated by Melba Maggay, Director of ISACC:

> If the national government is dysfunctional, never mind, as long as the local governments function. If we work on local governance the results are very immediate, so I feel whatever else happens on the national level, as long as you have all the grassroots governance improving something will happen. If you are Mayor you are in charge; if you are in the Senate you're just shuffling papers ... After the Captain of a local barangay[7] became a Christian we did some 'Excellence in the Workplace' training for the local officials and within weeks

---

[7] A barangay is the smallest political unit in the Philippines.

you could see a change: there's less corruption, the street gangs are no longer having gun wars and the crime rate has gone down.

Three other Evangelical informants mentioned positive experiences of reforming local government through some kind of Evangelical influence. Ph5, a member of staff of a Christian anti-corruption NGO, described her experience of conducting a programme on participatory local governance:

> There are a lot of Christians in politics at the local level, so in January 2007 we conducted a Good Governance Forum. This time it was attended by Muslims and Catholics as well. The speaker said: 'We'll talk about the Kingdom of God. Good governance is defined by what the Bible says.' Even the Muslims and Catholics really appreciated it, they were saying: 'We didn't know that good governance is instituted by God - for you to administer justice, to help the poor. You are not just public servants, you can be God's servant!' Toward the end, there was intense prayer from a leader from Assemblies of God (a charismatic type of church): 'Please stand up, this is the message of God for you today!' The participants were all crying and saying: 'Yeah, we will commit, we will commit.' And the very Mayor, maybe in his late twenties or early thirties, said: 'I want to replicate this in my place. This is beautiful.'

Ph11, an Evangelical lecturer in politics, said that:

> In 10 years the Mayor of Marikina, who is now the Metro-Manila Governor, changed the political culture of Marikina. It's a very small, very clean community, like the Singapore of the Philippines. When you look at him and his wife, it's because they take their spirituality seriously. The national scene doesn't look too good, but in local government we have a lot of Mayors who did very well.

Robert Nacianceno (Ph23), who was working for this reform-minded Metro-Manila Governor at the time of interview, felt it is easier to improve governance at local than at national level, and that his Evangelical faith had made a difference in his work:

> It should be easier for local government to implement a decision that there should be good governance, because they have local autonomy, they have their own constituency, they can decide how to spend their own funding ... Before I started in 2005, I asked God that I'd be able to do my job in a godly way. At first I felt like Daniel entering the lion's den. But God handled the situation for Daniel and I am pleasantly surprised that some of the things that we hoped to achieve, God has made ways of surpassing those things, to my own amazement and awe. We're able to do ten times more than we used to, because God has given us people of skill. The guy who is in charge of finance is a Methodist, and the one who is in charge of planning is also a Christian.

Promoting Civic Oversight

Evangelical informants mentioned a variety of activities aimed at promoting civic oversight. They include awareness-raising through prayer bulletins, educating voters and citizens about their rights, and organising micro-finance schemes to free rural communities from economic and political control by local oligarchs.

Ph5, a member of staff of a Christian anti-corruption NGO, described how she had used prayer bulletins to get Evangelicals interested in advocacy:

> The Evangelical community was very conservative in the early '80s. So to get them to be interested in national issues I produced a prayer bulletin. It's one way of slowly educating the church, to pray for our country. It's not confrontational, because when they hear about advocacy they get afraid: 'Oh, we're going to get in touch with a lot of radical issues, we are not interested in that.' But this goes with the flow of the life of a church. Who's going to argue about prayer? Some people would say: 'I never knew the gravity of the situation in our country', so that's already a good response at that time. I started with sex and violence in the media, because it's a moral issue. I would expect churches would easily write on that, because it's a moral issue. Maybe if I will advocate for an issue like human rights violations, it's harder.

Election fraud is widely seen as an important area for combating corruption. Ph16, a leader of the Christian Reformed World Relief Committee, described how he thinks the focus of Evangelicals in relation to elections has changed over time:

> For many years we asked: 'Which leader will be nearest to biblical requirements for a leader?' but we were not changing anything. So now we say 'Let's continue doing that, but now look at the systems'. For example we'd like to look at the list of voters in a community and mobilise the community to clean that list, then engage in the vote counting. In Mindanao the churches were very interested to be involved politically. More than 200 key leaders in one city who were Evangelicals came to that workshop. If we can put these things together and focus on certain communities who are ready, people will say: 'This community managed to have clean elections'.

Ph12, an Evangelical attorney, described the education of Evangelical voters, in preparation for the mid-term election (in May 2007), as a 'massive mobilization'. As one part of this, World Vision was partnering with the Alliance of Christian Development Agencies to run voters' education workshops for Evangelicals. Ph9 described them thus:

> The workshops focus on the biblical framework for good governance, in the light of God's kingdom. We highlight why Christians should participate in elections and advocate for clean and honest elections in the light of God's word. We use

the Election Code to raise awareness about what's acceptable and what's prohibited, for example the size and location of advertisements.

In addition to their strategy of converting senior government officials, FOCIG runs public information campaigns:

> We inform the public about the procedures you have to follow when you transact business for critical services from the government, like getting your passport, your driver's licence, a loan from the government banks, filing your taxes, starting a business. We tell people that they have rights, that they can contest them based on the rule of law, that they don't have to resort to under-the-table transactions.

Melba Maggay, Director of ISACC, described her approach as 'empowering the grassroots' which to her as a Christian is 'the only way you can conserve the concept of People Power':

> ISACC is developing an infra-culture for governance. It means teaching people to be a little more conscious of their rights; changing the culture of 'learning to be in your place', that we learned from the Spaniards. We say to people: 'We are all equal in the image of God'. Before, people didn't think they had rights, but increasingly there's a lot of organising happening in these communities. It begins to change some of our voting patterns, some of our cultural behaviour which is not conducive to democratic habits. It is not yet influencing the power structures; I think that will take another generation. But at least you have a more aware citizenry, you have plenty of people's organisations and they're very articulate, getting assertive increasingly about their rights.

Evangelical views on Catholic and liberal
Protestant efforts to oppose corruption

Melba Maggay thought that although the Catholic Church was 'a major instrument of injustice during the Spanish times' it has changed 'in the last 25 years or so':

> After we threw out the Spaniards and started Filipinising, it was under pressure, particularly when the American Protestants came in the 1900s. And they started having American Catholic missionaries also - before, they used to get just Spanish and Belgian priests. It forced the Catholic Church to purify their ranks, to re-think their identity as a church.

Three Evangelical informants felt that in recent decades the Catholic Church has performed better than Evangelicals in challenging corrupt leaders in the Philippines. Ph11, an Evangelical lecturer in politics, commended Catholics for being 'more politically engaged than the Evangelical sector'. Ph17, an Evangelical professor of history, commended the Catholic Church for being 'very strong about addressing corruption – trying to find ways of monitoring and minimising corruption, for example by tracking the purchase of textbooks, looking into the Dept of Education, tracking the nitty-gritty details'. Jovita Salonga felt that 'the Catholic Church has been more resolute, more determined, than the Evangelical churches in regard to pursuing good governance'. He attributed this to division between different denominations: 'Evangelicals in UCCP were against Marcos, but the Methodist church by and large supported him, because the Methodist church was more influential in the north, where Marcos was born'. Only one informant, Dolores Español, expressed a negative view about the way the Catholic Church uses its influence in relation to governance: 'The majority of the members of CBCP favour the current Administration, despite the serious allegation of corruption, and very few – just a handful of the members of that big group - are opposed to the Administration's corruption.'

Likewise, several Evangelical informants thought that liberal Protestants, represented by NCCP, had performed better in this regard than Evangelicals. Ph11, an Evangelical lecturer in politics, commended NCCP for being 'far, far more advanced when it comes to political and social engagement in the social field' and Ph4, an Evangelical author, observed that 'the liberal Christian groups in this country are more advanced as regards social justice and social concern'. Several Evangelical informants commented that socio-political involvement tends to be seen as 'Left-leaning', and therefore suspect. According to Ph9, the churches of NCCP are 'not accepted by the main Evangelical denominations'. They are 'more into advocacy and community development, but the problem with them is they are Left-leaning, and not many of us like to work with them, because of that label'. Ph16, a leader of the Christian Reformed World Relief Committee, said: 'NCCP have a history that they were identified with the Left, which creates a divide amongst the Protestants'. Reflecting this Evangelical tendency to label political involvement as Left-wing and suspect, Melba Maggay, Director of ISACC, recalled that:

> In ISACC we were part of the anti-Marcos resistance from day one – which the Evangelical church couldn't understand. It's alright to feed the poor, but if you're political, you're a Communist. After campaigning against the Clark Air Force base, people asked me 'What kind of Christian are you? Because we have heard that those who are born again get born against all that's progressive in this country'.

Ph3, an Evangelical theologian, felt that 'more Christians are aware that we should aim for equity, for social justice. But in terms of really doing it, it's still very few and far between'. Ph4, an Evangelical author, agreed that 'there is awareness, but the implementation of it, the commitment to it, is lacking'. Ph9, an Evangelical who works for the Alliance of Christian Development Agencies, said:

> We have not been able to strike a balance between being faithful to the Word and being able to create an impact in the community, without being isolated. To be pure, we always think in terms of being isolated, so we're not part of the

community. We're just gathered there in the church, without any influence or impact in the community - though slowly that's changing.

Ph16, a leader of the Christian Reformed World Relief Committee, said: 'Some churches are unresponsive to the situation in their community, they create walls to protect themselves from the realities. They say "There's the Red Cross, the UN, the government. Why should we do that?" So the community remains poor.' Regarding the nature of Evangelical social involvement, Ph5, a member of staff of a Christian anti-corruption NGO, said:

> More Christian NGOs are being organized and responding to social issues, and there are now Evangelical churches that are also into social issues. But I think most of them are still in the social welfare type of intervention: feeding programmes for the malnourished children, medical missions, helping the street children through feeding - but not really going to the root causes.

Shifts in Evangelical theology relevant to socio-political involvement

The impression formed from interviewing a variety of Evangelical informants was that they feel they have inherited from the USA a dualistic theology that discourages socio-political involvement; that some Evangelical leaders have been working for a generation to develop a different theology that supports socio-political involvement; but that they remain a minority in Evangelical circles.

In Melba Maggay's view, 'the Philippine church has captured a whole theological tradition that the gospel is for the soul, so we shouldn't have anything to do with politics'. Ph3, an Evangelical theologian, saw the USA as the source of this tradition: 'The seminaries were founded by missionaries from the USA and many of them do not have a background in the importance of Christians in society'. Ph4, an Evangelical author, commented on the influence of American and Chinese donors and teachers:

> In the conservative wing of Protestantism in this country, the issue still is the priority of the Great Commission over the Great Commandment. A lot depends on the theological orientation of the professors from the USA, because their theology is primarily focused on personal salvation, evangelism, church growth – but not in the area of social justice and advocacy. Chinese donors are very particular that the seminaries they are supporting should focus on church planting or evangelism. The moment the seminary fails to emphasise missions and evangelism, the Chinese donors will cut off the funds.

Some Evangelical leaders were upbeat about how far the Evangelical churches had grown towards embracing a theology that supports socio-political involvement. Melba Maggay, Director of ISACC, said that:

> Today, the church is getting more mature, finding its way out of the dualism. Among the thinking elements that theology is gone, among both Catholics and

Evangelicals. I think we have raised a critical mass now of serious Christians who see social involvement as part of their Christian duty. You still have tropical outposts of western pietism, but these are very small pockets now. The emerging leadership in our churches, both Evangelical and charismatic Catholic, now has a more integrated theology, and there's a great deal of practice as well. You have a whole generation of young leaders who were influenced by ISACC. Most of the major theologians that are emerging are ISACC people. We're still a minority within the Evangelical churches, but it's a sizeable, powerful and articulate minority.

Ph7, an Evangelical theologian, was similarly optimistic, but focused more on international forces that had brought change:

The change in attitudes among Evangelicals is palpable. Thirty years ago we'd have been regarded as liberals. I'm sure that the Lausanne Congress[8] has had a great deal to do with it - 1974, it's almost like yesterday. The Lausanne Covenant has been widely read and the mainline Evangelical denominations here would recognize that it is an historic document, so they would embrace the twin mission duties of not only evangelism but also socio-political involvement, which is to be salt of the earth and light of the world. Even the very right-wing, fundamentalist groups are beginning to thaw.

Likewise Ph11, an Evangelical lecturer in politics, thought that 'there is now a growing consciousness among faith-based Christian development organisations, as well as churches, on the need for more political and social engagement - that it is important to also educate our pastors in integral mission'.

However, several other Evangelical informants were less optimistic about the extent to which the Evangelical sector has changed. Ph3, an Evangelical theologian, said that:

Through ISACC's work, some churches have opened their minds to the importance of social work and justice. But most of our seminaries have closed their eyes to this - it's always the evangelistic, not the social, side of the gospel. I could not imagine seminaries or small Bible schools discussing the importance of social action.

Likewise Ph4, an Evangelical author, thought that 'the conservative Protestant community is still very behind, because their main concern is

---

[8] The 1974 Lausanne Congress was a gathering in the Swiss Alps of some 2,300 Evangelical leaders from over 150 nations. It produced the Lausanne Covenant, which includes the following statement on Christian social responsibility: 'We affirm that God is both the Creator and the Judge of all people. We therefore should share his concern for justice and reconciliation throughout human society and for the liberation of men and women from every kind of oppression' (Lausanne Movement 1974).

evangelism and church growth. In the area of social justice and advocacy I do not see any bright future. I don't see any trend of increasing'. Ph6, an Evangelical mission mobiliser, described how fellow Evangelicals had reacted when he helped to found Kapatiran, a new political party that seeks to promote Christian values:

> Evangelicals, by their theology, cannot imagine that you can be in politics and be a good Christian at the same time. Their image of politics is just so negative and dirty that they consider anyone who is a politician is corrupted by the system. They think that the separation of church and state also means the separation of Christianity and politics.

In the opinion of Ph19, an Evangelical who works for a secular anti-corruption NGO:

> There's only a minority of Christians in this country who would like to engage in good politics or good governance, who believe that part of their Christianity is a call to be involved in society. The belief that 'politics is evil, Christians should not be involved in that, Christians should just pray about all this evil' - that is a huge problem amongst Evangelicals in the country. Young people are being taught the theology of 'You can grow as a Christian and not care about the world. God doesn't care whether you're helping the needy people around you; as long as you're not hurting other people, as long as you're doing Bible study and praying, that is alright' ... You need a pastor who's going to tell the congregation: 'When you do not care about the poor around you and when you don't care about society, you're actually committing sin'. But no pastor would say that. It's very difficult to break that theology. It's strongly driven from the USA.

Ph22, a leader in the National Council of Churches of the Philippines (NCCP), said that 'a theology of "We don't care about this world because it's not our home anyway" is strong in the Evangelical community here. Some of them think we are so radical. I guess we are more prophetic'.

PCEC's approach to advocacy

Shortly before my visit to the Philippines Bishop Efraim Tendero, the General Secretary of PCEC, had celebrated his 50th birthday. President Gloria Arroyo had attended his birthday party and many Evangelicals were talking about it. Bishop Efraim was keen to give me a photo of the two of them together at his party, and said: 'We are praying for her and saying "these are our concerns for this nation"'. This close relationship between the Bishop and the President was reflected in Bishop Tendero's acceptance of an invitation to sit on the Presidential Commission for Charter Change. The Bishop described his participation on the Commission as 'one of our strongest, very concrete advocacies'. Ph14, an Evangelical bishop, summarised the conclusions of the Commission as follows:

There are three structural problems that we have found to be causing corruption and poverty in this nation. One is the system of government: the American Presidential bicameral system leads to too much corruption, so we are proposing to shift to a unicameral Parliamentary system. Number two is a shift of the structure of government from centralised to more decentralized, leading towards federalised government, strengthening local autonomy. And the third reform is taking away the restriction that foreigners can only own 40% of a big business, and they cannot own land. That really discourages investors, because they don't have full control of their business, and therefore only the few rich Filipinos can operate big businesses in the country.

Ph13, a senior Evangelical church leader, gave the following perspective on the theology that informs Bishop Efraim's involvement on the Commission:

The Philippine Evangelical theology of evil is basically centred on Satan and evil people. We have not studied the depths and impact of structural evil. We tend to fight evil, whether it's personal or structural, from the personal transformation side. Bishop Efraim has initiated a download among Evangelical leaders of what it is to address corruption in this country - developing a theology of structural evil. Evangelicals don't have enough understanding that it's the Executive that is lacking political will to impose reforms that would benefit Christians, Muslims, everybody. The church in the Philippines needs a healthy shove into the area of understanding public square advocacy, that is, engaging our faith while we're waiting for the coming of the Lord. Not just evangelism, but also discipleship, re-shaping the value systems so that this society can truly be the kingdom of the Lord in this world.

Ph14 described the results he hopes to see from this approach:

Politicians will take notice of the need to interact with Evangelicals. And that's very important, because after the election we want to call them to account for their programmes, their policies, their governance. By 2015 we want to see Evangelicals on the map in terms of addressing poverty and corruption, and seeing measurable results.

One Evangelical informant, Ph16, spoke positively about Bishop Efraim's involvement on the Commission:

There are many opportunities for PCEC to influence the Administration: there are now Evangelicals put in different Presidential Commissions, including poverty alleviation, for example. That also allows the churches to have access to development funds or development support. For example, we have a new project that we are doing in Mindanao in alliance with PCEC and through agreement with local government to build a thousand houses in a place where there are displaced people, informal dwellers. We wouldn't have done that if we were seen as an adversary of the government.

However, most informants, including most of the Evangelicals, expressed concerns. Several felt that Evangelicals in general were being seen as supporters of President Arroyo and were concerned about that. Ph5, a member of staff of a Christian anti-corruption NGO, said: 'PCEC is labelled by local churches as pro-government in a lot of ways, close to President Arroyo. People I talk to are not happy with that'. Ph16 said: 'From the perspective of many Evangelicals, PCEC is very closely aligned with the current administration. Maybe the leadership is not supported by the constituency'. Ph12, an Evangelical attorney, said: 'Several times I've informed Bishop Efraim that most of those in the Evangelical community think he is being too intimate with the Arroyo Administration. I told him if he really intends to be involved actively in politics, then maybe he has to consider stepping down from the leadership of PCEC'. Ph19, an Evangelical who works for a secular anti-corruption NGO, said:

> It's good that Bishop Tendero was there in the Constitutional Commission, at least there was a representation for Evangelicals. He could probably provide a biblical perspective in crafting the Constitution - but I think it has been too close for him. He's very much identified with the President. If you go a gathering of activists or NGO workers, and they realise that you're an Evangelical, they ask you: 'So, you're a supporter of the President?' That's the impression that people are getting. As a leader representing the Evangelical community, I think he has to be more careful.

Ph22, a leader in NCCP, said: 'I heard one of the pastors who's a member of PCEC saying "When Bishop Efraim says he's for Charter Change, that's not the position of PCEC. We're against it"'.

A second widely voiced concern about Bishop Efraim's proximity to President Arroyo is that he has been co-opted. Ph6, an Evangelical mission mobiliser, said:

> President Arroyo co-opted Bishop Efraim just before the 2004 election. She came to his office to get his support, and he had a chance to share the Evangelism Explosion with her, getting her to accept the Lord, and all this. And I'm sure it's for the hundredth time she did it. But he felt obligated now to consider her a disciple who he has to nurture. From his perspective he's just following up a person who he led to the Lord, but from her perspective I'm sure she's just using him. After the 2004 election President Arroyo tried her best to bring PCEC on her side and from my own analysis she succeeded. She got Efraim Tendero to be a member of the Constitutional Commission to change the Charter.

Ph3, an Evangelical theologian, said: 'The President co-opted him by appointing him as a member of the Commission on Charter Change. From there I could sense that he could not speak, he could not be a prophet'. Ph17, an Evangelical professor of history, commented that 'PCEC are so sickeningly pro-government. How can Bishop Efraim have sold himself to this administration?' Dolores Español said:

> Bishop Tendero's closeness to Arroyo will have no spiritual impact. That is baloney. She is just cynical. The Administration hope that being identified with a religious leader might bring some advantage to them. Their interest is just to get votes. Unless you change the leadership, no amount of Charter Change will ever improve governance. The people who are going to implement the Charter Change have violated the existing Constitution with impunity. The Charter Change is designed simply to hide the sins of the present Administration. Although PCEC now and then make pronouncements regarding corruption, they are not really very determined in reaching the point where these corrupt practices would be divulged to the public and condemned. I believe Bishop Efraim and others in PCEC are informed about the situation but they are at risk of being hauled to court for libel if they criticise the Administration. Or they get killed. They are aware of the risks of taking a strong position regarding corruption.

Ph22, a leader in NCCP, said: 'How can Bishop Tendero explain his conduct with President Arroyo? At one point he said "The church has to provide her with some spiritual guidance". I guess that's how he tried to rationalise the whole thing'. He went on to say: 'Bishop Efraim may have good intentions, but I doubt if President Arroyo does. She's a very wily politician. I hope the Bishop will be on guard, in order that PCEC will not be used for her political ends'. Ph24, Director of a secular anti-corruption NGO, said: 'Anyone who aligns themselves with the current Administration is getting the kiss of death. Religious groups will align themselves with Presidents and Administrations – and invariably the experience has been bad'.

In summary, the balance of opinion among these informants was that the leadership of PCEC has been co-opted by President Arroyo.

Evangelical silence in relation to extra-judicial killings

A leading news item during my first visit to the Philippines, in February and March 2007, concerned responsibility for hundreds of extra-judicial killings that had occurred since President Arroyo came to power in 2001. In February 2007 a government-backed inquiry, headed by the retired Philippine judge Jose Melo, found that 'elements in the military' were responsible for the deaths of some activists. In the same month Philip Alston, the UN expert on extrajudicial executions, concluded that: 'The Armed Forces of the Philippines remains in a state of almost total denial of its need to respond effectively and authentically to the significant number of killings which have been convincingly attributed to them.'

At the time of my visit PCEC was responding to these killings very differently from NCCP. The liberal Protestants who belong to NCCP are much more likely than Evangelicals to be politically active, and hence become targets themselves. Ph8, a member of staff of the National Council of Churches in the

Philippines, described the numbers of their members who were among the dead:

> UCCP is one of our most progressive churches; it's had the most number of killings. Of the 25 church people who have been killed, four of them are UCCP clergy and 11 are members of their mandated organisations or local church councils. All in all ten clergy and 15 lay workers or lay members have been killed. One of them was a former NCCP staff, one of my colleagues when I was in the parliamentary programme.

No informants were aware of any Evangelicals who had been killed. Ph9, an Evangelical who works for the Alliance of Christian Development Agencies, said: 'We are not a threat to the government so we don't get the same kind of treatment that NCCP does. When killings are done they are very vocal about it, unlike the Evangelicals'. Bishop Tendero had asked Ph7, an Evangelical theologian, to draft a document to say: 'This is where PCEC stands in relation to extra-judicial killings'. Ph7 described the background to Bishop Tendero's request:

> Bishop Efraim has access to the President. May be he is too closely associated with her. I brought that up with him six months ago. I said 'You must talk to the President about these extra-judicial killings. We cannot keep our silence'. The Bishop may feel that his hands are tied, partly because he's too closely associated with President Arroyo.

Ph16 said: 'PCEC can be limited in reacting to issues that confront the government directly, like the extra-judicial killings, because of the relationship with President Arroyo'. Ph11, an Evangelical lecturer in politics, said: 'I told Bishop Efraim directly that as a person of the church it is important to maintain a prophetic distance from the government'. Ph3, an Evangelical theologian, said:

> I'm disappointed with Bishop Efraim. I think he has sided too much with President Arroyo's Administration, so that he has lost his credibility to speak on critical issues, against what the President or her government is doing. So we don't hear from now. NCCP has done its part in speaking out against human rights abuses, but PCEC has not done their part, their voice has not been heard. Silent.

Summary

The reputation of Evangelicals for honest behaviour

Evangelical leaders in the Philippines think that Evangelicals have a reputation for honest behaviour. This view was shared by Dolores Español, Chairperson of Transparency International in the Philippines (an Evangelical who was formerly a Catholic) and Ph24, the Director of a secular anti-corruption NGO (a Catholic). Several Evangelical leaders were candid about failures of

Evangelicals to live up to their reputation, for example by paying bribes to escape a fine for a traffic violation, but this did not negate their view that the Evangelical minority is generally regarded as being more trustworthy than the Catholic majority.

Preaching about corruption

A prominent example of this strategy in the Philippines is FOCIG's strategy of trying to convert national government officials to Evangelical faith, then teach them to provide excellent public service. It is being used among the senior ranks of the army and the police. One general who was interviewed (Ph26) described instances in which he felt his new-found Evangelical faith had led him to resist misuse of public resources, such as overpricing of military equipment and using government vehicles to campaign for the President's election campaign.

Evangelical leaders in the Philippines hold very diverse views about the value of this strategy for reducing corruption. Assessments ranged from seeing it as 'the best contribution of the Evangelical community to eradicating corruption' (BJ Sebastian, an Evangelical businessman) to 'you can hardly transform a nation by making everyone goody two shoes' (Ph13, a senior Evangelical church leader). Specific concerns of Evangelical leaders about the FOCIG strategy include the risk of being co-opted by, and then being used to legitimize, corrupt governments; and the extent to which corruption can be reduced without systemic changes such as amending the Constitution.

Reforming government by having Evangelicals inside government

While the approach of FOCIG borders on this strategy, Evangelical leaders described two other strategies whereby Evangelicals might seek to improve governance through occupying positions within government: elect an Evangelical President; and encourage Evangelicals in local government to apply Christian values to their work. Evangelical leaders' assessments of the attempt by Brother Eddie Villanueva (a prominent Evangelical and leader of the Jesus Is Lord Church) to run for President in 2004 were mostly negative. There was greater optimism about the potential for Evangelicals to influence government at local level.

Promoting civic oversight

Many Evangelical leaders felt they have inherited from the USA a theology that discourages socio-political involvement, and some suggested that the Catholic Church and liberal Protestants have been more vocal than Evangelicals in challenging corruption. Some Evangelical leaders had been working for a generation to develop a different theology that supports socio-political involvement, and felt they had made some progress; but they also thought they remain a minority in Evangelical circles.

The leadership of the Philippine Council of Evangelical Churches is part of this minority. Their approach to advocacy has involved developing a relationship with President Arroyo and accepting an invitation to join her Commission on Charter Change. They believed their contribution to the Commission would help bring constitutional changes that are essential for reducing corruption. However, most Evangelical informants thought that President Arroyo has simply co-opted the leadership of PCEC, making it difficult for them to criticise her over issues such as extra-judicial killings.

Kenya Country Case Study

Introduction

Situated on the equator on Africa's east coast, Kenya has been called the cradle of humanity as it is home to some of the earliest remains of homo sapiens. Arab traders began frequenting the Kenya coast before the first century AD, and Islamic Arab and Persian settlements sprouted along the coast by the eighth century. During the first millennium AD, Nilotic and Bantu peoples started to move into the region, and the latter now comprises three-quarters of Kenya's population.

The colonial history of Kenya dates from the Berlin Conference of 1885, when the European powers first partitioned East Africa into spheres of influence. In 1895 Britain established Kenya as a Protectorate, mainly because of the decision to build a railway from Mombasa to Lake Victoria. Tribal lands were guaranteed, but all unoccupied territory became crown land. By the end of World War I there were more than 9,000 Europeans in Kenya, and much of the fertile highlands had been reserved for continual white settlement on long-term leases. Unable to sustain themselves by farming, many migrated to the towns in search of work. In 1920 Kenya was established as a British colony.

Africans were prohibited from direct political participation until 1944, when a nationalist organization, the Kenya African Union, was formed and campaigned for the redistribution of land. In 1947 Jomo Kenyatta, a prominent Gikuyu, became its leader. From October 1952 to January 1960, Kenya was under a state of emergency arising from the Mau Mau rebellion against British colonial rule, and Kenyatta was imprisoned for alleged complicity. However, the colonial authorities had to face the inevitability of change. The first direct elections for Africans to the Legislative Council took place in 1957. Kenya became independent in 1963, with Kenyatta, by then leader of the Kenya African National Union (KANU), as the first President. By the late 1960s Kenya was in practice a one-party state. Land redistribution, though biased in favour of the Gikuyu, quietened much of the clamour of Kenya's traditional leaders and Kenyatta's moderate, stable government attracted large-scale foreign investment.

His successor, Daniel arap Moi (a Kalenjin, and an Evangelical lay teacher in the Africa Inland Church) initially followed the same moderate political and economic policies. However, in June 1982 he made Kenya constitutionally a one-party state. Two months later an attempt by air force units to oust him was crushed by loyal troops. Facing a rising tide of criticism Moi jailed many of his leading Kenyan critics, but by 1991 the suspension of western economic aid and pressure from Kenyan churches, especially the National Council of

Churches of Kenya (NCCK), forced him to legalize opposition parties. Moi won a multi-party election in 1992 which was mired in a torrent of ethnic violence, much of it directed against the Gikuyu who had settled around the rift Valley and the coast. The decline in Kenya's economy under Moi's rule, after years of rapid growth between 1963 and 1973, have been attributed largely to 'corruption, mismanagement and structural distortions of the economy'.[1]

Table 6.1 Kenya values for selected indicators

Indicator (year)	Value	Rank, among the 77 countries included in the quantitative analysis
GNI per capita (2003)	$430	68 (Rank 1 = greatest GNP per capita)
Percentage of the population living on less than $1.25 a day at 2005 international prices (2005)	20%	60 (Rank 1= lowest percentage on <$1.25)
Gini coefficient of consumption (1997)	0.44	52 (Rank 1= lowest Gini coefficient)
Mining and large plantation or farm exports, as percentage of total exports (2000)	38%	60 (Rank 1= lowest percentage)
Control of corruption (pessimistic view) (2000)	-2.04	76 (Rank 1= greatest positive value)
Government revenue x corruption control (2000)	-40	72 (Rank 1= greatest positive value)

The 2002 election was won by the National Rainbow Coalition, a coalition of opposition parties and a KANU break-away faction. Mwai Kibaki (a Gikuyu and a Catholic) was elected the country's third President. Despite President Kibaki's pledge to tackle corruption, some donors estimated that up to $1bn was lost to graft between 2002 and 2005.[2] Six months after this field visit Kenya held presidential, parliamentary, and local government elections on 27 December 2007. When Mwai Kibaki was declared as the winner of the presidential election violence erupted in different parts of Kenya as supporters

---

[1]Peter Ndege 'Decline of the Economy, 1973-95' in Ogot and Ochieng (eds) *Kenya: the Making of a Nation. A hundred years of Kenya's history, 1895-1995* (Maseno Kenya: Institute of Research and Postgraduate Studies, Maseno University 2000), 221.
[2] British Broadcasting Corporation's 'Kenya country profile' Available at http://news.bbc.co.uk/1/hi/world/africa/country_profiles/1024563.stm Accessed 5 May 2010.

of opposition candidate Raila Odinga and supporters of Kibaki clashed with police and each other. The post-election crisis left about 1,300 Kenyans dead, and about 300,000 people were displaced.

Table 6.1 shows Kenya's position in respect of some selected indicators, including those relevant to the analysis of economic inequality in Chapter 2.

The author of the Kenya chapter in the 'Evangelicalism and Democracy' series includes Pentecostals within the Evangelical fold:

> Kenyan evangelicals may be divided into two categories. First, there are the leaders of the mainstream Protestant churches, who are also active in ecumenical bodies: the National Council of Churches of Kenya (NCCK), the All Africa Conference of Churches (AACC), and the World Council of Churches (WCC). They are heirs to the evangelical tradition founded by the early Protestant missionaries. Moreover, all mainstream Protestant churches are strongly influenced by the East African Revival, which has strong evangelical connections. Secondly, there are those who constitute the EFK. [3] With the exception of the Africa Inland Church, which has been in Kenya since 1895, these ministries arrived in Kenya within the last thirty-five years. The most numerous component within this category is Pentecostalism, which combines biblical orthodoxy with a charismatic form of worship and an emphasis on spiritual healing ... Since the founders of all Kenyan Protestant churches came from an evangelical background, this paper adopts an inclusive definition of evangelicalism that embraces all Protestant Christians. [4]

As for the proportions of the population in the major Christian categories, different sources agree that a little under one quarter of Kenyans are Roman Catholic. Following Karanja's practice of including Pentecostals in the Evangelical category gives a total of either 50.2 per cent or 52.9 per cent who were in the broad category of Evangelical in 2000. [5] Thus Kenya is a largely Christian country in which Evangelicals (broadly defined) outnumber Roman Catholics by approximately two to one. The largest Evangelical denomination is the Anglican Church of Kenya (ACK), to which nine per cent of Kenyans were affiliated in AD 2000. [6]

---

[3] By the time of my visit in 2007 the Evangelical Fellowship of Kenya (EFK) had changed its name to the Evangelical Alliance of Kenya (EAK).

[4] John Karanja 'Evangelical attitudes towards democracy in Kenya' in Terence Ranger (ed) *Evangelical Christianity and Democracy in Africa* (Oxford: Oxford University Press 2009), 67.

[5] Barrett, Kurian, Johnson eds *World Christian Encyclopedia;* Johnstone, Mandryk, Johnstone *Operation World.*

[6] Johnstone, Mandryk, Johnstone *Operation World.*

Table 6.2 Percentage of Kenyans estimated to belong to various Christian categories

Estimated percentage of the population in each group in AD 2000	Barrett et al. (2001)	Johnstone et al. (2001)
Christians	79.3	78.6
Roman Catholics	23.3	22.6
Evangelicals	22.4	35.8
Pentecostals / charismatics	27.8	17.1
Evangelicals plus Pentecostals / charismatics	50.2	52.9

The material in this chapter regarding the relationship between Evangelicals and corruption in Kenya is based on my interviews with 19 key informants in June 2007. Table C.2 in Appendix C gives brief details of the occupation, age, gender and religious affiliation of the key informants, and the dates and locations of the interviews.

The Reputation of Evangelicals for Honest Behaviour

Many Evangelical leaders described corruption within the church as a common problem. K2, an Anglican bishop, said:

> Corruption is found even in the church itself - in the elections of bishops and of church elders; and also with the money - it may not be banked. The corrupt people are members of the church, and some of them sit in the front pews. And some of the corrupt money finds its way in the offering bags, and also in fund-raising for constructing churches, schools and other developments. This makes it very difficult to know how to deal with, but we hope that the Lord will speak to those people. We are also corrupt. But this does not mean that we are done. Always, in any group, there is what we call a remnant who will make the truth a virtue.

K8, another Anglican bishop, reflected that 'I don't know whether we have a solution to corruption because even we in the church are caught up in the same mess'.[7] David Gitari, a former Anglican Archbishop of Kenya, said:

> If you go to people employed by the government for services they demand money and they think it is quite in order because they are spending a bit of their time to

---

[7] Gifford (1998:313) mentions that in the early 1990s the Anglican Church had two or three messy lawsuits before the Supreme Court: 'This means that the Church of the Province of Kenya is seen to have little authority to challenge the government over tribalism, spoils politics, unaccountability, transparency – so much so that some have suggested that its troubles have been fomented by security services precisely for this reason.'

help you, or they are helping you to jump the queue. In some cases even those with a Christian faith will ask for bribes, without seeing any contradiction.

K9, an Anglican Diocesan secretary, expressed similar views: 'Those who demand bribes are members of our church, but they think it's OK, because if my MP is doing it, if the Minister is grabbing land, it's OK.'[8]

While speaking to an audience of Evangelical bishops and pastors K5, a leader of the Evangelical Alliance of Kenya (EAK), suggested that petty theft of donated resources is common: 'During the distribution of food aid last year, how many of us did not take a bag or two of milk from the lorry for our families, and did not think of it as stealing?' When describing his experience of corrupt practices within the churches K19, an Evangelical lawyer experienced in working with churches, first mentioned nepotism in church appointments, then described a variety of other examples:

A major aspect of corruption is tax exemption. A good number of the clergy, across the board, would import, say, musical instruments worth KSh 5 million in the name of the church, exempt from duty, but when they landed here the clergy would sell them to a shop. And some Pentecostal pastors are well-to-do people, but they are not paying any income tax at all. I'd say that is corruption, because they were defrauding government of its taxes. Income tax is not a grey area. Another aspect of corruption in churches is procurement and disposal of assets. Some of the churches do not have a system and policies for this, so someone who is supposed to supply goods worth KSh 1 million will inflate the goods to KSh 1.5 million. However, there may not be too much bribery within the church, because it's easily identifiable as a sin.

Karobia, a leader of a small Evangelical NGO called Christians for a Just Society (CFJS),[9] referred to the way that pastors enrich themselves at the expense of their followers: 'Some of the richest pastors in this country are those that are working among the poorest people, preaching the prosperity gospel[10] and enriching themselves. People are being cheated on the tithing system, the same way they have been cheated on taxes.'

---

[8] This popular attitude to corruption reflects public perception of the Kenyan elite. According to Kibwana et al. (2001:6): 'Evidence from both documented literature and the views of citizens points to the general consensus that the Kenyan leadership does not just lack the moral courage and political will to fight corruption but views corruption as a legitimate way of life and virtually condones it.'

[9] CFJS aims to bring a Christian influence into the political arena, through encouraging upright people to stand for election and encouraging all people to vote. It is chaired by Dennis Tongoi, Executive Director of Church Mission Society, Africa. Among its other activities, CFJS has published a book (Tongoi and Kariithi 2005) on the role of the church in social transformation in Kenya.

[10] In the prosperity gospel, church members are taught that God will bless them with riches if they first give their money to the pastor.

The independent Evangelical and Pentecostal
churches are seen as the most corrupt

The picture suggested by several informants is that the independent Evangelical and Pentecostal churches have greater problems with corruption than the Catholic Church or the mainline Protestant churches. K5, a leader of EAK, said: 'The Ministry of Justice is targeting Evangelical churches for regulation because there are known to be problems of corruption.' K18, a leader of the Fellowship of Christian Unions, said that 'the bigger and wealthier Pentecostal churches are among the ones that are doing worst in terms of fighting corruption.' K19, an Evangelical lawyer experienced in working with churches, said:

> The mainline churches don't have problems with paying income tax because they have structures and a salary scale. But the Pentecostal churches do not have those things, so the pastors pay themselves whatever they pay themselves. And conflict of interests, for example where the one who is supplying to the church has a relationship with the bishop or the pastor, happens mainly in the Pentecostal churches because they don't have systems – though the mainline churches also have that problem, especially for employment.

K17, a leader of the Ecumenical Centre for Justice and Peace, also identified employment as an area for corruption in all except the Catholic Church: 'Apart from the Catholic Church, I think all the Protestant churches - Methodists, Presbyterians, Anglicans - have a problem when it comes to offering posts; but the Catholic Church would not be involved as much.'

K11, a senior leader of the Catholic Church in Kenya, was unusual among the key informants. Whereas the others were quick to acknowledge problems of corruption within their own churches, he said: 'We cannot afford in any way to be corrupt in our ministry. Therefore we must begin from inside so that we can be fairly sure that we will not stand accused.' It was unclear whether this reflected a degree of confidence about the reputation of the Catholic Church in Kenya, or merely reluctance to discuss any problems. The latter interpretation is suggested by his earlier comment that 'When you speak for the Catholic Church you have to be very discreet, and I would not want to draw a judgement on anybody.'

Loss of moral authority

Given the perceived extent of corruption in 2007 within many churches, it is not surprising that several informants thought that the church has lost the moral authority to speak out about it.[11] K17, a leader of the Ecumenical Centre for Justice and Peace, lamented that 'the church should be at the forefront to fight

---

[11] It is important to note that this was a fall from a considerable height. Gifford (2009:58) writes that 'in the Moi years ... the political leaders were largely discredited ... By contrast, religious leaders enjoyed enormous moral authority.'

corruption, but corrupt practices in the church make it lose the moral authority to fight corruption. Even in the education that I do to fight corruption, we lack moral authority'. Karobia, a leader of CFJS, expressed the inevitable consequence of the churches' loss of moral authority:

> Even though I firmly believe the church is God's agent for transformation, I'm very sceptical about whether the church will actually achieve that, because the church seems to almost always follow society. Corruption in the public arena led to corruption in the church, so I'm really sceptical about the church providing the solutions. It makes me very sad to know respected Christian leaders who have compromised: their organisations are now being investigated for corruption, and you're thinking, 'these are people who we thought were together with us'.

Symonds Akivaga, Senior Lecturer at the University of Nairobi, said: 'You see a lot of hypocrisy, people using the church and abusing the word of God. It is disturbing - you begin to wonder whether we believe in the same God'. K12, a Catholic lecturer in Law, said: 'Most leaders in the mainstream churches cannot easily address the people on any issue; they've lost credibility. The preachers don't have a moral platform; they have lost that moral ground'.

Perceived Causes of Corruption in Kenyan Churches

Material affluence modelled by western Christians, and fear of poverty

Several Evangelical leaders blamed corruption in Kenyan churches on material affluence modelled by western Christians. K2, an Anglican bishop, traced corruption to missionary roots: 'Corruption comes because people want to be rich. Most people in positions today in Africa were trained by missionaries in mission schools. They have seen the kind of life that westerners who were ruling this country used to lead.' K18, a leader of the Fellowship of Christian Unions (FOCUS), emphasised both the role of missionaries and of American broadcasters:

> A typical British missionary brought the Church of England to Kenya. The missionaries were generally fairly wealthy, they interacted with the colonial class, and they had to live at the level they had come from. Missionaries established schools and educated the people who took over government at independence. But they were taking over an aristocratic kind of system. All these early politicians, that was their education; they were made to long for a life where they had everything and they had servants. The life they had seen their masters living had now been given to them and they knew how to live it because they had seen it, and they longed for it.

> The church has remained looking out there. We are being educated by someone who is more affluent than us, who has the wealth to be able to send their message. Trinity Broadcasting Network (an American Evangelical broadcaster) has a very strong influence over churches in Kenya. The speaker will give examples about

when his automobile broke down, when he couldn't get his insurance, how his refrigerator was not working. And that has formed the mind of Kenyan Christians and Christian leaders. So now, picture this poor Kenyan who studied with a missionary, who came side by side with the colonialists. They have continued to get this same message. That's what we have here in Nairobi, that's the mentorship that has gone on.

Two Evangelical informants considered fear of poverty to be a cause of corruption. K3, a leader of the NCCK, said: 'Our preoccupation is fear of a future of poverty, so when you get into office your income doesn't matter; you are struggling to see if you can set aside something for later. So corruption is an expression of fear.' K2, an Anglican bishop, reflected that:

> Some of us were unable to have good houses, good clothes, good food, but through education you find that your standard has been raised. You get a job, and then you are afraid of drifting back to where you were. You are afraid for your children and your children's children – you don't want them to experience what you experienced. So the spirit of accumulation of wealth comes in, the desire to get rich quickly rather than step by step.

K1, a Programme Officer for Transparency International in Kenya, said: 'Coming from the experience of poverty in Africa, if you can get a way to move out of poverty then the end justifies the means. It's not usually through hard work; most of the time it's through corruption'. Perhaps related to the fear of poverty is the sense that wealth brings honour. K1 went on to say: 'The culture in Africa rewards people who have things, without questioning how they got them in the first place. When you go to church or the mosque you are given the first row, the wealthy person is well received'.

The prosperity gospel

Two Evangelical leaders mentioned the prosperity gospel as a cause of corruption in the church, especially in the independent Pentecostal and Evangelical churches.[12] K5, a leader of EAK, said:

> The Evangelical church has not been spared from corruption, especially because of the prosperity theology of health and wealth. The person who has prospered through this theology is mainly the pastor or the bishop, while the poor in our churches have continued to be poor. We changed the gospel from a gospel of salvation to a gospel of prosperity.

K18, a leader of FOCUS, gave his perspective on how the prosperity gospel undermines Christian ethics:

---

[12] However, it is interesting to note the observation of Lonsdale (2009:65) that 'in Kenya, charismatic congregations seem to be much less tolerant of the "gospel of prosperity" than elsewhere.'

The message is about what you get, not about sacrifice or ethics. You are uplifting the wealthy, saying the Father is one of silver and gold, creating a feeling among Christians that wealth is everything. Christians think that by evading tax they'll get wealthier faster; and riches, regardless of how they've been gained, are seen as a sign of God's blessing. So corruption in the church just thrives. You want people to give as much as possible so you spend all your time talking about how to release the money you have onto me, so that you'll get more. I don't have time to teach you that God's word requires that you do business right, that you pay your employee fair wages. That creates Christians who are so hungry for wealth, but are never taught about righteousness in so far as wealth acquisition is concerned. And that explains why the church does not even have fighting corruption as a serious agenda.

Lack of accountability for church leaders

Several informants identified a lack of accountability as a cause of corruption in churches. Karobia, a leader of CFJS, said 'There is no accountability at all for the tithes that the pastors get from their members every week. It is in many instances understood that all that money goes to someone's pocket. The people can't question, so they're being cheated on the tithing system.' K18, a leader of FOCUS, made similar observations:

A church member cannot question the church leader, because the church is a private enterprise. If you're a patron in a shop, you buy your commodity but you can't start questioning the shop owner. The fact that the charismatic Pentecostal Church in Kenya has become a private enterprise is a major, major problem. Churches are very strictly owned by an individual who has all power, who uses authority whichever way he wants, he has absolute authority over the matters of that church. That's the case with most of the new churches which are making the claim of Kenyans being very Christian. So you see the link between absolute authority and corruption. In the Anglican Church everything belongs to the institution, but among the Pentecostals church is private enterprise, where no one has the right to question me.

K19, an Evangelical lawyer experienced in working with churches, described how money given by western churches without adequate accountability requirements can promote corruption:

In church denominations that have 'Christian community work' among the poor you often find clergy coming to interfere, to get money from development agents of the church, and it's your own problem how you account for it. For example, if I'm the Bishop and you are the community worker, and I know there is money in your accounts because of donor funding, I just come and ask you: 'Can you submit KSh 500,000 to me? There is no receipt. You know how to account for that within your accounting systems'. That money, no one knows where it goes. That cuts across the denominations, and that is a form of corruption.[13]

In the opinion of Symonds Akivaga, Senior Lecturer at the University of Nairobi, 'most of the Evangelical churches are sponsored from abroad. Are they churches or are they commercial entities?'[14]

K19, an Evangelical lawyer experienced in working with churches, attributed the accountability problem at least partly to a lack of systems and policies:

> Every Sunday people are preaching 'Give money, and God will bless you'. They never come back and say: 'This is how much was given'. Members are straining, some are selling their properties to bring to the church, but no one knows where God takes these millions. They only see the pastor driving a very high-class vehicle and living a lavish life. You'll find clergy in the Pentecostal churches who are living a hundred times beyond the ability of the rest of the church members. They don't have policies or systems for determining the income and budget for procurement, so the pastor says: 'I want to drive a vehicle worth $10,000. I decide'. I'd call that corruption, because he was the one who decided; there was no tendering committee, no church board meeting that evaluated the ability of the church to buy it. Second, do they have limits that you can only use it for official purposes? If you use it for private purposes, do you have to chip in the fuel? There are some in the Pentecostal churches who have put in systems – but that is rare.

Quite apart from an absence of policies or systems, K3, a leader of the NCCK, thought that the lack of accountability might stem from the 'inability of Christians to be summarily harsh. If somebody has stolen you probably say something like "Relieve him of his duties, just leave him alone". You don't follow up with very punitive measures, so there's no serious consequence to corruption.'

---

[13] The potential for misuse of foreign donor resources may actually be greater in mainstream Evangelical churches than among the newer Pentecostal ones. Gifford (2009:242-244) points out that mainline churches have a major role as service providers and that 'the wealth brought in through Christian channels is practically incalculable.' He notes that 'the economics of [Pentecostal] Christianity are very different from the economics of the mainline churches', because the Pentecostal churches have a greater emphasis on raising money through local tithing.

[14] Gifford (1998:345) quotes Rev. Timothy Njoya, an outspoken Kenyan Presybterian, as making the controversial claim that 'over 90% of the clergy in Kenya today have no call at all. They come to the ministry because they could not have achieved a better career'.

African values

Two Evangelicals thought that the reluctance to hold leaders accountable stems not from any specifically Christian sentiments, but from African attitudes towards chiefs. K19, an Evangelical lawyer, said: 'The leadership is still very patriarchal, where the African chief says what is done, and who sits closer to the chief – that African chiefdom mentality is still running within the church context.'[15] Likewise Karobia, a leader of CFJS, said:

> The traditional concept of authority figures in Africa has perpetrated corruption. Africans don't question their leaders because our leaders are chiefs. If you're going to see him, you take him a cow or a goat - that also feeds into the corruption we have.

Three Evangelical leaders saw tribal identity as relevant to corruption. K2, an Anglican bishop, suggested that Africans do not regard favouring one's own tribe as corruption: 'Africans would not tolerate corruption. They can tolerate stealing, but this would be holy stealing where one tribe goes to another tribe to steal cows'. K17, a leader of the Ecumenical Centre for Justice and Peace, said: 'Corruption goes with tribalism. I was refused as a candidate in one of the dioceses, because I did not belong there! One of the people on the search committee asked me candidly, 'Why here, and not your home district?' K19, an Evangelical lawyer experienced in working with churches, echoed this:

> If you look at appointments of people to church boards, church committees, appointments of clergy at all levels, you often find that people prefer to appoint someone from their tribe. People feel more secure with a bishop or a provost or a moderator from home. That's corruption, and it cuts across the mainline churches and the Pentecostals. You find that there are denominations that are associated with a particular tribe, and people who have not come from that tribe will not get a chance to become teachers in the school, or NGO workers in a community service entity that is run by that church. If you asked the clergy who employed his relatives, or only employed people from his home area, they may not consider that as corruption – but it is. [16] And when it comes to voting, Christians do not vote as Christians, they vote as coming from a tribe.

---

[15] In his study of Episcopal leadership in the Anglican Church of Kenya, Bishop Mwangi (2008) describes the 'African chief' model of leadership as 'colonial', rather than traditional. In his view pre-colonial leadership in Africa followed the model of an 'elder', a role that included 'seeking justice for harmonious existence'. He distinguishes both of these models from Biblical leadership, which he describes as 'servant leadership'.

[16] This might not meet my definition of corruption if, within a particular tribe, having personal connections with those making the appointment are irrelevant to one's chances of success.

However, K2, an Anglican bishop, thought that corruption can arise not from having African values but from losing them:

> Corruption comes in when you have dropped your own values. Being content with what you have is there not only in the Bible but also in the African teachings. Because of westernisation some people have lost their cultural values, but they are not embracing western values so they are swinging somewhere in between. That person becomes dangerous.

K2 also observed that following rules rather than relationships when using money is alien to Africa:

> Many Africans are poor in keeping policies. They see administration as something coming from the West, especially when it comes to money. Money is there to be shared with my relatives at a time of need, so you can go to heavy borrowing, which you may not be able to pay back. You haven't used this money yourself, it has gone to relatives who are needy.

This approach to handling money is obviously contrary to the Weberian understanding of the proper use of public office: 'It is decisive for the modern loyalty to an office that, in the pure type, it does not establish a relationship to a person ... but rather is devoted to impersonal and functional purposes'.[17]

Co-option by the state

Several informants made critical references to the patronage that some Evangelical churches used to receive from President Moi. K5, a leader of EAK, recalled how independent Evangelical churches regularly received donations of land from President Moi:

> One church got a thousand lots of land from Moi, another got 300. Parklands Baptist Church was built on a children's park. We have only woken up now because we are nothing. Now we have to ask members for subscriptions because we can't get money from State House. We lost our moral ground.

K8, an Anglican bishop, suggested that the prosperity gospel provides a replacement source of income for churches that formerly received support from President Moi: 'Some of the prosperity gospel church leaders were supporters of Moi's regime. You wonder whether they received a lot of material support. Have they now started promoting the prosperity gospel because the current regime does not give them any material?' K1, a Programme Officer for Transparency International in Kenya, commented that 'according to the

---

[17] Heidenheimer and Johnston *Political Corruption*, 77.

Harambee Report a lot of the funds that came in through Goldenberg[18] went to moral institutions, to churches and to schools, so they lost their moral power.'

Preaching About Corruption

Many Evangelical leaders gave the impression that they believe that preaching can help fight corruption. K2, an Anglican bishop, said: 'The church is combating corruption through preaching. We preach against corruption every Sunday and we have Bible studies.' K13, a senior leader of the African Independent Pentecostal Church of Africa, said that in his church 'we educate the congregation on the effects of corruption on mankind' and 'preach against corruption and its ills.' K17, a leader of the Ecumenical Centre for Justice and Peace, said:

> In almost 60 per cent of the sermons, corruption will be mentioned. In every pastoral letter that will be issued, whether it is by the Catholic Church or the other churches, there is a line trying to talk against corruption. When corruption is mentioned in sermons the response of the congregations is quite positive.

My visit to Kenya in June 2007 coincided with a three-day workshop on corruption for about 50 bishops and pastors, organized by K5, a leader of EAK. The speakers were mostly staff of the Kenya Anti-Corruption Commission (KACC, a government agency)[19] who had been selected for this audience because they were Evangelicals themselves. In his opening remarks at the workshop, K5 said: 'If corruption is to be fought it will take the involvement of Evangelicals in Kenya. Only the gospel is going to change Kenya'. This optimism about the power of preaching was echoed by Dr Smokin Wanjala, Deputy Director of KACC. After noting that the event was 'one of KACC's best-attended workshops', he told the audience:

> Scripture is the best basis for fighting corruption. The church has a fundamental role. At the end of the day it is men and women who must change their hearts and minds in order to defeat corruption. Ultimately if we cannot base our war on a moral platform we cannot win the war.

---

[18] 'Goldenberg' refers to a Kenyan corruption scandal during the 1990's in which millions of dollars were paid for non-existent exports of gold and diamonds (Wrong 2009:62).

[19] Wrong (2009:327) gives a sobering estimate of KACC: 'In Kenya, as in many other countries, KACC is part of the grand corrupters' game, providing them with another bureaucratic wall behind which to shield, another scapegoat to blame for lack of progress.' This follows her description of the way in which Justice Ringera, the head of KACC, exonerated the former justice and finance ministers David Mwiraria and Kiraitu Murungi despite John Githongo's tape-recorded evidence implicating them in the Anglo-Leasing scandal, allowing President Kibaki to reappoint Kiraitu to his cabinet (Wrong 2009:269-73).

The highly religious nature of the proceedings was striking. Every speaker from the government agency began their presentation with the following short liturgy:

Speaker: 'God is good ...'
Audience: '... all the time'
Speaker: 'All the time ...'
Audience: '... God is good'

When Dr Ken Obura, a staff member of KACC, spoke on 'The Role of The Church in The Fight Against Corruption' the language of his presentation was more religious than practical, as illustrated by his concluding points:

Does our church belong to God or is it our personal investment? To whom do we give glory: politicians, rich members, or God? Is our church clothed in righteousness or dirt? As Ministers do we feed God's sheep or persecute them instead? Do we make God's temple holy or defiled? The Church must find and crystallize the theological basis of condemning and fighting corruption'.

To encourage participants to find this theological basis, participants were then invited to form small groups in which they brainstormed Bible passages that they considered relevant to corruption, and identified practices in their churches which might be considered corrupt in the light of them. In conversation over lunch Dr Arbogast Akidiva, Principal Officer for Education at KACC, shared his thoughts about the workshop:

KACC is spurring on the church, telling them: 'This is your calling, to call people back to righteousness. You can do wonders with the living Word.' ... This is an opportunity for the church to engage in a little reflection and introspection. We're interested in having the church do a systems audit. What are some of the structural things that would encourage corruption? KACC has a standard audit approach that's available upon request. We come and do examinations, not investigations, to assist them. How I wish some of these bishops and pastors would invite KACC to do a systems audit.

My own observation during the workshop was that Dr Akidiva was not being inundated with such invitations. During plenary discussion a number of bishops and pastors objected to the suggestion that there is any corruption in their churches, and praised their members for the financial sacrifices they make.

Several other informants, who were not connected with the KACC workshop, also expressed optimism regarding the churches' potential contribution to fighting corruption through preaching. K19, an Evangelical lawyer experienced in working with churches, was confident that appropriate teaching about corruption would reform the church, and put the church in a position to challenge the government:

If someone developed a theological reflection course on tendering, disposal of assets, misuse of church property, they can easily help the church leaders. I've participated in developing such a curriculum for 17 theological institutions from eastern and southern Africa and when we addressed those issues with the church leaders and theologians you could see them saying: 'Oh, this is where we've been making our mistake'. If you can help the Pentecostals see that what they are doing is corruption, and therefore it is sin, they will easily change because they want to avoid sin - so there is hope. So I'm sure that with good theological training and reflection the church is open to be challenged on these things. Some of them are very sensitive, like ethnicity and nepotism, but if you address them from a theological perspective, they are open. And if they are able to address corruption within the church, then they can challenge the government on some practical aspects. The President, the Vice President, the Ministers, the top professionals, they all come to churches.

K1, a Programme Officer for Transparency International in Kenya, said: 'If we have a bold approach the moral power of the religious community is second to none'. K12, a Catholic lecturer in Law, said that 'religion is a power, it's a force in this country. The moral argument can be boosted if there's evidence of change'.

Reforming Government by Having Evangelicals Inside Government

Given Daniel arap Moi's long period of rule as President of Kenya and his identity as an Evangelical, this section begins with a description of the ways in which key informants reflected on the relationship between his political actions and his faith. It concludes with a description of two strategies that were suggested whereby Evangelicals might combat corruption from within government.

A wide variety of Evangelical leaders thought that Moi was a corrupt President. K5, a leader of EAK, said: 'The corruption mess in Kenya was made by an Evangelical: Moi.' David Gitari said:

The 24 years of Moi's reign was a disaster for Kenya. He went to church every Sunday, and the first news on the radio and the TV during his time was where Moi worshipped on that Sunday. He was a Christian on Sundays, but from Monday to Saturday he did the most terrible things in this country. I wouldn't be surprised if some murders were instigated by him. Moi was the greatest hypocrite of all time ... Moi always had crates of KSh 1,000 notes wrapped in their thousands and people came to collect money for their fund-raising. It is most unfortunate that elections in this country are now a matter of money, and it is Moi who introduced it. You cannot be elected unless you have money, and Moi was the prime source of money to his friends.

K8, an Anglican bishop, shared this strongly negative view of Moi: 'President Kibaki is a very good person, but he is working against the forces of evil that lasted for over 24 years under Moi. That period was enough for corruption and other injustices to entrench themselves.' K18, a leader of FOCUS, said: 'Moi was meant to be an Evangelical, but you see what he was at … it's the same thing of absolute power and corruption.' K3, a leader of the NCCK, thought that Moi had been much more corrupt than Kibaki:

> Under Moi, business entities were running but they were always declaring losses, and giving nothing to the Exchequer. Kibaki's government has put all government servants on performance contracts, reorganized the system, and all of a sudden each of these entities is making a profit. If Kibaki's government was more corrupt than Moi's government, all the sectors of the country would not be performing.

However, none of Moi's Evangelical critics suggested that he was not a Christian. Among the key informants only K12, a Catholic lecturer in Law, suggested that Moi's professed Christian faith was insincere:

> Moi went to church very regularly and made a big deal of saying: 'I'm God-fearing, I can't do evil.' Church leaders who were close to him said: 'This guy cannot kill an insect, he's so good, upright and sensitive – there's no corruption here'. I always dismissed this as a quest for legitimacy.

Two Evangelical leaders implied that the discordance between Moi's faith and his actions as President was the result of his personal failings. David Gitari said that 'Moi was the greatest hypocrite of all time' (but did not suggest that he was not a Christian). K13, a senior leader of the African Independent Pentecostal Church of Africa, said: 'Moi let his people steal, he did not try to stop all this stealing.' Other explanations focussed on the difficulties of applying Christian principles in political life. K9, an Anglican Diocesan secretary, said:

> Moi was a very good person, he wanted things to be done right, but the government is large and he couldn't control things, things went on without him knowing. He lost control of his own lieutenants who were doing things on the ground. They were more corrupt than he was.[20] He indirectly encouraged corruption - he turned a blind eye and pretended nothing was happening. Moi is a Christian, but he's also a politician. His full time is being a politician – maybe his hobby is being a Christian.

David Gitari, the retired Anglican bishop who had described Moi as a hypocrite, also expressed great sympathy for politicians in his position:

---

[20] This seems too soft on Moi. Wrong (2009:284) notes that the Kroll investigation into the Goldenberg scandal 'shed devastating light on the systematic looting conducted by Moi's family and friends. The former president's sons Philip and Gideon were reported to be worth £384 million and £550 million respectively, with the assets held in an array of international real estate, bank accounts and shell companies'. According to Lonsdale (2009:61), the Goldenberg scam made Kenyans as a whole 30 percent poorer.

When we are discussing politicians we should sympathise with them, forgive them for their shortcomings. If the Vice President was corrupt, we should not leave him there but ways and means must be found in which we can do the right things. Even if you're not going to sack your Vice-President, maybe you can give him another job. Don't put him to shame.[21] It's a question of sympathising with those who are in power, knowing that they are also human beings, knowing that there are some dilemmas that might be so difficult for them. So we sympathise – but we don't just let them do whatever they want.

K3, a leader of the NCCK, expressed similar sympathy towards Christian politicians who fall short of expectations:

I suspect the corruption in predominantly Christian countries has to do with withdrawal. We all know that no one can be 100 per cent perfect, but if a person goes into politics we expect him to be 100 per cent, or he's nothing. If he loses five per cent we'll hit him so hard he may quit Christianity.

Strategies for helping Christians oppose corruption from within government

Against this sobering history of corruption having grown under an Evangelical President, Evangelical leaders suggested two possible strategies for opposing corruption from within government. The first involves helping Christians connect their faith with public life and the second involves replacing democracy with an ethical dictatorship.

K18, a leader of FOCUS, and K16 and Karobia, the leaders of CFJS, talked about ways in which they have tried to help Christians connect their faith with their behaviour in public life. K18 described how he challenges Christians who are already in government and are involved in corrupt practices:

Some of the government officials who had a Christian past do not know what to do with themselves. The only point where you can handle them is to say: 'You were the Vice-President of your Christian Union. What has become of you? What became of your Christian conviction?'

---

[21] This unwillingness to condemn corruption may be linked to national pride. Lonsdale (2009:61) writes that 'Most believed he [Moi] had been personally and profitably involved in the grand fraud [Goldenberg]. Yet, an ecumenical gathering of church leaders declared that to put the ex-president in the dock would demean national honour.' Kibwana et al. (1996:vii) observe that 'Citizens who dare raise a voice and chronicle episodes of runaway corruption within their country are dubbed unpatriotic elements who are motivated by foreigners to tarnish the good image of the government.' The NGO which published that report was shortly afterwards deregistered by the government which, in an explanatory letter, had the temerity to claim that 'Your activities have been most injurious to the public interest, in so far as you have exposed to ridicule and contempt the image and integrity of the Kenya government' (Kibwana et al. 2001:vii-viii).

Both he and the leaders of CFJS referred to efforts to help Christians think through the issues before they enter public life. K16, a leader of CFJS, reflected that:

> Many people go into the public sector as Christians but don't know how to leave as Christians, because you go to a job and everybody's corrupt, so how do you begin to address that? It's not just saying: 'Go and address corruption.' We need to teach people how to do that.

K18, a leader of FOCUS, said the approach of FOCUS is to 'bring together Christians who want to go for electoral posts, to begin fellowship and forming values.' Karobia described the naivety with which he thinks many well-intentioned Christians aim to reform politics:

> In the 2002 general elections we had a fellowship of 17 or 18 Christians who wanted to run for office. CFJS tried to come together with the churches to provide the thinking needed on how to stand for the faith, how to campaign. A lot of them were new to the whole political game, to involvement in political parties, to developing independent constituencies or support bases etcetera, to the point of being naïve. When you face off against someone that's not so clean, but has rendered public service for a long time, he has learned in the trenches. So when you just come out and say: 'I'm going to get him out because he did this deal', the other side is that he's taken a long time to become the politician he is. It doesn't take only a year, just because you say 'I love Jesus'.

Notwithstanding these reservations, Karobia was convinced that 'more Christian professionals need to go into politics. The church needs to proactively come in, with their resources, systems, support and infrastructure to provide the capacity.'

Unfortunately, what may be much more evident than these laudable efforts to connect Christian values with public life are the efforts of politicians to use churches as vote banks. K16, a leader of CFJS, said: 'The gap between the spiritual and the social has now been bridged, in fact people have gone the other way: we have bishops vying for political posts. So the new issue is to find Christians to stand for integrity.' Karobia outlined two examples that were current in June 2007:

> Bishop Margaret Wanjiru of Jesus is Alive Ministries is one of the wealthiest bishops I know. She wants to vie for the Starehe city centre constituency for this year's election.[22] Bishop Pius Muiru of the Maximum Miracle Centre wants to

---

[22] Gifford (2009:151) quotes her as writing in 2006: 'Christ shed his blood from his hands and feet so that we may be rich ... The Calvary package not only included salvation but also included the prosperity and inheritance of our hands and feet'. She was elected as MP for Starehe in 2007, but her predecessor has claimed there were

become President. He's been asking people to change their constituency so that they can vote in his specific constituency.[23] The highest level of corruption is where a spiritual leader uses his spiritual authority to make people vote for him.[24]

Karobia reflected on how little popular understanding there is of the ethical politics he seeks to promote: 'Bishop Muiru's supporters don't see it. They're not thinking: "That's abuse of power". They're thinking: "This is our guy, we're with him".'

The second suggested strategy for combating corruption from within government is to replace multi-party democracy with an ethical dictatorship. Karobia suggested that:

> Since multi-party politics came up, people are not significantly more engaged and involved in the parties. In fact, there is a lot of apathy and people are not following parties but specific individuals. Tribalism has worsened. Democracy doesn't work in this country. What you need is an ethical dictator. To deal with corruption in the church, and for the church to help with corruption in society, we need visionary dictators.

K17, a leader of the Ecumenical Centre for Justice and Peace, said:

> Ministers should not be elected leaders, but the people with the kind of qualifications and competence. The high people involved in grand corruption live in their own cocoon, in their own clubs where they discuss their own things. Only they themselves can eliminate the grand corruption, so a change of heart and attitude is needed. President Kibaki wants to get rid of corruption, but he inherited leaders who were very much involved. He will find it difficult to sack a Minister who is involved with corruption, because he will think first about that Minister's block ethnic vote: 'If I sack him, what are the repercussions?' His own position would be at risk.

Promoting Civic Oversight

This section describes informants' comments regarding the churches' role in promoting civic oversight. Although a few positive examples were mentioned, most of what was said concerned reasons why the churches, particularly the Evangelical churches, have been weak in this area.

---

irregularities in polling, and the matter was being fought in court as of April 2010 (Sam Kiplagat 'MP falls short in vote recount' Daily Nation 16 April 2010).

[23] Gifford (2009:166) states that 'the entry of Bishop Margaret and Muiru into politics brought a surprising backlash against both, and an airing of all sorts of reservations around the whole phenomenon of the new [Pentecostal] Christianity. The criticisms were directed far beyond Wanjiru and Muiri alone.'

[24] But note that this does not fit my definition of 'corruption'.

Loyalties in Kenya are tribal, not national

Before engaging with the churches' role in civil society, it is pertinent to describe the informants' comments regarding the level of collectivity with which Kenyans tend to identify. K3, a leader of the NCCK, said:

> The kind of allegiance that Britain requires from its citizens is the same allegiance that the Kenyan tribe requires of its citizens. If it is my tribe against your tribe, I will stand in solidarity with my tribe. Whenever there's been an external threat the country has stood as a country: in the fight for independence, and when Uganda threatened to annexe part of Kenya, Kenyans stood as a nation. The problem is that they have never sat down in more sober times to discuss how to co-exist.

Karobia, a leader of CFJS, thought that Kenyans continue to see the state as alien:[25]

> During the fight for independence, when you fought the government you were fighting the white man – so you were a hero. If you destroyed government property, it was the property of the oppressor. We have not yet achieved the socialisation necessary for people to accept that this is now our country. We must take responsibility for that road, that streetlight, that community land – that's ours, not the government's.

K17, a leader of the Ecumenical Centre for Justice and Peace, described how the primacy of tribal identity affects governance and anti-corruption efforts: 'If I am related to the accused I would want to protect them. For example, when a judge is accused of corruption you would find people saying, from tribal inclinations: "No, they are trying to attack our own person".'

Until he resigned in January 2005, John Githongo was Permanent Secretary in the Office of the President in charge of Governance and Ethics. While in that post he exposed a $100 million fraud (the Anglo-Leasing scandal) that was allegedly perpetrated by Ministers of President Kibaki's government. Some of those implicated in the scandal belong to the same ethnic group as Githongo (Gikuyu).[26] In a lecture in Oxford he described the common reaction of fellow Kenyans to his actions:

---

[25] Paul Gifford comments that 'the African state from birth was essentially an agency for control and extraction. There was never any merging of state and society as common expressions of shared values. Thus there has been little in the way of legitimacy, or popular commitment to public institutions' (*African Christianity*, 4).

[26] Ben Sihanya writes: 'The public and commentators emphasise that both parties in the corruption drama [those being accused by the public of massive corruption and those appointed to fight corruption] largely hail from the same ethnic group or region – are Kikuyu or Meru – and belong to the "Mt. Kenya Mafia" of popular discourse.' Chweya L, Tuta JK and Akivaga SK *Control of Corruption in Kenya: Legal-political dimensions 2001-2004* (Nairobi: Claripress 2005), xvii.

The most persistent accusation made in my regard over the past seven rather interesting months has been of betrayal. That by allowing the exposure of certain activities this has amounted to the betrayal of my country. When I ask some of those who hold this view with the greatest conviction more closely what their real problem is they almost always point out that the greatest betrayal I have committed has been against my tribe; my ethnic group; my kith and kin. For there is an unspoken pact that says when graft is perpetrated by ones kith and kin it is allowable; that every tribe has its turn to eat ... The issue of ethnicity and inequality is the elephant in the room and it has proved too big to sweep under the carpet. This has been the most enduring lesson on my part in the fight against corruption thus far.[27]

In June 2007 K1, a Programme Officer for Transparency International in Kenya, gave the following interpretation of events:

You have boldness from John Githongo, because of his integrity and his desire to see the national agenda thrive. For a normal person it would be "How can you do this? You are exposing your fellow tribesman!" A sense of national identity has not taken root.

All these comments reinforce the view that loyalties in Kenya are primarily tribal, not national. This may not hinder efforts to make local leaders accountable, since they may share tribal identity with those they represent; but without a stronger sense of national identity it is hard to see how civil society could generate the pressure needed to constrain national leaders to act in the national, rather than tribal or personal, interest.[28]

Some Evangelical activities aimed at engaging communities for better governance

Several Evangelical informants described activities in which their churches or organisations had participated in civil society to promote good governance. K14, a member of staff of EAK, described EAK's civic education initiative in two constituencies in the run up to the 2007 general election. These constituencies had often experienced tribal clashes during previous elections:

People no longer ask whether an individual has the best qualities of a leader, but how influential that leader is and how much has money he has. The majority are

---

[27] John Githongo 'Inequality, Ethnicity and the Fight against Corruption in Africa: A personal perspective'. Lecture given at the Oxford Centre for Mission Studies on 15th August 2006.

[28] The churches are certainly not immune from this. Lonsdale (2009:66) writes that 'if theological differences were not enough to cast doubt on the capacity of Kenya's Christianities to inspire good governance or effectively reprove the bad, there is the still more disabling fact that in the popular mind, many of its churches bear an ethnic, not national, character.'

involved in organized thuggery and killings so that only those associated with that leader end up voting. They kill the election in that area. To restore hope among the community we are focusing on the historical trends of these two constituencies since independence: What kinds of leaders have they had and what impact have they caused in the community? To sensitise the pastor or bishop on the need to empower their people amidst the state of hopelessness over many years, we are being helped by the scriptures: for example, Luke 4:18 is about preaching good news, opening the eyes of those who are blind, setting free the oppressed. When the eyes of the leaders are opened they realise they can empower their people to elect the leaders who have integrity, who will be accountable to them. By the end of the training people are asking: 'Who are the good leaders who have these qualities?'

K2, an Anglican bishop, saw Anglican churches playing a useful role in the government's Constituency Development Fund initiative, in which some funds for schools, health centres and roads are decentralized to Parliamentary constituencies: 'That has decentralized corruption to the constituencies. We have told the church not to be left out, but to be members of the Constituency Development Committees and to be a voice for the voiceless, for the poor, for orphans.' K17, a leader of the Ecumenical Centre for Justice and Peace, described the current activities of the Centre: 'In seminars we discuss with people the causes and effects of corruption, and how they can fight corruption. Our 2006 calendar has got these themes, so the people can be reminded of it the whole year. Karobia mentioned the anti-corruption initiative of CFJS in the late 1990's:

> We said: 'If you're a Christian and you are in this battle against corruption, sign a card with this pledge: "I won't give a bribe, I won't take a bribe, I will expose bribery"'. People put those cards in their offices where people could see them. It was very well received, both by business people, political guys, people in the public arena who knew of CFJS or supported it.

Evangelical views on Catholic and Anglican efforts to oppose corruption
Two Anglican leaders thought that the Anglican Church and NCCK have been strong advocates for good governance. K8, an Anglican bishop, claimed that 'the mainline churches under the umbrella of NCCK were the only advocates of justice and righteousness during Moi's time.'[29] K9, an Anglican Diocesan secretary, said: 'The Anglicans and Catholics have been notorious in speaking out. They've got capacity, structure and educated people.' However, David Gitari thought this history had faded:

---

[29] The crucial role of the churches has been thoroughly documented by Githiga (2001).

We seem to be lacking courageous bishops to continue that tradition.[30] Protestants are so divided. There are those who belong to NCCK, the Pentecostals and EAK, and they all hold different positions.[31] The Catholics are better organized because it is the Bishops' Conference which issues statements, not just one Bishop.

According to K16, a leader of CFJS, 'The Catholic Church has always beaten Evangelicals in terms of raising the flag whenever there is corruption and wherever the government is not doing its work.' His colleague Karobia echoed these comparisons, placing the mainline Evangelical churches somewhere between the independent Evangelical churches and the Catholic Church:

Evangelicals have been a bit behind, truly. The mainstream denominations, through NCCK, have been proactive - Mutava Musyimi has been keen on that. But it's less than the Catholics, because the Catholic Church have their own resources while NCCK depends a lot on donor funding.

K18, a leader of FOCUS, said: 'The Catholic Church has been fairly influential, because they succeeded in not living too far from the people they are ministering to; they have succeeded in going very deep and very far.' [32]

Two non-Evangelical informants, however, saw a decline in the Catholic advocacy role since Kibaki (a Catholic) had become President. Symonds Akivaga, Senior Lecturer at the University of Nairobi, said:

The Catholic Church used to be very vocal on behalf of the voiceless on issues like human rights and child abuse. They aired their views very strongly. But now these things are articulated with less vigour than in the past. There's a clear linkage between the church and politics in this country. The Catholic Church came out very, very strongly against Moi's regime, but the current regime faces no criticism from the Church. There seems to be a marriage of convenience between the two.

These criticisms were echoed by K12, a Catholic lecturer in Law:

The Catholic Church in this country is thoroughly divided in its attitude towards this government. Some of the top leaders are with the government on things that are completely unethical and irrational, like stalling the Constitutional Review. They don't seem to be engaging this government the way they've engaged other

---

[30] Gifford (2009:220) writes that 'co-option has been far more characteristic of Kenyan Christianity than the "prophetic Christianity" of Gitari, Okullu, Njoya and Muge'.

[31] Lonsdale (2009:63) writes: 'Among the severest divisions of opinion are those that reflect on how far faith is concerned at all with secular governance and social justice.'

[32] These assessments in 2007 seem to forget that, during the Moi era, it was Evangelical leaders who spearheaded opposition to the President, with the Catholic Church becoming involved later, and hesitantly (Gifford 2009:35-6).

governments in the past. This is why people are saying 'What is in it for you?' It isn't principle, surely. I'm a Catholic, and the Chair of the Episcopal Conference spoke the language of the government, not the language of the Catholics. On the issue of anti-corruption, Anglo-Leasing and stuff, they've been very mild.

Theological hindrances to Evangelical engagement in advocacy

K3, a leader of the NCCK, described how Kenyan Evangelicals have generally approached political, economic or social issues solely from a spiritual perspective:

> You would diagnose poverty as a curse, and believe that if your members can come to the Lord and start giving, the poverty will go away. The more you give, the more you get out of poverty - it invites the blessing of God. The same would have happened to the political sphere: 'It's God who appoints leaders. When we pray God hears us and God will appoint the leaders; voting is almost inconsequential'.

David Gitari traced the roots of a theology of separation to the East African Revival movement:

> It has played a major part in the church not getting involved in politics to a point where the church can fight those in power. It was inward-looking. It mainly spread among the Anglicans, Presbyterians, Methodists and some of the other mainstream denominations. They came up with the very strong idea that a born-again Christian cannot be a politician. In fact a member of the Revival who goes into politics is called a cold, or lukewarm, Christian – because they cannot see how a politician can be a Christian. So this discouraged many people from going into politics ... The Revival, though it did a lot of good work, was misleading. We must see the Revival as one of our hindrances in challenging corruption in this country.

K16, a leader of CFJS, described his perspective on how Kenyans tend to see the role of the church:

> There is a huge dichotomy in this country between being a Christian and being actively involved in social justice issues. There has been very little teaching from the pulpit on how Christians can engage on social justice issues. People feel the work of the church is to preach to people on a Sunday, and hope that they will learn a bit about God so that you can pray for them. Social justice issues are the responsibility of the private sector, or the government, or civil society, or non-government organisations.

Symonds Akivaga, Senior Lecturer at the University of Nairobi, however, articulated a Marxist explanation for Kenyan Evangelicalism's other-worldly theology:

It is said you can never conquer people physically unless you have also conquered their minds, their spirits. That's where religion became important. Everybody seems to think that the missionaries came here basically to spread Christianity, to evangelize. But one has to look at that with a little bit of care because in every situation they went to, the whole idea was to mollify a people. The role of the Christians was to tell the Kenyans: 'You can suffer down here, but your kingdom is in heaven'. So colonialism and Christianity were part of the same fellow, two sides of the same coin. That is not to say that there were no missionaries who were pro the Africans' aspirations; there were a lot who started schools[33] and welfare organisations, which later became the political organisations. But on the whole, religion in this country became a major pacifier.[34]

Material hindrances to Evangelical engagement: co-option and repression by the state

Several informants recalled how President Moi had used his powers of patronage to try to co-opt churches. K8, an Anglican bishop, claimed that 'a lot of money from Moi's regime went to create divisions among the churches.' According to David Gitari:

President Moi belonged to the African Inland Church (AIC). After the queue-voting business he told them to pull out of NCCK and instead of saying: 'We're not going to be controlled by the President', they pulled out. Then whenever AIC applied for a plot to build a church, they were given. Whenever we applied, it became a problem. If we imported cars and asked for exemption from import duty, the government refused. If AIC applied, they were given.

He expressed concern that once again the church had been co-opted: 'I fear today that even though Kibaki is much better than Moi, churches might not be willing to challenge him because they are getting some benefits from his Presidency.' K19, an Evangelical lawyer experienced in working with churches, endorsed this view: 'Currently we have several church leaders who are being paid by the politicians so that they don't harass them or challenge the government departments, but give high praise to the government.' K18, a

---

[33] A good example is the missionary Carey Francis, who was Headmaster of the Alliance High School. Greaves (1969:190) records that President Kenyatta sent a personal message to be read at his Service of Remembrance: 'I feel a profound sense of loss, and wish to record my sincere appreciation for the great work that Carey Francis, one of the greatest educationists that Kenya has ever had, did for Kenya and her people.'

[34] Lonsdale (2009:68) contrasts Kenya's 'emancipation theology' with Latin American 'liberation theology': 'Clean contrary to Latin American liberation theology, with its biases toward the poor and against the structural sin inherent in the alliance between corrupt local states and international capital, Kenya's theology of emancipation is suspicious or contemptuous of the poor, or of African humanity more generally, with its supposed liability to indulge in violence and anarchy and is inclined to be indulgent of and respectful toward the state.'

leader of FOCUS, saw corruption in the Pentecostal churches as a reason for their silence on social justice issues: 'All the big Pentecostal names have acquired land plots from powerful politicians, so they are not able to speak.'

Several informants described how fear of repression by the state has deterred people from fighting corruption, particularly during Moi's Presidency. David Gitari became an outspoken critic of President Moi when he introduced queue-voting in 1986. He said: 'I became so vocal about queue-voting that in 1989 thugs, organized by the government, came to my house to kill me. The following morning the police came to tell me "This is the work of the Minister for National Guidance".' Moving to more commonplace forms of intimidation, he described how a Christian friend who was a Returning Officer during Moi's Presidency agreed to stuff ballot boxes:

> He was given the ballot papers by the District Commissioner and told to put a mark for the favoured candidate; so by the time he reaches the polling station he has already voted for hundreds of other people. I asked him: 'Why did you do that, as a Christian?' And he said: 'I have to take care of my daily bread.' In other words, 'I don't want to be sacked, otherwise my family is going to suffer.' He was a Christian, but he was full of fear. You get very, very few people who are prepared to stand for the truth.

K13, a senior leader of the African Independent Pentecostal Church of Africa, said: 'Grand corruption is being done in Parliament or government departments by big men who should be feared. If they say something, everybody has to obey. They cannot be investigated. For your safety, even if you know something you will stop.' K1, a Programme Officer for Transparency International in Kenya, said: 'When we have a strong moral power coming from the churches, it raises the benchmark. The challenge is we have not seen that over the years because of the culture of fear, the history of dictatorship, detention without trial.'

K12, a Catholic lecturer in Law, identified a newer way in which churches can be co-opted: by getting them to legitimise government anti-corruption activities:

> In the recent past the church has been co-opted in two different ways, either into the corruption game, or into the anti-corruption measures. Some church leaders have been recruited by the state to try to fight corruption. For example, Mutava Musyimi at NCCK is leading the Steering Committee of the Kenya Anti-Corruption Campaign. He has been a vocal Christian leader who had built his name as a reliable person, but more recently he's been known as someone who's been co-opted by the state in its political games – he has a very big legitimacy problem. As a result the church is not as vocal and consistent on the anti-corruption crusade as they were in the Kenyatta period and part of the Moi government.

Symonds Akivaga, Senior Lecturer at the University of Nairobi, said:

It is doubtful whether the church can combat corruption, because the church leadership is moving closer to the political leadership. If they are in agreement, they'll articulate what the political leadership says; if they totally disagree, they'll just remain silent ... Most churches in Africa would tend to be supportive of what the government is doing, not because of the doctrines of the church but because of the interests of the churches. Given the poverty of the country, most people want to pursue their own self-interest ... In the 1990s you had a very centralised regime that could either destroy you, or build you through patronage. If church leaders wanted their church to grow, to be protected, then the best thing for them to do was to be on good terms with the government and not provoke it. Very many pseudo-churches started purely with the intention of being pro-government and getting resources from the government.

Despite these informants' sobering depictions of how the church's role in speaking out against corruption can be undermined by dualistic theology, co-option and fear, three informants expressed reasons for hope. Karobia, a leader of CFJS, said:

The prophetic role must continue to be played, because the government listens to the church. They cannot ignore the church. The church voice is vital to any political leader – in fact, between now and the elections you'd be surprised how many political leaders are going back to the churches, helping churches raise money, so that they can move voters from the church. They recognise that the country is actually very religious, and anybody who wants to make any political gain must be on the side of the church. So the church can use this opportunity to guide its members on how to vote, and to let the politicians know that unless they shape up they will not have the support of the church.

K18, a leader of FOCUS, was optimistic about the impact of Evangelical work amongst students: 'Most of the Evangelicals that speak out, like David Gitari, were influenced by the student ministry in Kenya; and this talk about corruption has become much more common.' Given his prominent role as an advocate for better governance, it seems fitting to give the last word in this section to David Gitari: 'If you are consistent, even those in power will end up respecting you very much. Even those District Commissioners who used to be very tough with me, after they retired they came and praised me: "Thank you for your stand."'

Satisfying Elite Interests

The interview with Karobia, a leader of CFJS, was unique, in that he was the only informant in any of the four case-study countries who suggested a strategy for fighting corruption that incorporates satisfying the interests of a corrupt elite. He outlined his analysis, and corresponding strategy for dealing with corruption, as follows:

The 'Asian Tigers' had a lot of internal energy; visionary leaders, mobilizing a lot of capital; and a culture of saving a lot of money. But when you look at some of their methods, it was cronyism: so-and-so comes from a wealthy family, and we're going to entrust him to run three or four family corporations. There's no discussion! But that's what built South Korea. They have corruption, but they organized it in a certain way. You're stealing, but you have a vision for multiplying jobs, growing the economy, you don't finish off the enterprise. If you steal just for yourself, they'll kill you.

Our form of corruption in sub-Saharan Africa isn't visionary corruption. It's like the story of the goose: you can choose to eat the eggs or eat the goose. We seem to keep on eating the goose, so there are no more eggs to eat. Whether it's a public company or a parastatal, we just run it down, finish it off. We cannibalise, get the monies and take them abroad.[35] So one of the solutions that is being put to the government is to say: 'Keep the money, but invest it here. Don't invest it in the Channel Islands or Switzerland. Invest here.'

Summary

The reputation of Evangelicals for honest behaviour

Evangelical leaders were quick to acknowledge that Evangelicals are 'caught up in the same mess' of corruption as everyone else. Examples of corruption that were mentioned included nepotism in appointing clergy and lay staff, tax evasion, petty theft, and clergy enriching themselves at the expense of the poor in their congregations. They described corruption as being greatest in the independent Evangelical and Pentecostal churches, and less in the mainline Evangelical churches. The Catholic Church, which is outnumbered approximately two to one by Evangelicals, was seen as least corrupt, at least in respect of appointments to church posts. This picture stands in stark contrast to the Philippines, where the Evangelical minorities enjoy a reputation for honest behaviour.

Causes of corruption in the church that were suggested by Evangelical leaders include the material affluence that was and is modelled by western Christians; fear of poverty; the prosperity gospel (in which church members are taught that God will bless them with riches if they first give their money to the pastor); a lack of accountability for some church leaders; African values such as tribal identity; and co-option by the state through offers of land and tax breaks.

Preaching about corruption

Not surprisingly, given the damaged reputation of Evangelicals in Kenya, the focus of preaching about corruption around the time of this visit was on reform

---

[35] This observation reflects comparisons between Africa and South Korea made by Chabal and Daloz (1999:107-8).

within the Evangelical sector. Recognising the extent of corruption in the independent Evangelical and Pentecostal churches, in June 2007 the Evangelical Alliance of Kenya organized a workshop on the topic for Evangelical bishops and pastors. The Evangelical leaders of this workshop expressed great optimism about the potential for Evangelical preaching to fight corruption, if only the Evangelical churches could address the corruption within their own ranks. The workshop was littered with phrases such as 'only the gospel is going to change Kenya' (K5); 'you can do wonders with the living Word' (Dr Arbogast Akidiva); 'scripture is the best basis for fighting corruption' (Dr Smokin Wanjala) and 'the church must find and crystallize the theological basis of condemning and fighting corruption' (Dr Ken Obura).

Reforming government by having Evangelicals inside government

Most informants saw Daniel arap Moi, an Evangelical, as having acted corruptly during his 24 year rule as President. However, only one informant (K12 - a Catholic) suggested that Moi's profession of Evangelical faith was insincere. Two Evangelical leaders (David Gitari and K13, a senior leader of the African Independent Pentecostal Church of Africa) implied that the discordance between Moi's faith and his actions as President was the result of his personal failings, but a slightly greater number focussed on the difficulties of applying Christian principles in political life. Some Evangelical leaders suggested that these difficulties could be addressed by bringing aspiring Christian politicians together for training and values formation, but two (Karobia and K17, a leader of the Ecumenical Centre for Justice and Peace) thought that radical systemic change would be needed, from democracy to a system of ethical dictatorship.

Promoting civic oversight

Evangelical leaders described some contemporary initiatives to help civil society improve governance, such as EAK's civic education initiative in selected constituencies. Some Anglican Evangelical leaders (K8 and K9) also recalled the courage of NCCK and the Anglican Church as 'advocates of justice and righteousness during Moi's time'. However, David Gitari commented that 'we seem to be lacking courageous bishops to continue that tradition'. He and several other Evangelical leaders saw the Catholic Church as ahead of Evangelicals in promoting civic oversight, though two non-Evangelical informants thought the Catholic Church has become less vocal since Kibaki, a Catholic, became President in 2002.

Reasons suggested by Evangelical leaders for Evangelical weakness in this area included dualistic theology, and co-option and repression by the state, particularly under Moi. Several informants pointed out a fundamental difficulty in relying on civic oversight to regulate the Kenyan state: most Kenyans feel greater loyalty to their tribe than to the state - but favouring one's own tribe over another is seen as corrupt.

Satisfying elite interests

Finally, the Kenya country case study was unique, in that it was only here that an Evangelical leader (Karobia) suggested a strategy for fighting corruption that incorporates satisfying the interests of a corrupt elite: let them steal, but persuade them to be less destructive, by investing the proceeds within Kenya rather than abroad.

Niels and Amyjay Riconalla at the Manila office of the
Fellowship of Christians in Government.

President Gloria Arroyo attending the fiftieth birthday party of Bishop Efraim Tendero,
General Secretary of the Philippine Council of Evangelical Churches.

Judge Dolores Espanol, Chair of Transparency International in the Philippines.

Jovita Salonga, former President of the Philippine Senate.

Anglican Archbishop David Gitari at his home in Kenya

Daniel Arap Moi, former President of Kenya and
Evangelical lay teacher in the Africa Inland Church.

Dyness Kasungami, Human Development Advisor for DFID in Zambia and former Chair of the Zambian Fellowship of Evangelical Students.

Frederick Chiluba, former President of Zambia and an Evangelical lay teacher.

Zambia Country Case Study

Introduction

The period before the nineteenth century remains relatively obscure. Zambia (formerly Northern Rhodesia) was occupied by the UK during the late nineteenth century, conceived originally as a tropical dependency rather than as a settler colony. The British system of indirect rule initially allowed great freedom to local rulers, but in the late 1920s copper was discovered in the north. By the beginning of World War II, in 1939, Zambia had become a major producer of copper. The copper industry brought an influx of European technicians and administrators who became a dominant force in Zambian life.

Yet copper exports did not confer much prosperity. The mineral rights were owned by the British South Africa Company, which duly exacted royalties. Taxation was levied on what profits remained, but half was retained by the British government, which made only tiny grants for economic development. In 1938 these arrangements were criticized by a visiting financial expert, Sir Alan Pim. In a report to the Colonial Office, he urged more public investment in roads, schools, and health services, for Africans as well as whites. Missionaries ran many primary schools, but in 1942 only 35 Africans were receiving secondary education.

After the Second World War the new Labour government in Britain began to promote the formation of African trade unions. Following a major African strike in 1952, the real wages of African mine workers at last moved upward. In 1956, however, the copper boom came to an end. While many Africans were thrown out of work, whites in Northern Rhodesia became increasingly aware of how far the federal tax system channelled copper profits into Southern Rhodesia. In 1958, a new generation of leaders led by Kenneth Kaunda, a former teacher and civil servant, founded the Zambia African National Congress and its successor, the United National Independence Party (UNIP).

Following UNIP's massive campaign of civil disobedience in 1962, a 1964 election based on universal adult suffrage gave UNIP a decisive majority, including the support of nearly a third of the white voters. Later that year Zambia obtained independence from Britain under the Presidency of Kenneth Kaunda, who ruled until 1991. According to one historian, although Kaunda imposed a one-party state from 1972, he 'not only admitted to the existence of the problem of corruption but also took a very dim view of it ... Consequently, corruption among the upper echelon of political leaders was insignificant.'[1]

Economically, Zambia is one of the most unequal countries in the quantitative analysis of 77 countries in Chapter 2. Table 7.1 shows Zambia's position in respect of some selected indicators, including those relevant to the analysis of economic inequality in Chapter 2.

Table 7.1 Zambia values for selected indicators

Indicator (year)	Value	Rank, among the 77 countries included in the quantitative analysis
GNI per capita (2003)	$350	71 (Rank 1 = greatest GNP per capita)
Percentage of the population living on less than $1.25 a day at 2005 international prices (2005)	64%	76 (Rank 1= lowest percentage on <$1.25)
Gini coefficient of consumption (1998)	0.53	68 (Rank 1= lowest Gini coefficient)
Mining and large plantation or farm exports, as percentage of total exports (2000)	56%	70 (Rank 1= lowest percentage)
Control of corruption (pessimistic view)[2] (2000)	-1.82	68 (Rank 1= greatest positive value)
Government revenue x corruption control (1999, 2000)	-35	66 (Rank 1= greatest positive value)

The author of the Zambia chapter in the 'Evangelicalism and Democracy' series includes Pentecostals within the Evangelical fold: 'I include Pentecostals in the Evangelical category for the purposes of this chapter, whether or not they are members of the Evangelical Fellowship of Zambia'.[3] As for the proportions of the population in the major Christian categories, different sources agree that about one third of Zambians are Roman Catholic. Following Isabel Phiri's practice of including Pentecostals in the Evangelical category gives a total of either 34.5 per cent (Barrett et al. 2001) or 43.9 per cent (Johnstone et al. 2001) who were in the broad category of Evangelical in AD 2000. Thus Zambia is a

---

[1] Bornwell Chikulo 'Corruption and Accumulation in Zambia' in Hope and Chikulo eds *Corruption and Development in Africa: Lessons from country case studies* (London: Macmillan 2000), 175.

[2] For a detailed account of the operation of corruption in Zambia see Afronet (2002).

[3] Isabel Phiri 'President Fredrick Chiluba and Zambia: Evangelicals and democracy in a "Christian Nation"' in Ranger *Evangelical Christianity and Democracy in Africa*, 101.

largely Christian country in which Evangelicals (broadly defined) slightly outnumber Roman Catholics.

The largest Protestant denomination is the United Church of Zambia (UCZ). It is a member of the Council of Churches in Zambia (CCZ), an umbrella body that represents the mainline Protestant denominations. The majority of independent Evangelical and Pentecostal churches are members of the Evangelical Fellowship of Zambia (EFZ). The Zambian Episcopal Conference (ZEC) speaks for the Catholic Church.

Table 7.2 Percentage of Zambians estimated to belong to various Christian categories

Estimated percentage of the population in each group in AD 2000	Barrett et al. (2001)	Johnstone et al. (2001)
Christians	82.4	85.0
Roman Catholics	33.5	33.5
Evangelicals	12.5	25.0
Pentecostals / charismatics	22.0	18.9
Evangelicals plus Pentecostals / charismatics	34.5	43.9

The relationship between the churches and corruption in Zambia has been influenced by the rule of Frederick Chiluba, an Evangelical, who was President of Zambia from 1991 to 2001. Chiluba did not occupy State House until three months after his election, after a group of 50 charismatic friends and associates had performed a 'cleansing service' at State House. The link between church and state was further strengthened when an 'anointing' service was organized for President Chiluba by the three main Christian bodies: CCZ, EFZ and ZEC. On December 29, 1991, President Chiluba declared Zambia a Christian nation (though with full religious freedom for all faiths). Standing between two pillars at State House, Chiluba said:

> The Bible, which is the word of God, abounds with proof that a nation is blessed, whenever it enters into a covenant with God and obeys the word of God. 2 Chronicles 7:14 says 'If my people who are called by my name will humble themselves and pray and seek my face and turn from their wicked ways, then will I hear from heaven and forgive their sin and will heal their land.' On behalf of the people of Zambia, I repent of our wicked ways of idolatry, witchcraft, the occult, immorality, injustice and corruption. I pray for the healing, restoration, revival, blessing and prosperity for Zambia. On behalf of the nation, I have now entered into a covenant with the living God...I submit the Government and the entire nation of Zambia to the Lordship of Jesus Christ. I further declare that Zambia is a Christian Nation that will seek to be governed by the righteous principles of the

Word of God. Righteousness and justice must prevail in all levels of authority, and then we shall see the righteousness of God exalting Zambia.[4]

Notwithstanding this declaration, ministers and senior officials in Chiluba's government were suspected of large-scale corruption, for example by profiteering through the privatisation of the Zambia Consolidated Copper Mines and the liquidation of Zambia Airways.[5] In early May 2007, about five weeks before the field visit on which this chapter is based, Chiluba himself was found guilty of stealing $46m of government money in a civil case heard in a London high court. A Zambian court had ruled in 2006 that Mr Chiluba was medically unfit to stand trial on corruption charges, so the London case, in which the lead defendants were two London-based law firms accused of laundering the money, was brought on behalf of the Zambian Attorney General. The Guardian newspaper of 5 May 2007 reported the judgment as follows:

> In a damning 220-page judgment Mr Justice Peter Smith accused ex-president Frederick Chiluba of Zambia, who left office in 2001, of shamelessly defrauding his people and flaunting his wealth with an expensive wardrobe of 'stupendous proportions'. The judge reserved his most abrasive remarks for Chiluba, whose corruption trial in Zambia has been repeatedly postponed because of his ill health. He refused to give evidence to the court. Mr Justice Smith singled out as 'the most telling example of corruption' his $500,000 purchase of hundreds of suits and monogrammed shirts from an exclusive boutique in Switzerland, as well as 72 pairs of handmade, high heel shoes to extend his 5ft stature. 'This was at a time when the vast majority of Zambians were struggling to live on $1 a day and many could not afford more than one meal a day. The people of Zambia should know that whenever he appears in public wearing some of these clothes he acquired them with money stolen from them.'

That is the context in which I interviewed 23 key informants in June 2007 about the relationship between the churches and corruption in Zambia.[6] Table C.3 in Appendix C gives brief details of the occupation, age, gender and religious affiliation of the key informants, and the dates and locations of the interviews.

The Reputation of Evangelicals for Honest Behaviour

The situation suggested by both Evangelical informants and others is that the reputation of Evangelicals in Zambia is being damaged by corruption in new

---

[4] Gifford *African Christianity*, 197-8.
[5] Gifford *African Christianity*, 206-7.
[6] More recently, a Zambian court has cleared Mr Chiluba of the same charges following a six-year trial, after a magistrate ruled the funds could not be traced to government money (Guardian newspaper of 17 August 2009).

Pentecostal churches. There was also some concern that corruption may have started to affect the traditional Evangelical churches.

Several Evangelical leaders criticized the activities of new Pentecostal churches in Zambia. Z10, an Evangelical bishop, thought the problems with church corruption are greatest 'in the new Pentecostal churches'. Z1, a lawyer and a Pentecostal, thought that corruption has 'affected the new Evangelical churches more than others'. Commenting on the mushrooming of Pentecostal and Evangelical churches, Z5, a senior leader in UCZ, thought that they are 'not founded on Christ but on man-religion, and probably the interest is financial gain' and that 'what's happening at the moment is actually embarrassing the church'. Z3, a UCZ pastor, had concluded that 'There's an economic rationale to a lot of the Pentecostal growth. It's like the way you see the small businesses on the streets – the churches are similar'. This view was endorsed by Dyness Kasungami, Human Development Advisor for DFID and an Evangelical: 'If I don't have access to public resources I will start a church, which gives me access to another set of resources ... The whole motive of starting the church or the ministry is really just to have access to resources'.[7] Z1, a lawyer and a Pentecostal, was not sure how widespread financial abuse is within the Pentecostal churches. At one point she said that 'There have been quite a number of churches where pastors have been thrown off their throne because they used church money for personal gain', but later suggested that 'it's a few bad eggs that have spoiled this image, it's not a lot of them, most of the churches are very sincere'.

As for the situation in the more established Evangelical churches, Z21, a leader in the Council of Churches of Zambia, thought that financial abuse has occurred only 'very few times' in the traditional churches because 'pastors are allowed to preach, but Boards are responsible for finances'. However Z1, a lawyer and a Pentecostal, thought that corruption 'could be happening in the traditional churches, but we don't know. In the charismatic churches everybody talks, so it comes out in the papers'. Worryingly, Dyness Kasungami thought that although lack of accountability started with the newer Pentecostal ministries, 'slowly it has worked back into the traditional churches ... I go to UCZ. Increasingly when you try to ask "How do you use the money that we give you through offerings?" you're asking the wrong question'.

Two non-Evangelical informants also thought that financial abuse is seen as more common in the new Pentecostal churches than in mainline Protestant or Catholic Churches. Z22, a leader in the Zambian Episcopal Conference, commented that a lot of Pentecostal church leaders 'are simply impostors, they are not even there for the right reasons', though he thought that financial abuse

---

[7] Gifford (1998:314-5) comments that 'many African NGOs, like the modern African Christian churches ... exist only to the extent that there is a donor somewhere prepared to fund their activities. This is a crucial element of Africa's contemporary NGO and church scene, and to neglect it is to give an incomplete picture of contemporary African Christianity'.

in churches with structured institutions is only 'occasional'. Z2, a leader of Transparency International in Zambia, said:

> We see people coming up with churches, not with the real motive of teaching the religious fundamentals or changing people. The message might be very good but the actions of the leaders are completely different. The mainstream denominations like the Seventh Day Adventists, ZEC, they seem to stick to their principles. But the Pentecostal churches, which are mushrooming at a very fast rate, they seem to build the formation of the churches mostly on aspects of their leaders getting at least comfortable lives ... They start up a church, then they create an international affiliation with other churches in the US. Then you'll see a lot of pastors coming from the US to preach, to make donations and to provide support to those church leaders, to go for studies to the US or to have exchange programmes. Those leaders ended up becoming more wealthy than their members. That's the kind of picture we have seen from the 1990's up to date ... Church leaders sometimes make pronouncements acknowledging that there could be problems even within their ranks as well, but it's in his church over there, not my church ... Church members will not fight wholeheartedly against corruption. They will look out for some immediate benefits, because they see their leaders living very comfortable lives ... So it's a bit difficult to see the church actually contributing very effectively to the fight against corruption.

Perceived Causes of Corruption in Zambian Churches

An easy way to explain away the problem of corruption within the church would be to claim that the corrupt individuals are simply not Christians. However, only two informants suggested this. Z16, a UCZ pastor, suggested that, although most Zambians assume they are Christian because they are baptised or have grown up in a traditional Christian setting (such that 'you might even offend somebody if you suggest they must be saved'), nonetheless 'they have no fear of the Lord'; and, as noted above, Z22, a leader in the Zambian Episcopal Conference, thought that a lot of Pentecostal church leaders are 'simply impostors'. Explanations for church corruption that were given much more frequently than people simply not being Christians concern poverty; lack of accountability, particularly for donations from western churches; and theologies that facilitate corruption.

Poverty

Given the very strong macro-level correlation between poverty and perceived corruption (see Figure 2.11 in Chapter 2), it is not surprising that informants' personal experience also suggested poverty as a cause of corruption. Z13, a University chaplain, said that:

> Day to day corruption among church members is very common because right now jobs are very rare in this country. I remember one minister saying to me "You people are saying that I'm only employing my relatives. But if I don't employ

them, who will?" We have preached about corruption to members of our churches, but some people say "If we don't do that, how are we going to see our children work? How are we going to make ends meet?"

Dyness Kasungami noted that 'The poorer people get, the more they struggle to access resources, the less attention they'll pay to corruption'. Z15, a member of staff in the Auditor-General's office, commented that:

American Pentecostal churches at times donate books like a Bible that comes free for us to distribute to our fellow Christians. But I've observed in certain cases that once these books come we tend to sell them. Then the money that is realised from that is spent personally. We always ask what is the reason for that, and the answer is poverty ... The efforts of the churches to control corruption are always outdone by the poverty levels. Families are very poor in most cases. People need to go to school, better housing, better facilities. This tends to make us not lean much on Christian principles. People think 'the more I become honest, the more poor I will become'.

However, Z10, an Evangelical bishop, observed that although people are vulnerable 'because of the poverty levels which cripple the church, the church pastor not getting adequate remuneration', he has also 'seen people that are not that poor who are still susceptible and open to such kind of temptations'.

Lack of accountability for church leaders

Several Evangelical leaders commented on the relative lack of accountability structures in the independent Evangelical and Pentecostal churches. Z3, a UCZ pastor, said:

Evangelical churches don't have a structure to which they're accountable - even Evangelical Alliances tend to be loose alliances where you don't feel obliged to subject yourself to any review. The church I belong to (UCZ) is not corrupt-free, but it has a structure, so you can only go so far as an individual before the whistle is blown. I've served on the EFZ board and it's very difficult. The churches are all very juvenile in their approach to ministry and a danger to themselves.

Z15, a member of staff in the Auditor-General's office, commented that: 'Resources in the churches are mostly managed just by church leaders. So people look at how best to get those positions - it's financially motivated. Essentially we're talking about theft'. Three informants commented that, even where churches have accountability structures in place, they may not be effective because the leaders resist them. Z16, a UCZ pastor, commented that:

In UCZ the accountability structures are there, but it also depends on the individual person in charge and how they feel responsible over what they are in charge of. Leadership in our culture is still centred around persons, more than the institution ... When the members say 'There's no money in the church – where has our money gone? Can we have your reports?', usually you'll find that there are no reports. It's just between the minister and his treasurer. That has brought a lot of conflict in Evangelical circles, within UCZ.

Dyness Kasungami said:

> They'll have their own audit structures within the church, but the truth is that they do not work, because it's like the government: there'll be networks and by the time people come in to audit they know what they'll find and they'll know how to get round it, so it will not really work ... Even in Lusaka, somehow we allow our leaders to get away with it. We give them the money, but we can't ask what happens to the money. And when you're asking, you become the problem ... I know a number of my friends who've either been chased, or totally, totally sidelined in some of these churches because they were asking for accountability.

Dyness had formerly been Chair of the Zambian Fellowship of Evangelical Students. She drew striking parallels between the cultures of government and church in Zambia:

> Accountability does not exist in public life. This morning we were discussing the problem of health workers and the level of absenteeism and late-coming for work. For me those are very simple standards. If I'm a Christian and I'm living faithfully I should be faithful in all of life ... sometimes they stay away to go to church functions, unfortunately. If I try to extrapolate that, the people in the civil service are the same people that are in the church, and so accountability will not exist in the church either.

Z7, Director of a Zambian anti-corruption NGO, wondered:

> To what extent do the leaders in our church understand that money has been given for X,Y and Z and therefore as a church leader I'm accountable to this or that person that sits on a committee? At the last AGM in my church there were two strange budget lines in the audited financial report. One was 'church expenses' and the other was 'sundry expenses'. A member asked about these but he hit a brick wall, he got no answer.

Western church donations without accountability

Some Evangelical leaders thought that corruption in the church is exacerbated by northern churches that donate money without sufficient accountability. Various Evangelical leaders described giving by western churches as 'good' (Z5), 'extremely noble' (Z7) and representing 'real international connections that are paying dividends' (Z11), and Z20, a leader in a Zambian Christian NGO, thought that misuse of money donated from northern churches is 'not a very common problem'. However, two Evangelical leaders expressed concerns about the way that donations from western churches may be misused. Dyness Kasungami saw damaging similarities in the ways that government and church in Zambia relate to donor support:

For me who works in the donor sector dealing with government during the week, and on Sunday I go to church, the pattern is replicated. It starts with moving from 'I am responsible to work so that I can meet the basic needs of me and my family', to accepting the support of donors who say 'You seem to be failing to meet your needs, therefore I will support you'. Then it moves to a point where the donors are almost responsible for me. But for me who receives, as a government official for example, I'm not obliged to pass on the benefits to the people on behalf of whom I'm receiving this support... The same thing goes into the church, so where initially we could look after ourselves, now we need the brothers and sisters who are better off to help us. And when the help comes, I don't pass the help on to the beneficiaries, or I decide how much I'll pass on - the rest is controlled by me. So even within the church, not only is there dependency but also a lack of accountability.

Z7, Director of a Zambian anti-corruption NGO, said that 'British churches have slowed down their levels of assistance to the Zambian churches because of the high levels of corruption in the church'. Nonetheless, 'because of the AIDS situation lots of people are giving donations' despite the fact that 'the levels of accountability, even in the church, are horrible'.

Several Evangelical leaders criticised western churches for not assessing potential recipient organisations adequately and for failing to establish adequate financial accountability systems. Z10, an Evangelical bishop, said that:

Unfortunately, donor organisations tend to be naïve. They sometimes don't know what happens on the ground. The fact that someone's carrying a business card and has a big title does not mean that they are necessarily accountable people, morally upright and trustworthy persons here on the ground. And so the donors must do their homework. They must get clarity about what these people are asking money for, how will they use it. How will they know that it has been used for the purpose that was intended? The donor agencies need to get on the ground and understand what's really happening.

Z17, a Pentecostal pastor, observed that:

Our brothers from abroad don't really look at who they're giving things to, their Christian character. If someone just writes a project proposal and sends it over to them, maybe they just look at the merits of the case that has been presented. They don't even want to get a referee from somewhere to say 'This person is fit to run such an organisation and to receive funding'.

Z8, a former Vice President of Zambia, urged donor churches to help develop systems for accountability:

Americans more than anybody else are not used to supporting systems outside their country. They support individuals who they believe they can work with, who believe in what they're doing. Money comes from the US in huge quantities to these church organisation or individuals and they do not have the capacity to manage those resources in a manner that is internationally acceptable. It's no fault of their own, but they just don't have the system so when the money comes, if there's $10,000 to the pastor and the church says "This is for you and what you're doing in Zambia", he has to decide how much does he give to his family, how much of it does he use for the poor, how much does he use to buy equipment. It's basically his own decision. On the other hand, if those donor churches would demand financial reports it helps the recipient churches to make sure that they can account for every dollar they spend – and some churches do that.

Z11, an Evangelical bishop, reflected that his advice that 'whoever is making donations in the west should be able to call for accountability' is 'not very popular in civil society'.

A Catholic perspective on the Evangelical sector was given by Z22, a leader in the Zambian Episcopal Conference, who said:

> If I'm a pastor and then I apply to a church in Europe or America, who trusts that I'm going to do something, if I tell them that I'm going to start an orphanage and they send me $40,000 and I may build a house for myself and my wife and bring in my nephews and nieces, and then I say these are the orphans I'm looking after.

'Touch not God's anointed' and the prosperity gospel

Informants described two types of theology that undermine accountability and honest behaviour. The first teaches that since the pastor has been anointed by God he should be accountable only to God and not subject to any scrutiny by others in the church. The other theology teaches that God wants all Christians to become rich through giving to support Christian work, which in practice means giving to His local representative, the pastor. Z16, a UCZ pastor, thought that in Evangelical circles it is common to find the attitude 'I am the anointed of the Lord, you cannot speak against me or question me. I am the final authority'. Z1, a lawyer and a Pentecostal, said:

> If there's nepotism or misuse of money by the pastor there'll be a lot of murmuring, but nothing will be done about it. It won't be like "We've got to get him out", but a lot of people will be talking. They won't be happy with it, but they will think "What do we do?" The pastor or priest, whoever is in charge, is revered, you don't attack him. "Touch not my anointed" is the scripture quoted. You could get away with stuff for a long time before the church is fed up with you.

Dyness Kasungami referred to tele-evangelists who say 'You don't touch the man of God, you don't question the man of God'. She said:

> I've been in congregations where they've said, 'According to the Bible you should not be questioning your elders about where the money went or how the money is spent. You should trust the leaders'. The man of God is exalted to the level where you don't question, because according to the Bible you give the

money and then they decide. At most you can pray for wisdom for them so that they'll allocate the money well. They are new churches.

On the issue of prosperity theology Z5, a senior leader in UCZ, described prosperity theology as 'dangerous' because 'it leads to corruption'. Z13, a University chaplain, described the following tactics as part of the 'gospel of prosperity':

> Our friends run sometimes their ministries or churches single-handedly. If I have a partner outside the country I will tell him I have so many people, these are the problems I'm facing, I'm banking on starting an orphanage for street kids – so why don't you send money? Sometimes you find with these people that they buy themselves posh cars, because they believe that God is a rich God, and He wouldn't see us be poor.

Z15, a member of staff in the Auditor-General's office, suggested that church members like to have pastors who are reasonably well-off: 'a pastor has to live at a level that is well above the abject poverty level ... We Christians also want to have a pastor who is looking nice, who is well dressed. It's important to the congregation'. However, Z3, a UCZ pastor, was less convinced that church members are happy to enrich their pastor:

> I've been long enough in both Evangelical and mainline churches (25 years) that I've seen a shift. People start off preaching prosperity, but after a while you realise that only the leaders get prosperous ... I've seen people beginning to lose faith, at least those who go to those kinds of churches. They'll give the best that they have to the man or woman of God, and expect a return for that ... I can see how prosperity attracts a lot of people because people are in need and if possible they want to have a magic wand and get what you want right now.

She described some pastors' plans as 'crafty':

> They realised with time that prosperity teaching doesn't go very far, you can only do it so many times. There are many crafty pastors who change their style. Some of the pastors who earlier on were teaching a straightforward prosperity message, they might begin to talk about projects, things that will bring wealth to the church, and blackmail people into giving to the church. It might be a church building - they can slant their message to suit the audience. The people might think that they're going to benefit in the long term, but the pastor might benefit more.

Co-option by the state

Z7, Director of a Zambian anti-corruption NGO, saw government donations to churches as a strategy for weakening their moral authority: 'Governments in Africa realise the potency of the churches, so they've been finding a way of crippling them and making them dysfunctional'. Z8, a former Vice President of Zambia, described this effect on the churches:

The compromise that came through receiving money from the President compromised one of the strongest voices to challenge corruption, which is the Evangelical voice. Up to this day the Evangelical movement has not recovered from that lack of engagement at the time when they should have challenged Chiluba about corruption. In Zambia the church's moral authority has been eroded because we were compromised publicly and when the country expected us to speak we couldn't speak, even on matters that were of an urgent nature.

A slightly more hopeful voice was expressed by Z21, a leader in the Council of Churches of Zambia, who thought that although 'parts of the body of Christ, for the sake of money, compromised their values of Christianity... now the problem is better - we are working very closely now with some of those churches'.

Finally, only one informant made any reference to 'dualism' (in which Christianity is seen as having relevance to the spiritual, but not to the other, dimensions of life). Z16, a UCZ pastor, referred to a 'dichotomy of belief' in which although 'most of our members think that church is a holy place' so that 'we must be holy when we're inside the church building', Christian faith is concerned only with 'issues of spirituality, not so much how you live your Christian life outside the church'.

Preaching About Corruption

The most forthright example of preaching about corruption was the description given by Z18, a Pentecostal pastor, of his pastoral visits to government offices:

> I encourage them to repent and believe in Christ and work like a servant of God. I say to them 'If you work because you trust the President and start to cheat people, remember that one day judgement will come and you're going to perish forever.'

Two Evangelical informants thought the churches were quite active in preaching against corruption. Z6, a newspaper journalist, said: 'The church has got a strong voice against corruption ... The church has done its part and it continues to do so'. Z1, a lawyer and a Pentecostal, thought that:

> The majority of churches have played a subtle role by teaching 'Let's live Christ-like lives' ... Everybody's being reminded 'You accept a bribe today, you're not only stealing from the government, but you're literally stealing your children's future. You'll have sold out your country'.

However, a slightly more common view was that the church has said rather little about corruption. Having acknowledged that 'church structures themselves are not very accountable' Z16, a UCZ pastor, said:

> I find that we are silent on the issue of corruption. I haven't heard a concerted effort to speak against corruption. We keep quiet, lest the politicians should point

their fingers at us and say 'Can we audit your books?' Politicians may say we don't have proper, accountable structures.

She had even found opposition to raising the topic: 'Even if personally I would want to go out and speak about corruption, in my church set up the elders may ask me "Minister, this is not even on our agenda. How has it come into our context?"' Z21, a leader in the Council of Churches of Zambia, said 'we need to break the silence on corruption'. She was optimistic that 'the message has gone through to churches that corruption is our issue ... once it entrenches in the minds of people in the churches, especially in the leadership, then we will definitely start to deal with it'. Z20, a leader in a Zambian Christian NGO, commented that 'There's been very little engagement by the church as far as corruption is concerned. The church doesn't speak loudly against corruption because the finger will be pointed at it very, very quickly'.

Z14, a Catholic member of staff in the Auditor-General's office, was 'really taken aback' when I asked about the relationship between the church and corruption because she had 'never really thought about it':

I haven't seen any activity in that area – I'm a Catholic, but I've also attended Pentecostal churches. I haven't heard anybody talk about it - it's supposed to be part of Christianity – to have integrity, to be upright, not to be corrupt. It's all part of biblical teachings, but I haven't heard any teaching in church about corruption, though it might crop up in some examples in sermons. But I've never heard a sermon just on corruption.

Why do the churches not preach about corruption more than they do?

An obvious answer to this question, already mentioned by Z16 and Z20 above, is the concern of churches that they themselves will be found wanting if they raise the topic of corruption. However, a number of informants suggested other possible answers.

First, several informants thought that Zambians do not see corruption as wrong and may regard attempts to fight corruption as a foreign agenda. Z10, an Evangelical bishop, suggested that 'The main hindrance for the church being fully able to participate in the fight against corruption has to do with perspective, a lack of understanding of the fact that the Bible speaks against corruption, that it's a vice within society'. Z16, a UCZ pastor, said 'We are a very hospitable people and I don't think we like to see evil in other people. We don't really get pierced to the heart with things that we should be concerned about, like corruption.' Z19, an Anglican church leader, thought that 'most Christians are very reluctant to wage war against something they've seen that is not right. So the church has not spoken enough against the vices of corruption'. Z12, a senior member of staff at the Zambia Anti-Corruption Commission, felt that 'the biggest challenge in fighting corruption is to get the public to believe that it is an evil and that it's detrimental to their welfare'. One senior Evangelical leader (who did not want this comment to be attributed) said that 'Zambian culture is tolerant of evil. We are not able to confront one another.'

Father Peter Henriot, Director of the Jesuit Centre for Theological Reflection, suggested three reasons why corruption is sometimes tolerated:

(1) it is expected that those who have a bit of authority have a right to claim something for themselves, even outside the laid-down rules;

(2) it is accepted that those who are in serious need are not doing anything wrong to compensate for low wages;

(3) it is anticipated that strict accountability and transparency is sometimes too much of a demeaning demand on high officials (how often do we hear "trust me" as a substitute for following the rules!).

These attitudes towards corruption were evident in two Evangelical leaders' descriptions of reactions to the conviction on corruption charges of former President Chiluba. Z16, a UCZ pastor, thought that many Zambians are grateful to Chiluba and say things like 'What have you done for me, you who is condemning him? He's made mistakes but we all make mistakes, look at the good that he's done, at least he's given me shelter'. Z1, a lawyer and a Pentecostal, said:

Most people couldn't care less, they're too hungry to be bothered about Chiluba and corruption. They don't understand why there's a hullabaloo. 'He stole, so what?' They're used to the tyranny rule of the headman.

Two church leaders thought that fighting corruption might be seen as a foreign agenda. Z3, a UCZ pastor, warned that:

Corruption still tends to be defined in very western terms. When you say someone is practising nepotism in our context, how much of that is just being nice to the people you live with in your community? ... Anything that doesn't have ownership doesn't help. Any assistance that comes to fight corruption and is western-driven, no matter how knowledgeable the person is, I would think it's misplaced.

Though he personally disagreed with the following view, Z20, a leader in a Zambian Christian NGO, thought that:

There's a perception by most of our educated people that because of what we went through – colonisation and things like that – we are much better than the North and there's very little we can learn from them. And that perception is really killing us, because there's a lot we can learn from the other side in the area of good governance.

A second suggested reason for the churches' limited emphasis on corruption is lack of training. Z21, a leader in the Council of Churches of Zambia, noted that 'issues of corruption, other social issues, are not really tackled when church leaders are being formed ... so the church keeps quiet when they don't understand'. However, she felt that educated lay members have become dissatisfied with this:

> In our pews now are sitting well-educated people who ... want to connect what this Christianity has to do with my life now. 'We fully understand the implications of salvation then, but how about now while we move towards salvation?' And many churches are not equipped to face that challenge and that is why they are not doing anything about it.

She expressed gratitude for the opportunity to learn from organisations like Transparency International: 'We do a lot of listening and understanding: what is corruption and how can it be curbed, because it's not part of our learning'.

Preaching from the pulpit is felt to have little impact on corruption

Only one informant (Z17, a Pentecostal pastor) expressed confidence in the power of preaching to change corrupt behaviour: 'we have been preaching the gospel, and that's the only way that people can be helped – by a change of heart, a change of mind'. However, several informants expressed concern at the apparent lack of impact of preaching. Z10, an Evangelical bishop, noted with concern that:

> Earlier this year there were some revelations that some government Directors and Permanent Secretaries, the people that run the day to day machinery for the public service, were engaged in high levels of corruption, there were large amounts of money being misappropriated. These are people who would be frequenting churches. The question I asked at that time was "What is the impact of the church in these lives?" Because if it is now seen that the corruption is really strong and has proliferated at that level, then these individual Christians are not applying their faith.

Z16, a UCZ pastor, even thought that 'the church is to blame for the economic and political situation, because in church we have everybody, be they a politician, a doctor, a nurse, they are all there'. She continued:

> What is the message that we're preaching, and what impact is it having on their lives? Because if it has impact on their lives it should reflect in their workplaces and their homes, but it doesn't. If I go to the council today or to the government ministry, those people are Christian. But for him to give me my file, he'll want me to give him money for a drink or for lunch: 'I'm the power, the authority here. If you do not do what I say you will not get what you want from me'.

Z1, a lawyer and a Pentecostal, observed that 'at the lower level you've got people teaching about a Christ-like way of life' but immediately questioned 'whether people are listening, or adhering to it'. Z6, a newspaper journalist, thought that 'the church has got a strong voice against corruption, but we haven't seen a reduction in terms of corruption levels'.

Reforming Government by Having Evangelicals Inside Government

In early May 2007, about five weeks before the field visit on which this chapter is based, former President Chiluba had been found guilty in a London high court of stealing $46m of government money. Given Chiluba's identity as an Evangelical, this section focuses on the different ways in which his actions were being interpreted.

Dyness Kasungami thought that 'despite all the things that have come out, there are still people within the church that would stand by him now. They do not believe that he did any wrong. Partly it is because they were beneficiaries'. This reluctance to believe that Chiluba stole from his own people was evident in comments from several Evangelical leaders. Z13, a University chaplain, said 'we have not seen the figures, so we can't exactly say that he misappropriated the money. He really gave out the money to the church and to the public ... Chiluba helped the church so much'. Z5, a senior leader in UCZ, commented: 'from what I've read so far it sounds a very complex network. It's not clear whether he embezzled large sums of money for himself'. Reflecting on coverage of the trial before the judgement was announced, Z19, an Anglican church leader, thought Chiluba had been dealt rough justice:

> They didn't give Chiluba much time to exculpate himself, or a fair platform where he could be tried fairly, without interference from the current President and his people. Whenever he's speaking, he refers to Chiluba as a thief – but he's still innocent until the law proves otherwise.

Z15, a member of staff in the Auditor-General's office, thought that although the money Chiluba handled 'didn't go through a formal process', nonetheless it was 'given to churches ... It was given to the needy'. Z20, a leader in a Zambian Christian NGO, expressed frustration at this reluctance to criticise Chiluba:

> I don't think I've heard an Evangelical voice talking about what should be done about Chiluba's corruption. Whether it's because it was done from Britain and we feel embarrassed and ashamed that we cannot rule ourselves, I don't know. Or whether it's because Mr Chiluba is a Christian and also he gave a lot of donations to the churches, whether the churches are now feeling guilty by association, I really don't know. It has been a bit frustrating for me that the church has not said anything tangible.

For Zambian Christians who do think Chiluba was corrupt, a simple way to explain away his corrupt behaviour is to deny that he is a Christian. Two Evangelical leaders and one Catholic informant clearly thought in this way. Z21, a leader in the Council of Churches of Zambia, thought that 'Chiluba's Christian Nation Declaration was a way of hoodwinking the Zambian people, because the majority are Christians. He was manipulative, he knew exactly what he was looking for, he knew what he was doing'. Z4, a retired military officer, said:

People in the town where Chiluba lived deny that he was ever a Christian. Quite clearly, his strategy was to create a Christian identity for himself to win votes. There were some true Christians with him at the beginning and he dispensed with them ... True Christians don't do that.

Z22, a leader in the Zambian Episcopal Conference, said that:

Chiluba claimed he was an Evangelical. And he started weekly prayers at State House to pray for himself and the government. I asked my bishop to stop going there because I said 'You are playing into the hands of a political gimmick'. Meanwhile Chiluba was sticking his fingers everywhere, and we knew it. He's been a shrewd manipulator from way back, before he became the President.

However, a larger number of Evangelical leaders who thought Chiluba had acted corruptly nonetheless thought his profession of Christian faith was genuine. Z10, an Evangelical bishop, thought that Chiluba was 'sincere, well-intentioned - but misguided'. Z11, another Evangelical bishop, agreed: 'When you talk to former President Chiluba, he's knows what salvation is all about. He knows what prayer is. There are failings in his life, fine, but when you talk about his faith, regeneration, his Christian testimony, then he's clear'. Z17, a Pentecostal pastor, said 'I think Chiluba was definitely a born-again Christian. The man seems to love the Lord a lot. Of course you may see some flaws, some faults – but then no one is perfect'. Z20, a leader in a Zambian Christian NGO, was unequivocal in saying that 'Chiluba is a Christian'.

Z8, a former Vice President of Zambia, thought Chiluba had 'presided over one of the most corrupt administrations in the continent' but nonetheless described him as 'a man who fears God'. He went on to pose the obvious question: 'Why would a man who fears God, a man whom people thought was going to be the redeemer, preside over one of the most corrupt administrations in the continent? Not only preside over it, but be implicated in it himself.' Z11, an Evangelical bishop, blamed Chiluba's carelessness and fallen human nature:

It's very clear that Chiluba meant well, as evidenced by his first term of office. In his second term, you begin to wonder whether he was distracted. It was like 'I'm going out anyway', so he became careless, he lost it. He was distracted in the sense that there were a lot of forces at play. Maybe it's in the fallen nature that these things were surfacing'.

Z8, a former Vice President of Zambia, gave two different explanations for the contradictions between Chiluba's faith and actions: failing to think through the connections in practical terms,[8] and being outnumbered by corrupt colleagues in Cabinet. On the first explanation Z8 said:

---

[8] Both David Martin and Paul Gifford point out that Evangelical theology provides little help. 'As Evangelicals experience the intricate dynamics of the political sphere, they have no traditions to use as guides ... In the absence of sophisticated norms deployed by

I think that he did not intentionally begin to allow corruption. I think he was counselled into corruption. The system of government counselled him 'Look, this is the way that things are done. So in order to protect yourself you must do this'. Because a President is really like a dog on a leash, he's led to places, he's driven to a place, he makes a speech, they put him in the car, they take him to State House and lock him up there until they open the following morning. It's a prison. You've got to be strong enough to think for yourself. The Presidency and the Vice-Presidency are the only jobs in government where you're not expected to think, because you've got people to think for you. If there's a speech someone will write it for you. If you have to make a decision they'll give you a note of what to say. So you've got to be strong enough to be able to connect your values and your Christian faith to government. And my conclusion is that my elder brother in the faith failed to practically connect his faith to everyday life of government. The reason could be that it was a new concept, a totally new concept. By failing to connect to government, the government system connected to him and that's how he fell into the trap of corruption.

On the issue of being outnumbered in Cabinet, Z8 said:

You don't run government alone as President. It's a consensus issue, a compromise issue. You may have two Christians with values and 21 other Cabinet Ministers. Either this Christian President must dictate what he believes are the good and right values, or if he's going to be a democrat, he's going to allow everyone around his Cabinet table to make proposals. And usually the decision that wins the vote may not necessarily be Christian, or even in the interests of the nation. A Christian President's morals can obviously rub off onto the other members of cabinet, but these are developed men and women whom he cannot change in one or two years. They believe what they believe, they're corrupt at heart, they don't know what he's talking about, so they're going to do what they think is right.

Promoting Civic Oversight

Two Evangelical informants described activities aimed at engaging communities in better governance. Z5, a senior leader in UCZ, mentioned some activities of his church's Mission and Evangelism Department:

---

high-status ecclesiastics and religious intellectuals, Evangelicals are exposed to the vagaries of circumstance equipped with little more than native good sense and the limited inferences they can draw from the Bible. They lack markers to stabilize their responses' (Martin 'The Evangelical Upsurge', 40). 'The Evangelical sector of Christianity does not really have a theology of good government; for them all that is needed is to have Christian leaders (frequently themselves) either in positions of influence or as advisors to those who hold such positions' (Gifford *African Christianity*, 216-7).

It educates the masses, our members, on the dangers of corruption, because we feel that if that kind of education and awareness can reach the masses and the grassroots then we should be able to arrest this scourge of corruption. For instance, during elections people would be given food, materials (T-shirts) or cash by someone soliciting for a vote. People wouldn't understand the dangers of obtaining those items and the implications it has for the development of the country, because you have the wrong people going into government and they'll continue to use the same way to corrupt people throughout.

A more sophisticated approach is the Mapalo Initiative in Ndola. Mapalo is a slum community of 60,000 people. The Jubilee Centre, an Evangelical NGO whose stated mission is 'to empower churches, communities and their leaders to realize their full potential', worked with community leaders to identify local priorities such as roads, a high school, a hospital, piped water and better drainage, then brokered the signing of a social contract between the electorate and all their political candidates:

After the 2006 general elections, our elected Ward Councillor and Member of Parliament hereby pledge to work with us to address the above problems affecting our community during his/her tenure in office, agreeing to make change in most of the stated areas within the first three years of his/her term, diligently consulting our community on the various issues of governance which affect us. This social contract has been entered into between the candidates and the electorate.

Signed,

At the time of the field visit in June 2007 it was too early to assess how successful this approach had been, but it certainly demonstrated that at least a few Zambian Evangelicals are trying to engage communities for better governance.

Evangelical views on Catholic efforts to oppose corruption
Notwithstanding these Evangelical efforts at local level, leaders of mainstream Protestant church groups, Pentecostal pastors and leaders of anti-corruption bodies all agreed that in Zambia the Catholic Church is more effective than other churches in advocacy for better governance at the national level.[9] Z3, a UCZ pastor, said:

The Catholics are better placed structurally than the Protestants, for example through their Jesuit Centre for Theological Reflection. They raise issues that are

---

[9] Paul Gifford (*African Christianity,* 224-6) comments that 'only the Catholic Church receives sufficient resources to be able to maintain its institutions, and therefore preserve discipline and function with reasonable efficiency ... Zambian church statements display an economic awareness that equivalents in Ghana and Uganda lack. This quality is probably attributable to the Jesuit Centre for Theological Reflection'.

pertinent to the fight against corruption, and engage the public and the government, and lobby through parliament. Then there's the Catholic Centre for Justice, Peace and Development, that engages very creatively and meaningfully. They raise questions very professionally with the Zambia Revenue Authority and through Parliament. We do not engage as Protestants at a level where you can challenge the structures meaningfully.

Z16, a UCZ pastor, said:

The Catholic Church are very consistent in their theology and in their issuing of statements concerning affairs in the nation, but the rest of the church has no consensus in what we say. The Catholic Church, because of their system, what they say carries a lot of weight. Even from the Evangelical point of view we tend to listen when the Catholic Church speaks out on an issue. We feel they've spoken on behalf of the people.

Z5, a senior leader in UCZ, said 'We're very grateful to the Roman Catholic Church; they were the first to come out and begin to give direction, especially during the 2001 elections'. Z21, a leader in the Council of Churches of Zambia, contrasted Evangelicals negatively with the Catholic Church:

Zambia Episcopal Conference (the Catholic body) and the Christian Council of Zambia (mainstream Protestant) speak with one voice, currently on the Constituent Assembly. The Evangelical Fellowship of Zambia is very slow, they been playing distance for some time – though they are part of the Oasis Forum ... At one time we mounted a huge campaign at the Parliament, lobbying for them to enact a Constituent Assembly, but the Evangelicals said categorically that they would not participate. So sometimes they'll come, sometimes they won't. The Executive Director is very keen, but the membership are dragging their feet about participation.

Z10, an Evangelical bishop, said 'sometimes the church is aloof, not wanting to get their hands dirty: "Politics is a dirty game, so let's keep away"'. Z17, a Pentecostal pastor, thought Evangelicals should emulate the Catholic Church:

The Catholics are really helping shape the thought of the nation. They really come out very strongly to speak against any social evil. The Roman Catholics issue pastoral letters that address corruption, HIV/AIDS, abuse of power etc. They also run Radio Ichelengo – for a month they were addressing the issue of corruption, trying to sensitise the public on the evils of corruption. This is where the Evangelicals need to go too.

Z20, a leader in a Zambian Christian NGO, lamented that the church does not see governance issues as 'part of the mission of the church, as something we should be addressing long-term as a spiritual issue where we are doing discipleship and developing people, encouraging them to take responsibility for themselves, holding communities accountable and holding government accountable'. Dyness Kasungami had formerly been Chair of the Zambian Fellowship of Evangelical Students (ZAFES). She reflected that 'ZAFES has focused on corruption and integrity issues a little. We try to raise some social issues, but it's not as much as you'd expect'. Z22, a leader in the Zambian Episcopal Conference, gave a Catholic perspective:

> More and more churches are beginning to buy into this idea of economic justice, that we cannot leave economic issues to the state alone, that all of us are stakeholders ... But a good number of Evangelical churches still have to make sense of that.

A live issue during my visit to Zambia was debate regarding Evangelical involvement in the Oasis Forum, a body that was pressing for changes to the Constitution that would limit the powers of Zambia's President. Three Evangelical leaders thought it was appropriate for Evangelicals to be involved in this Forum, but two disagreed. Z11, an Evangelical bishop, remarked that the current Constitution has:

> failed in many respects and the only way we can succeed is to have better structures in place. We do not need a good man, we need structures that will hold anyone accountable, regardless of whether they are evil .... The executive has too much power.

Z17, a Pentecostal pastor, was full of admiration for this stance, saying that:

> because the President is all-powerful, if he is engaged in corrupt activities it will be very difficult for any organ of state to deal with him until he leaves office. Any President could take advantage unless the Constitution is worked on. That's really where the church has come through, for 3 or 4 years now. They've been telling the government to change the Constitution.

Z21, a leader in the Council of Churches of Zambia, was proud that 'The church has been in the forefront of advocating for a new Constitution in that hope that, when we have a new Constitution, issues of corruption might be minimised'.

On the other hand, criticisms of Evangelical involvement were expressed by Z16, a UCZ pastor, who thought that 'the Evangelical Fellowship of Zambia's stand has been compromised in the sense that they belong to the Oasis Forum that is talking specifically about the Constitution'. Z7, Director of a Zambian anti-corruption NGO, thought the churches' role should be limited to prayer and mediation:

> Talking about the Constitution is political and can be partisan. We don't want a situation where the church is pitted against government ... The moment the church becomes part of the hullabaloo of discussions of any particular issue then the church will not be able to mediate ... Rather than the church hitting headlines,

what the church should have done is organized nationwide prayers for the leadership of this country wherever they are, whether in opposition or government. The church leadership should set themselves apart.

Theological hindrances to Evangelical engagement in advocacy

Both Catholic and Evangelical informants thought aspects of prevailing Evangelical theology hinder engagement in advocacy. The prosperity gospel has already been mentioned as a cause of corruption in the church. It was also seen as an impediment to proper civic engagement. Z22, a leader in the Zambian Episcopal Conference, described the prosperity gospel as 'very magical. It stops people from getting engaged with the issues'. Z20, a leader in a Zambian Christian NGO, said that:

> The church here sees poverty as a personal problem. Particularly the Evangelical church doesn't see poverty as anything to do with the systems that are in place. The churches that are strong and have resources see poverty as a personal problem of bad decisions, laziness, lack of faith, not having a relationship with Jesus. So they don't see corruption as affecting the level of poverty in the nation. This perspective comes from Nigeria and the US, it's a version of the prosperity gospel that attributes poverty to personal sin and lack of tithing.

Z21, a leader in the Council of Churches of Zambia, also attributed the reluctance of Evangelicals to engage in advocacy to their understanding of the Bible's teaching about submission to government: 'it may be because they think their role is to work with the government of the day, not to criticise them, because the Bible says "Honour the leadership"'. Dyness Kasungami described this theology as 'wrong' and thought that 'if you submit yourself to the government of the day, whether that government is living up to its standards or not, you're really condoning corruption'. Father Peter Henriot, Director of the Jesuit Centre for Theological Reflection, has described this theology as a 'pernicious heresy':

> There still exists a pernicious heresy in some church circles that true Christians should never challenge civic authority. I call this view pernicious – harmful, destructive, insidious – because it would silence, shut up, the voices of Desmond Tutu against apartheid in South Africa, Martin Luther King against segregation in the USA, John Paul II against communism in Poland, and the mother bodies of Evangelicals, Protestants and Catholics (EFZ, CCZ and ZEC) against "third-termism" in Zambia. And I call it heresy because it deliberately mis-reads, mis-interprets, scripture. In taking up the famous passage from Romans 13, it focuses on verses 1 to 2, that speak of authority being put in place by God and that whoever opposes authority opposes God. But it ignores the key phrases of verse 4 that make very clear, very clear indeed, that the one in authority is God's servant "working for your own good." In other words, if the ruler is not working for the good of the people, is not promoting the common good, is not serving the national interest, she or he simply loses legitimacy, no longer has authority and should not be obeyed. Certainly he or she should not be respected!"

Poverty and naivety have made churches vulnerable to co-option by the state
Beyond theology, a powerful practical reason why some churches have refrained from criticising the government is that they have been co-opted through financial gifts. Although Christian leaders expressed doubts about the impact of their preaching on corruption, the government appears to believe they have political influence worth paying for. Z11, an Evangelical bishop, described his experience of this:

> I personally was offered Kw.150 million to do some campaigning during the election. They said 'There are no strings attached. We just feel that people are being misinformed, and we feel that if you, with your deserving reputation - you can correct them and tell them the right thing'. I turned it down, I refused. I told them I'm not available for purchase. But not much later, after I turned it down, I began to see on TV bishops (from the independent Pentecostal churches) who began to campaign and speak the language of the President. They would say 'We don't want people who have more than one wife to become President. We don't want smokers for President' and stuff like that. Knowing what I'd been offered, I knew that they'd been paid. I've had several offers. One time I was coming from the church and I was approached by three gentlemen sent from State House. They said, 'What do you really want, and we are willing to give it to you? Anything.'

Z12, a senior member of staff at the Zambia Anti-Corruption Commission, said: 'In the 2006 election some independent churches were paid by political parties. The leaders have access to the media, they are able to stand before their congregations, so they use all these platforms to drum up support'. Z4, a retired military officer, thought that it was mainly the Pentecostal clergy that were 'pocketed': 'the Catholic Church was able to stand their ground against Chiluba, very strongly. But the Pentecostals were split', the inevitable result being that 'the church has been weakened because of political influence'.

Poverty and naiveté were the explanations given for the ease with which many churches have been 'bought' by politicians. Z17, a Pentecostal pastor, said:

> The church has been compromised because it lacks financial capacity. If I am building a church in my community, I don't have the money to raise that structure. And then the government comes in and says 'We're going to help you. How much money do you want?' If I get that money from the government, next time I have to speak for the voiceless I'm not going to bite the finger that feeds me.

Likewise Z8, a former Vice President of Zambia, said that a 'lack of resource and creativity in the Evangelical world has made the church to be very dependent on western dollars, so they are very vulnerable to being bought'. Z5, a senior leader in UCZ, thought that 'if people are empowered economically they'll be able to resist such kind of temptations'.

Several informants maintained that when churches received money from President Chiluba they believed it was legitimate and well-intentioned. Z19, an Anglican church leader, said 'the recipients of money from Chiluba's Slush Fund saw it as a way of helping the community, they didn't know there was an improper motive behind his giving'. Z13, a University chaplain, reflected that:

> I didn't understand where Chiluba was getting the money from. I thought maybe he was lobbying outside the country. It helped a lot of churches, schools and other organisations ... Since those programmes affected ordinary people we thought it maybe was good ... We thought it was coming from the right source. But the church should have had a prophetic voice, rather than just accepting everything.

Z6, a newspaper journalist, said 'Innocently the churches would think that the President is just donating to a very good cause so they wouldn't reject it'.

Fear of the state

A final reason why Christians might be reluctant to advocate for better governance concerns their physical safety. One informant described the following experience:

> I've been shot at. I was driving home at night in Lusaka. I was just getting home, and a car was trailing me. I would stop and give them an indication that they should pass, they never passed. Then I realised I was in danger. So I quickly turned, facing them, and I tried to rush to the police. As I passed them they fired. I thank God that I'm still alive. In the morning I picked out the cartridge and took it to the police and they said it was one of the police or the military weapons that had been used. What had happened that particular morning makes me certain that it was pre-arranged. Some of my colleagues had a meeting with one of the Commissioners in the Constitution-making process and this man was asking about me and saying 'How well do you know this man? He is hated so much by the President'. They told me that in the morning and in the evening the shooting happened.

Another informant gave the following account:

> If all the churches would get together and address these evils, I think our voice would be massive. Many believers in Zambia share my view, but then the problem is we fear the government. Sometimes they would call you to the Intelligence Office to quiz you on certain statements you might have made. It's intimidating, with very subtle threats. They say 'You've been speaking against the President, saying that he's sick and he couldn't rule the nation. You are church men – how can you speak like that?' They wouldn't divulge their sources of information. To be singled out as a pastor, to be called to appear before an Intelligence Officer who comes from Lusaka, that can give you a few shivers. There were no direct threats, but they said 'If you want to continue, we can prosecute you for defamation of the President'. They can even apply some economic embargoes against you. If you are running a firm and you supply to

government then they will not buy anything from you. That's how they keep people in line. If your relatives hear that you've been called to appear before these people, they'll tell you to shut up: 'You may lose your life'.

Summary

The reputation of Evangelicals for honest behaviour

Evangelical leaders described corruption as more prevalent in the new Pentecostal churches than in either the traditional Evangelical churches or the Catholic Church, though one Evangelical leader (Dyness Kasungami) expressed concern that the problem may be growing in the traditional Evangelical churches. Only one Evangelical leader (Z16, a UCZ pastor) suggested that corruption in the church occurs because the people involved are not Christians. Causes suggested by other Evangelical leaders were poverty; lack of accountability for church leaders, particularly for donations from western churches; theologies that facilitate corruption ('Touch not God's anointed', and the prosperity gospel); and co-option by the state. In contrast with Kenya, no informants suggested that tribalism is a cause of corruption in Zambia.

Preaching about corruption

Several Evangelical leaders thought the churches have been rather silent on the subject of corruption. Suggested reasons for this include awareness that the church's own house is out of order; a cultural 'tolerance of evil'; a perception that fighting corruption is a western agenda; and lack of relevant training for church leaders. Several Evangelical leaders expressed doubts about the extent to which preaching about corruption changes people's behaviour, and there was no sign of anything similar to the Evangelical Alliance of Kenya's initiative to address corruption within the Evangelical sector in Kenya.

Reforming government by having Evangelicals inside government

Some Evangelical leaders were reluctant to accept the 2007 London court judgement that former President Chiluba, while professing to be an Evangelical Christian, had stolen $46m of government money; other Evangelical leaders were frustrated by this reluctance to accept the judgement. Among the Evangelical leaders who accepted the court's verdict, only two (Z21, a leader in the Council of Churches of Zambia, and Z4, a retired military officer) thought that Chiluba's profession of Evangelical faith was insincere. Z8, a former Vice President of Zambia, gave two different explanations for the contradictions between Chiluba's faith and actions: failing to think through the connections in practical terms, and being outnumbered by corrupt colleagues in Cabinet.

Promoting civic oversight

Most informants saw the Catholic Church as leading the Evangelical and Pentecostal churches in this area, though there were notable exceptions such as the Mapalo initiative, in which an Evangelical NGO is helping a poor community to hold their political representatives to account for electoral promises. Evangelicals were divided over whether it is appropriate to lobby for changes to the Constitution that would limit the powers of the President. Suggested reasons for Evangelical weakness in promoting oversight by civil society included theologies that emphasise submission to the state and see poverty as the result of individual sin; and co-option and repression by the state.

Peru Country Case Study

Introduction

Situated immediately south of the equator, Peru's diverse geography comprises three regions: arid coastal plains to the west, rugged Andean mountains centrally, and tropical forest lowlands to the east. Most Peruvians are either Spanish-speaking mestizos - a term that usually refers to a mixture of indigenous and European/Caucasian - or Amerindians, largely Quechua-speaking indigenous people. Peruvians of European descent make up about 15 per cent of the population. Peru's distinct geographical regions are mirrored in a socio-economic divide between the coast's mestizo-Hispanic culture and the more diverse, traditional Andean cultures of the mountains and highlands.

When the Spanish landed in 1531, the territory that today is Peru was the nucleus of the highly developed Inca civilization. Centred in Cusco, the Inca Empire extended over a vast region from northern Ecuador to central Chile. In search of Inca wealth, the Spanish conqueror Francisco Pizarro, who arrived in the territory after the Incas had fought a debilitating civil war, conquered the weakened people. The Spanish captured the Inca capital at Cusco by 1533, and consolidated their control by 1542. Gold and silver from the Andes enriched the conquerors, and Peru became the principal source of Spanish wealth and power in South America. Peru's wars of independence (1820-24) achieved emancipation by 1824, though independence was not recognised by Spain until 1879.

The military has been prominent in Peruvian history. Coups have repeatedly interrupted civilian constitutional government, most recently during the period 1968-80. Peru's governments during the 1980s were democratically elected, but natural disasters, a fall in international commodity prices to their lowest levels since the Great Depression and rampant corruption led to worsening living conditions for Peru's poor and provided a breeding ground for social and political discontent.[1] The emergence of the terrorist group Sendero Luminoso (Shining Path) in rural areas in 1980, followed shortly thereafter by the Tupac Amaru Revolutionary Movement (MRTA) in Lima, sent the country further into chaos.

Concerned about the economy, the increasing terrorist threat from Sendero Luminoso, and allegations of official corruption, voters chose a relatively unknown mathematician-turned-politician, Alberto Fujimori, as President in

---

[1] Peter Klaren *Peru: Society and nationhood in the Andes* (Oxford: Oxford University Press 2000).

1990. He immediately implemented drastic economic reforms to tackle inflation, but found opposition to further drastic measures, including dealing with the growing insurgency. On April 4, 1992, Fujimori dissolved the Congress in an 'auto-coup', revised the constitution, and called new congressional elections. Large segments of the judiciary, the military and the media were co-opted by Fujimori's security advisor, Vladimiro Montesinos. The government unleashed a counterattack against the insurgency that resulted in countless human right abuses and eventually quashed the Shining Path and MRTA. Fujimori's constitutionally questionable decision to seek a third term in AD 2000 brought political and economic turmoil, and a bribery scandal that broke just weeks after he began his third term forced him to call new elections in which he would not run. He fled to Japan and resigned from office in November 2000. He returned to Peru in 2007, and in 2009 he received prison sentences of 25 years for ordering kidnapping and murder, seven-and-a-half years for embezzlement and six years for corruption.

Although some commentators have claimed that Evangelical participation was decisive in Fujimori's 1990 victory, the Evangelical author Dario Lopez has pointed out that Evangelicals were only about five per cent of the population and that the Evangelical candidates for Congress with Fujimori's party received a total of only about 100,000 votes, far below the potential of the Evangelical electorate.[2] Of the 19 Evangelicals elected as supporters of Fujimori in 1990 only one, Gilberto Siura from the Peruvian Evangelical Church (IEP), continued after the 'auto-coup' of 1992. In Lopez' assessment:

> Gilberto Siura became well known nationally as one of the most conspicuous defenders of the regime and affirmed that his presence in congress was clearly part of the will of God. But despite the fact that all the evangelicals elected to congress in 1992, 1995 and 2000 were pro-Fujimori, it would seem that in the country at large there were both evangelicals (a majority of them) who supported the Fujimori regime, and other evangelicals (a minority which grew as the authoritarian character of the regime became more evident) who were opposed.[3]

Subsequent administrations under Alejandro Toledo (2001 – 2006) and Alan García Pérez (2006 – present) have not been associated with the Evangelical constituency, though Pastor Humberto Lay, a minister of the Emmanuel Bible Church, ran for President in 2006. He was unsuccessful, gaining only four per cent of the vote and only two seats in Congress.

Table 8.1 shows Peru's position in respect of some selected indicators, including those relevant to the analysis of economic inequality in Chapter 2. Economically, Peru is among the most unequal quartile of countries included in

---

[2] Dario López 'Evangelicals and Politics in Fujimori's Peru' in Paul Freston (ed) *Evangelical Christianity and Democracy in Latin America* (Oxford: Oxford University Press 2009), 131-62.
[3] López 'Evangelicals and Politics in Fujimori's Peru', 135.

the quantitative analysis. It also has unfavourable values for most of the indicators of the proposed determinants of economic inequality, particularly for 'mining and large plantation or farm exports'. The model in Chapter 2 suggests that economic inequality in Peru is more a consequence of what the country produces than of corrupt government, but that the net effect of government is, nonetheless, to increase economic inequality.

Economic inequality increased under Fujimori in the 1990s, and this trend is expected to continue, given the country's dependence on capital-intensive natural resource exports in a context of a large pool of very low-income earners.[4] Peru, like most Latin American states, is 'intermediate between the successful East Asian states ... and the rent-seeking and predatory African states ... The Peruvian state is less predatory and there are developmental islands of efficiency in an otherwise weak and ineffective public sector.'[5]

Table 8.1 Peru values for selected indicators

Indicator (year)	Value	Rank, among the 77 countries included in the quantitative analysis
GNI per capita (2003)	$2,150	43 (Rank 1 = greatest GNP per capita)
Percentage of the population living on less than $1.25 a day at 2005 international prices (2005)	8%	50 (Rank 1= lowest percentage on <$1.25)
Gini coefficient of consumption (2000)	0.48	61 (Rank 1= lowest Gini coefficient)
Mining and large plantation or farm exports, as percentage of total exports (2000)	65%	74 (Rank 1= lowest percentage)
Control of corruption (pessimistic view) (2000)	-1.07	39 (Rank 1= greatest positive value)
Government revenue x corruption control (2000)	-19	43 (Rank 1= greatest positive value)

---

[4] Crabtree J and Thomas J *Fujimori's Peru: The political economy* (London: Institute of Latin American Studies 1998), 265-8.

[5] Cameron M and Mauceri P *The Peruvian Labyrinth: Polity, society, economy* (Pennsylvania: Pennsylvania State University Press 1997), 226-8. The inequality-increasing effect of petty corruption in Peru, whereby low income users of public services pay a larger share of their income than wealthier ones, and are also more likely to be discouraged and not to seek a service at all (Kaufmann et al. 2008:18), was noted in Chapter 2.

The Peru chapter in the 'Evangelicalism and Democracy' series does not discuss the relationship between Evangelicalism and Pentecostalism.[6] However, the author clarified his view of this when I interviewed him: 'In Peru, Evangelical and Pentecostal are the same, there's no difference' (Pe8). As for the proportions of the population in the major Christian categories, different sources agree that Peru remains predominantly Roman Catholic, but have widely differing estimates of the numbers of Evangelicals and Pentecostals / charismatics (Table 8.2). Despite these differences, it is clear that the majority of Peruvians are Roman Catholics and that Evangelicals are a fairly small minority. The National Evangelical Council (CONEP) is a representative body of Evangelicals in Peru, formed in 1940 by Protestant missions and their national churches. The majority of Protestant churches are still connected with it. The largest Evangelical denominations are the Peruvian Evangelical Church, the Assembies of God and the Seventh Day Adventists.[7]

Table 8.2 Percentage of Peruvians estimated to belong to various Christian categories

Estimated percentage of the population in each group in AD 2000	Barrett et al. (2001)	Johnstone et al. (2001)
Christians	97.2	90.1
Roman Catholics	95.7	69.0
Evangelicals	4.4	8.7
Pentecostals / charismatics	13.4	6.2
Evangelicals plus Pentecostals / charismatics	17.8	14.9

The material in this chapter regarding the relationship between Evangelicals and corruption in Peru is based on my interviews with 33 key informants in April and May 2008. Table C.4 in Appendix C gives brief details of the occupation, age, gender and religious affiliation of the key informants, and the dates and locations of the interviews.

The Reputation of Evangelicals for Honest Behaviour

Most informants thought that Evangelicals in Peru have a reputation for honest behaviour. Starting with Evangelical leaders based in Lima, Pe33, a leader of CONEP, said:

> If a hundred Catholics beat their wife, that's normal. If an Evangelical beats his wife, it's news. The surprise that is generated from this sort of event reflects that

---

[6] López 'Evangelicals and Politics in Fujimori's Peru'.
[7] Barrett, Kurian, Johnson eds *World Christian Encyclopedia*.

what the Evangelicals preach, and are expected to live, is different. People see Evangelicals as people who generally live what they preach.

Pe2, another leader of CONEP and a former Senator, said: 'Base social organisations that work in communities always choose an Evangelical to be the Treasurer, because they know they will not steal the money and there'll be a report on everything that comes in as income for the organisation.' Pe11, a senior leader of the Pentecostal Church of Peru, claimed that 'the difference in corruption between Catholics and Evangelicals is pronounced. Here, everybody is "Catholic", it's just a nickname. Corruption in the Evangelical church represents less than ten percent of what you'd see in the Catholic Church'. Pe27, a senior leader of the Presbyterian Church, thought that 'in any small community the Evangelicals are always more trusted. Evangelicals are still considered to be the moral reserve of the country. The difference between Evangelicals and Catholics is still very marked'. Pe12, a leader of Paz y Esperanza (an Evangelical NGO), said:

People still tend to believe that Evangelicals are more honest than others. The Evangelical doesn't drink or smoke, so because he isn't enslaved by those things he behaves better, he is more committed to work, he doesn't accept immorality (at least publicly).

Pe9, a leader of the Evangelical student organisation in Peru (AGEUP), said: 'That image of being very good and respectable brings many Catholics to the Evangelical faith. The Catholic community doesn't live its religious faith - though now, with the charismatic movement and Liberation Theology movements, more are committed, more personally involved'. These favourable perceptions of Evangelicals were echoed by Evangelical professionals in Cusco.[8] Pe16, an Evangelical lawyer in Cusco, said:

Corruption in Peru is general in the whole society, and almost everybody is Catholic. But the level of corruption in Peru is low among Evangelicals, because the word of the Lord is our rule. People who have accepted Jesus Christ as their Saviour are more committed with their work of the Lord, and they want to do their best, wherever they are.

Pe17, an Evangelical Professor in Cusco and former City Councillor, said: 'To say "I am a Catholic" means nothing, but to say "I am an Evangelical" is different. People know that Evangelicals are well organized, they help each other, they are people with honesty'. He gave examples of Evangelical participation in community programmes to install drinking water systems or implement 'glass of milk' programmes. In his opinion, Evangelical churches

---

[8] Cusco is an Andean city of 320,000 people, once the foremost city of the Inca empire.

had demonstrated that 'they have more responsibility, they manage in a better way, they have no corruption'.

Two Evangelical pastors in Andahuaylas[9] expressed similar views. Pe20, an IEP pastor, said: 'The community knows that a Christian doesn't drink, and can look after the money. Yes, they trust the Christian people.' Pe19, a leader of the IEP synod in Andahuaylas, said: 'There is a big difference between the Catholic Church, and the Evangelical Church here. For Catholics it is normal if someone gets drunk. The next day he can just go to the priest and be sorry for that.'

Although all these favourable opinions about the reputation of Evangelicals were expressed by Evangelicals, several sources suggested that these opinions are held by non-Evangelicals as well. The recent voting behaviour of the mainly Catholic electorate in Andahuaylas suggests they are inclined to trust Evangelical Mayors. Pe19, a leader of the IEP synod in Andahuaylas, described how, although Evangelicals comprise only about only one percent of the local electorate, seven of the nineteen Mayors elected in 2006 are Evangelicals: 'People don't trust in their leaders, they are fed up with them because every time they are corrupt, and I think that is why they gave an opportunity to Christians to see if they can do something'. Pe27, a senior leader of the Presbyterian Church, described how the Mayor in his district of Lima believes that Evangelicals can change society:

> The Mayor is not an Evangelical, but he said, 'I am doing a lot of different things for this community, but the ones who can truly change it, who can bring really lasting change are you Evangelicals, and I need that change too'. It's in that sort of an exchange that the church can be involved in the fight against corruption.

A Catholic perspective was provided by Pe30, a Catholic law lecturer in Lima:

> Evangelicals are still a minority compared to Catholics, and the perception is that Evangelicals tend to believe more in what they believe, and be more committed in that way, and so they probably tend to be more honest - though Catholics have a small nucleus that is very committed. In the Catholic Church, you would expect to see promotion of honesty in the mass, in the catechisms, in pastoral care - but very few times have I seen that sort of exhortation or recommendation, except maybe in the committed minority groups.

In the other three case-study countries, the Chairperson or Director of the national office of Transparency International (TI) expressed a clear opinion regarding the reputation of Evangelicals in their country. Unfortunately, I was unable to get a comparable opinion in Peru. Pe29, a leader of Proethica (the national office of TI in Peru) said that he did not know 'how the Evangelical religion runs'. He did, however, express a negative opinion about the role of

---

[9] Andahuaylas is a small Andean town of 30,000 people.

Catholicism: 'You go to church on Sunday, and if you steal a lot of money, you confess with the priest, pray one hundred Hail Marys and you are forgiven, you go to heaven. I don't like religions'.

Evangelical behaviour does not always match their good reputation

Despite this generally favourable perception of Evangelicals, most Evangelical informants described ways in which some Evangelicals fail to live up to their reputation. Pe31, a leader of the Bible Society and a former Senator, reflected that 'there have been well known cases of corruption in the Evangelical churches. It is very sad that we can find the same pattern of problems of society in the churches'. The range of behaviours mentioned by informants in the context of 'corruption' was quite wide. The examples mentioned included misuse of church resources; misuse of public resources; paying bribes; growing and trafficking illegal drugs; and failing to act justly. Starting with misuse of church resources, Pe10, a leader of Paz y Esperanza, said:

> We still have the legacy that Evangelicals are seen as honest - you are faithful to your wife, you do not drink alcohol, you don't do to parties, you are people without sins - but I'm not sure whether that would apply to handling of money. Maybe at the beginning, but we had a lot of problems with pastors misusing funds.

Pe6, a leader in a large Evangelical INGO, recalled that 'We gave money to some churches for their projects for children and we had a lot of problems with how some of them would use the money. There were people who took the money for their own family'. Pe8, a Pentecostal pastor and author in Lima, echoed this: 'In one or two places there were corruption cases in the Evangelical church, using money for yourself and your family and not for the church'. However, he also thought that this is 'not a common problem'. Although Pe7, an IEP Pastor in Cusco, acknowledged that 'you do see corruption in the Evangelical sector, especially in the area of controlling money', he had to go back to 1980 to think of a clear-cut example (which was of a pastor who had 'forged documents to get funds'). Pe20, an IEP pastor in Andhuaylas, described other examples of misuse of church resources:

> Perhaps half of the 150 IEP churches in Andahuaylas are built on someone else's land, without any legal paper. After four or five years the owner of the land, a Christian, says, 'That is not yours, it's mine.' The other thing I saw is that the Treasurer lends the church's money to people and keeps the interest for himself.

There were also mentions of abuse of public resources by Evangelicals. Pe17, an Evangelical Professor in Cusco and former City Councillor, recalled the results of polling about 300 Evangelicals who worked as Mayors, city councillors or local government employees: 'About 100 of them said that they knew of other Evangelical colleagues who had fallen into corruption, trying to get money in an easy way, illegally'. Pe18, an Evangelical lawyer in Cusco, recalled her experience of an Evangelical who was an Academic Chief: 'If he knows that there is a scholarship he keeps it to himself and says "That's for me" '.

Several informants thought that paying bribes was quite normal for Evangelicals. Pe2, a leader of CONEP and a former Senator, said: 'Evangelicals pay bribes for passports or driving licences; if the police stop an Evangelical driver for something, the driver knows that handing over a bill will solve the problem'. Pe8, a Pentecostal pastor and author in Lima, agreed: 'It's normal for Evangelicals to pay bribes to policemen, and Evangelical policemen may take bribes. Pastors think it's not done by Evangelical people, but that's not true. The pastor just doesn't know'. Pe10, a leader of Paz y Esperanza, recalled:

> One Evangelical pastor came to me and asked if I had friends in the army: 'My son is eighteen years old and we don't want him to join the army. It doesn't matter if we have to pay something'. He was a good pastor, a very honest person – but he didn't have in his mind that that was corruption. Evangelicals don't see paying bribes as a sin, they see it as a way to a deal with certain issues - such as getting your passport in one day not two days.

Pe27, a senior leader of the Presbyterian Church, described the involvement of Evangelicals in growing and trafficking illegal drugs:

> I was at a conference of about eighty pastors in the jungle, and I asked, 'How many of you grow coca, the plant?' I watched the people looking at each other and at last one pastor said, 'I grow coca.' And then another pastor said, 'I do too,' and another, and maybe five came forward, but then, asking around later, it came to light that practically all of them grew coca. They said that if they sell coca to the national coca industry, which is a legal establishment, they earn very little; but if they sell to the drug traffickers, they can cover their families' needs.

A minority of Evangelical informants thought that Evangelicals had lost their reputation for honest behaviour. However, this was not a result of the variety of failings just described, but rather the high profile behaviour of some Evangelical politicians. Pe8, a Pentecostal pastor and author in Lima, said: 'There may be stereotypes that an Evangelical is a good person who doesn't steal money, but after Fujimori it's not necessarily the same, because in Fujimori's time there were many cases of corruption with Evangelicals inside the government'. He concluded that 'The perspective about Evangelicals changed. There were not many Evangelicals who supported Fujimori, but they were a visible group, the media was aware of them'. Pe31, a leader of the Bible Society and a former Senator, noted with regret that:

> I don't believe that Evangelicals are seen as more honest than Roman Catholics now. When I was younger, it was a fact – 50 years ago. The change has been caused by the behaviour of some Evangelicals in politics: lying, misuse of money, and mismanagement of power.

Pe6, a leader in a large Evangelical INGO, agreed: 'There's no difference in the integrity of different denominations of Christians. In politics we need to know the individual, because a lot of people just saw the opportunity to be in power and receive good money, but with no experience'.

To conclude this section, most Evangelical informants said that Evangelicals in Peru have a reputation for honest behaviour. The willingness of Catholics to vote for Evangelical Mayors, and the opinion of the one Catholic informant who expressed an opinion on the matter, support this view of the reputation of Evangelicals. Graham Gordon, responsible for the Advocacy and Communications department of Paz y Esperanza, gave the following interpretation of how this reputation can co-exist with knowledge that Evangelicals sometimes fail to live up to it:

> The expectation is that Evangelicals will have greater integrity than Catholics, because the expectation of the Catholic Church in terms of integrity is very low. However, the recognition of hypocrisy within the Evangelical church is also very strong. Disappointment comes as the other side of the coin of expecting integrity. From the Catholic Church, if someone doesn't behave in a particularly integral way, it's expected to a certain extent – maybe not from their leaders, but from the general members of the Catholic Church. The general members of the Evangelical church, because they preach so much against sin, and about pure lives and being honest - when someone is not honest that's a greater disappointment for everyone else involved.

Perceived causes of corruption in the church

The causes of corruption within the church that were suggested by Evangelical leaders were lack of accountability, and the prosperity gospel. Pe2, a leader of CONEP and a former Senator, said:

> Corruption equals accumulation of power minus vigilance, and we see that situation in many churches, especially independent churches with a tendency towards neo-Pentecostalism. There are churches where only the pastors know how much money comes in, and they are not accountable to anyone on that.

In the opinion of Pe33, another leader of CONEP, 'some Evangelicals see democracy as dangerous, because it's too open, it's too controlling, and it requires everything to be transparent'. Pe7, an IEP Pastor in Cusco, described his experience:

> There are lots of problems where the organisational structure concentrates all the power with the pastor. I worked in a church for two years where the pastor received funds to build the church and to do social work, but he never showed accounts – that was a frustration for many of the members'.

Pe4, an Evangelical pastor in Huanuco, observed that 'there tends to be more corruption in churches that don't have a structure to deal with funds' and described a 'huge difference' in the way churches respond to different types of failing: 'adultery creates a huge scandal, but if the case is about corruption it's not highlighted as much, it's easier for that to slip under the wire'. Pe9, a leader of the Evangelical student movement in Peru, agreed: 'There are churches where there's no system for controlling the use of resources. The leadership decides everything and the church isn't well informed. So we can't present ourselves as being model citizens'. Pe12, a leader of Paz y Esperanza, thought that the teaching in some churches discourages accountability: 'They teach that we shouldn't be self-critical. That message promotes a situation where we don't say anything if there's corruption within a church'.

Only three informants made any reference to foreign donations as a possible contributor to corruption in the church. Pe11, a senior leader of the Pentecostal Church of Peru, said: 'Overseas money can corrupt the church. Some Evangelical churches here have partnered unofficially with some NGOs, and the money has come into their pockets, not where it was intended'. Pe6, a leader in a large Evangelical INGO, said:

> We had most problems with autonomous churches that don't have regional or national mother authorities, because the accountability was not there. Now we try to be sure that there are accountability systems: that there's a Board, the pastor or project director is not going to put his family on the project. If you create an environment with a little room, it's your fault.

Pe31, a leader of the Bible Society and a former Senator, echoed a complaint expressed by Lawrence Temfwe in Zambia: that donors sometimes cause corruption by failing to cover the local costs of administering projects they wish to sponsor. He said:

> Bigger organisations – some churches and foundations - pay very little money for administration. Indirectly this creates corruption, because it is inevitable that if they have too little money for administration, they will need to take money from the projects. It may be against the will of the donors, but they are forced.

The prosperity gospel was suggested by three informants as a cause of corruption in Evangelical churches. Pe11, a senior leader of the Pentecostal Church of Peru, said: 'People don't measure the excellence of ministry by your relationship with God, rather by what you've got – your car, your house, your clothes. That contributes to corruption'. According to Pe2, a leader of CONEP and a former Senator, 'prosperity theology has been emphasised quite a bit in recent years. If you're poor, it's because you're in sin. The symbols of a Christian life are material goods and riches, and that prepares the ground for corruption'. Pe33, another leader of CONEP, described one particular manifestation of this theology:

> You can see elements of corruption in the prosperity theology, because it's understood that prosperity is a chain: if two of us are under another person's

coverage, we tithe to him, and therefore we can have other people under our coverage, and they owe us tithes. It's a chain of power that benefits the person who's on top, so it starts the process of manipulating others. The person who's on top of the pyramid isn't accountable to anybody except God. The theologies of power and prosperity are taking root in many different Evangelical traditions.

Preaching about Corruption

Pe2, a leader of CONEP and a former Senator, said: 'Themes of corruption, the violation of human rights, the fight against poverty, have not always formed part of our theology. There are very, very few sermons preached on the topic of corruption'. Pe6, a leader in a large Evangelical INGO, said: 'Churches talk about being honest, but they don't direct their teaching to corruption. We talk about honesty and ethics, but not corruption directly'. Pe31, a leader of the Bible Society and a former Senator, said: 'The churches have a very deteriorated understanding of sin: it is just drinking, smoking, dancing. They don't relate social life with the gospel. There is almost no preaching about corruption'. Pe12, a leader of Paz y Esperanza, said: 'There's no Evangelical preaching about corruption. The emphasis is just what is intimate, the family. There's little attention paid to what happens in the public sphere'. Pe18, an Evangelical lawyer in Cusco, agreed: 'The message is about the family, how to be with the husband or the wife, with the children, and afterwards in the society. But I think we really don't talk much about corruption'. Pe25, a leader of a Christian NGO in Andahuaylas, said: 'Every preacher needs to teach about discrimination, values and corruption. Sometimes there are just spots of teaching about that, but not generally'. Pe9, a leader of the Evangelical student movement in Peru, said:

> When you go to an Evangelical service, in general you're not going to find a message that connects the Word to problems of corruption, poverty, injustice, human dignity or problems within the country, because a good part of the church sees that as political discourse, and not as a valid message that comes from the Word of God. We Evangelicals in Peru need to preach the gospel to each other, taking into account the realities of the country, just as Jesus did in his time, because we have been taught a gospel that doesn't come from the Bible.

Finally, Pe15, a Lutheran leader in the Institute of Communication Studies (an NGO advocating for human rights), said:

> Unfortunately the main topics of preaching often have nothing to do with the realities of society and when they do get to talk about corruption they use it to proof-text that we are getting towards the end times, that Jesus is about to appear and we'll all head off.

The potential contribution of preaching to fighting corruption

Some Evangelical leaders – mainly those who lead churches or theological institutions - expressed optimism about the impact that preaching would eventually have on corruption. For example, Pe14, a leader of an Evangelical seminary in Lima, said:

> The best way for churches to combat corruption is through Bible teaching, with an emphasis on God's law and Jesus' ethical teaching. If the church is trained that way, and the pulpits reflect it, then that will become the norm for Christian conduct.

Pe26, pastor of an IEP church in Andahuylas, said: 'One of the things we do to fight corruption is to preach about the truth the Bible says, that to do those things is not good before God'. Pe27, a senior leader of the Presbyterian Church, anticipated that Bible teaching would produce Evangelicals who seek to serve others, which in turn would result in better social and legal control of corruption:

> We need to work within the church very strongly before we can work outside of the church. We need sanctity within, before we can pray and then act against corruption outside. And, in order to achieve that, the Evangelical presence has to be very consistent with the Word of God, so that new generations are prepared to really serve; and with the passage of time, those things can become social norms and be instituted as laws. And that means that we need to revise our Sunday school materials.

Pe1, an Evangelical doctor and former Councillor in a small city, disclosed a similar expectation when he explained his interpretation of the different levels of trust he had experienced in London and Lima:

> In London people trust each other. Here mistrust is just at the surface of the skin. For almost 300 years in Europe Christian values permeated the lives of people, so that even post-Christians lived according to those values, even without thinking. That's still not happening after two or three generations of Christians in Latin America – it will take a bit longer.

Pe10, a leader of Paz y Esperanza, thought many Evangelicals believe that producing more Christians will automatically reform society: 'As a result of church growth in the 1990's the idea from big sectors in the church is that as we have more Christians in Peru we will have social change.'

However, Evangelical informants who arguably had the greatest experience in trying to fight corruption were less sanguine about the contribution that preaching might make, at least in its current form in Evangelical churches in Peru. Pe31, a leader of the Bible Society and a former Senator, lamented that 'the preaching and teaching of the gospel is not affecting many people's personal behaviour, or the social ethic. The churches are growing, but society is not changing very much'. Pe2, a leader of CONEP and a former Senator, said: 'There continues to be an emphasis that when an individual person is converted, things like corruption automatically disappear. But we are recognising that the processes are not like that, because there are customs that also have to be changed'. Pe33, a leader of CONEP, made similar criticisms:

> The problem in our churches is that we are primarily expert in individual formation, and it's assumed that through training and forming people, the systems will change in due course,[10] when what is needed is a greater and heavier public participation. I don't think, like some pastors say, that when Peru is Evangelical it'll be paradise ... It's not only the people; it's the systems that the people have produced. The political system is corrupt. So we need to make not moral decisions but political decisions to eliminate a system that's corrupt. The churches need to act in the social-political realm, participating in networks and alliances with other socio-political actors.

Reforming Government by Having Evangelicals Inside Government

Many informants mentioned the involvement of Evangelicals in Fujimori's government, and all who did so looked back on it as a negative experience for both the country and the church, because they thought most Evangelical politicians had failed to challenge corruption and human rights abuses. This had left some informants sceptical about the contribution of Evangelical politicians at national level. For example, Pe33, a leader of CONEP, said:

> People think that if we have Christians in Congress we can bring influence and change society. But we have had experiences of Evangelicals in Congress who have become corrupted. So we don't need Evangelical political parties, nor do we need to be in the government, to work towards this goal.

Pe8, a Pentecostal pastor and author in Lima, said: 'It's typical in Latin America that when Evangelical leaders come to the political arena they have problems, especially with corruption'. Pe12, a leader of Paz y Esperanza, said:

> Unfortunately, I don't think Evangelical politicians have much potential to fight corruption. The experience in Peru has not shown that at all, especially the experience of the past two decades. In Fujimori's second government, from 1995-2000, five Evangelical Congressmen that were from Fujimori's party were sometimes the primary defenders of actions that were against human rights, and were responsible for covering up government corruption. We'd suppose that if

---

[10] David Martin describes this as a general characteristic of Evangelicalism: 'Its individualistic approach supposes that political improvement depends on the multiplication of persons of moral integrity; the preferred discourse is through personalized images rather than structural arrangements and forces' (Martin 1999:40).

someone is Evangelical they're supposed to be against everything that's wrong and corrupt, but that hasn't been our experience.

The Evangelical leaders who mentioned the Presidential candidacy in 2006 of the Pentecostal pastor, Humberto Lay, assessed it negatively. Pe8, a Pentecostal pastor and author in Lima, recalled that Humberto Lay's campaign had been tainted by allegations of corruption within his own party: 'Lay paid his son about $30,000 to print political pamphlets. The judge said "No problem", but for many months this was important news.' Pe9, a leader of the Evangelical student movement in Peru, said: 'The Evangelical church will get involved in politics when there are elections and the church has an Evangelical candidate, just because they want power. There's not a vision of getting into politics with an agenda to serve.' Pe10, a leader of Paz y Esperanza, recalled that:

> At the last election an Evangelical party got four to five per cent of the votes in the country – but without a clear understanding of the big problems in Peruvian society or any political alternative agenda, just the idea that if a righteous person is at the head of the government everything in the country will be changed.

Graham Gordon recalled the reaction of Evangelicals in the small town of Moyobamba to Lay's lack of political experience:

> When somebody asked Humberto Lay what his political experience was he said he'd had 25 years' experience of managing a large church. Anyone who's got any kind of political experience knows that that's not enough, but lots of Christians at that meeting said 'Yes, we've got to give him a chance, he's better than the rest.'

Despite these negative assessments of Evangelical Congressmen, and of Humberto Lay as a Presidential candidate, a number of Evangelical leaders envisaged the possibility that Evangelical politicians might perform better in future. Pe17, an Evangelical Professor in Cusco and former City Councillor, said: 'Evangelicals have to be in political situations in those levels, to contribute to fighting corruption, making better laws.' Suggestions as to what have been the 'missing ingredients' to date tended to focus on the failings of the individuals, such as lack of understanding, commitment, training or experience, rather than on systemic problems, such as a lack of critical mass of reformers. Pe10, a leader of Paz y Esperanza, said: 'We really don't have a good Evangelical Congressman with a clear view about society, connected with his values, able to transform society', implying that such an individual might one day emerge. Emphasising the need for personal commitment, Pe15, a Lutheran leader in the Institute of Communication Studies (an NGO advocating for human rights), said:

> If, and only if, they are deeply committed to changes within the country, and if they have a very political perception of the problems, then Evangelicals within

government can have a useful role in fighting corruption. In some cases where we've had Evangelicals as senators, they keep quiet about many cases of corruption despite the fact that they are leaders and have a voice, so you can tell that they are very connected to what their party says, before anything else. But there are others from other parties, for example an indigenous leader from the Methodist church, who criticises government and has a very different position. Pedro Arana, the President of the Bible Society, tries to be consistent between what he says and what he does. When he was in Congress he played a good role. And Carlos Garcia, who was the Second Vice-President under Fujimori's presidency, was the only Evangelical in Congress who was openly opposed to Fujimori.

Pe7, an IEP Pastor in Cusco, said:

Many Evangelicals who came to be Congressmen didn't have experience or abilities, and many succumbed to political power. There hasn't been any training to prepare such people, but recently Dario Lopez and Victor Arroyo have started offering trainings for people who are, or aspire to be, part of the government. The Evangelical student group has also focused on training people who are interested in getting into politics.

Pe16, an Evangelical lawyer in Cusco, said:

About ten people in the Congress who were Christians came into the cycle of corruption. They were good Christians, well formed, intelligent, but they didn't have any experience in politics, they were leaders only in the church. It was a big shock for them. To influence society we need brothers and sisters who are called to work in politics, and who have gained experience as leaders of communities before going into politics.

Only two Evangelical leaders mentioned lack of critical mass as an obstacle to Evangelicals seeking to improve governance from within government. Pe2, a leader of CONEP and a former Senator, said: 'It's good for Evangelicals to intervene in public life, though we have not seen any difference in the behaviour of the Restauracion National Congressmen. There are only three of them, so they cannot fulfil all that they intended.' Thinking along similar lines, Pe20, an IEP pastor in Andhuaylas, said: 'If we have a President from the church, what would happen if the Congress people are not Christian? That will be too difficult for him. We need more people, more votes, to have representation in the government'.

So despite the perception that most Evangelicals who have been involved in national politics have performed poorly to date, a number of Evangelical leaders envisaged the possibility that Evangelical politicians might perform better in future. Their suggestions as to what have been the 'missing ingredients' to date tended to focus on the failings of the individuals, rather than on systemic problems, such as a lack of critical mass of reformers.

Evangelicals in local politics

Evangelical leaders were more positive about the track record of Evangelical politicians in local than in national politics. Pe12, a leader of Paz y Esperanza, said:

> In some interior provinces some Evangelicals have had public office and have worked well compared to other authorities. They haven't embezzled public resources, they haven't organized big parties and abused alcohol. Evangelical politicians have performed better at local than national level because they feel responsible for their towns, they identify with the community. They are under greater surveillance by the Evangelical community: in communities where the proportion of Evangelicals is greater than in Lima, there's more incentive to preserve a good reputation.

Pe7, an IEP pastor in Cusco, said:

> Many Christians have become Mayors, or members of the Mayor's group, in small towns in rural provinces and we've seen very good results. The community often believe in them and trust them because of their values, ethics and testimony. The best way for the church to fight corruption is our own testimony of honesty in important roles, both surrounding the government as well as within the government.

Pe26, an IEP pastor in Andahuaylas, said: 'One way to fight corruption is to elect trustworthy people. If they are believers in Christ, we can trust them.' Pe19, a leader of the IEP synod in Andahuaylas, was convinced that Evangelical conversion of the Mayor in Tupor district had reduced corruption: 'After he became a Christian he cut all the corruption and the other leaders were very angry. But after a time they realised that they can do more things now with the money from the government, and they agree now'.

Nonetheless, there had clearly been some disappointments in the behaviour of Evangelicals in local politics. Pe20, an IEP pastor in Andhuaylas, said: 'There are more and more Christian people participating in politics – but not all of them with a good fight. Many of them go into politics because they want to get money for themselves.' Pe27, a senior leader of the Presbyterian Church, said: 'Many of those who were elected as Mayors stopped being Evangelicals. And so, whenever an Evangelical takes a role in the government we need to do it with a certain level of awareness.'

Just as with national politics, Evangelical leaders' suggestions as to why Evangelical politicians may disappoint tended to focus on the failings of the individuals, such as lack of understanding, commitment, training or experience, rather than on systemic problems, such as a lack of critical mass of reformers. Pe31, a leader of the Bible Society and a former Senator, lamented the lack of training for Evangelical politicians: 'The Evangelical influence in society is very weak. Discourse is one thing, action is another. We have several Evangelical Mayors, but we have no training for them in what it means to be public servants.' Evangelical church leaders in Andahuaylas had been organising events to train and encourage the seven Evangelicals who are Mayors in various towns there. Pe19, a leader of the IEP synod in Andahuaylas, said: 'The first thing we do to fight corruption is to get all of them together for prayer, and to train them biblically: talking about corruption, and how to lead the community in the right way with our Bible principles.' Pe20, an IEP pastor in Andhuaylas, described the same events in these words:

As a church we very often we try to get the mayors together, mostly for prayer. They come for two days, with their wife. We have a time of prayer, read the Bible, and ask them how life is for them, being a mayor. Is it easy or not? What is missing? For many it is a big problem that during festivals the community leader is obligated to drink, to go to the saints, or to sign things illegally without the committee knowing. If you say no, they hate you, and that is why we say: 'Never mind if you lose your election in the community, you are still a leader in the church, and you are free, you have peace in your mind. It is much better for you to maintain your faith for five years. That testimony will be so good for the church - and you might have authority for the next election'. According to the reports we have, they are doing well up to now, at least on the money matters. The Mayor can't see everything, but if he says: 'We are going to do this. It is going to cost this amount of money', then they are going to spend that amount of money.

Only two Evangelical leaders mentioned the systemic problems facing aspiring reformers. Pe19, a leader of the IEP synod in Andahuaylas, said: 'Here, the corruption is institutionalised at every level, so it will not be easy. Even if the top man at the regional level is a Christian, it will be so hard, so difficult, to cut the corruption.' Pe17, an Evangelical Professor in Cusco and former City Councillor, described a battle he had fought with his political colleagues:

During our first month on the city council, the other members said: 'Now we are going to get much money. If we got $1000 before, now we will get $1500'. I was the only one saying 'I am here not to get money, but to serve the people.' I called an ally in the press, and told him what was happening: 'It is legal, but it is not justice. Help me please'. Then for eight years we did not get any more money. At first it broke my relationship with the other 12 councillors, but after that they realised that it was a good lead.

In the experience of Graham Gordon the obstacles to reform can include not only the self-interest of political colleagues, but also the expectations of the Evangelical constituency:

In Moyobamba about ten years ago, an Evangelical councillor gave a very interesting example of how church members saw his role in the local government. They saw him as one of them, an insider, who was in local government to favour the church. For example, if somebody had a speeding fine they would give him a

ring to see if he could use his influence to get it waived. A Christian inside
government is seen as faithful if he helps you out, usually breaking the rules, and
not very faithful if he makes you as a Christian citizen follow the same rules as
everyone else.

Evangelicals as government employees

Given the emphasis of the Fellowship of Christians in Government on seeking
to fight corruption in the Philippines by converting government employees to
Evangelical faith, it was interesting to note that Evangelical informants in Peru
were rather sceptical about the likely impact of such a strategy. Pe27, a senior
leader of the Presbyterian Church, said: 'For an Evangelical who works in a
government office, especially in accounting or anything like that, it's two
options: if you want to work, you stay quiet.' Pe31, a leader of the Bible
Society and a former Senator, said:

> I don't know how Evangelicals can influence their environment, even if they have
> good conduct themselves. For example, a Catholic friend of mine who was the
> Social Security Secretary put an Evangelical in charge of the Discipline
> Commission - but he was afraid to discipline people.

Pe15, a Lutheran leader in the Institute of Communication Studies (an NGO
advocating for human rights), said:

> There are many Christians in the army, but I wouldn't say they are good
> examples. There is a general from Fujimori's era who changed over to the
> Christian and Missionary Alliance church, but despite him saying he's converted
> it hasn't changed his way of thinking as a very oppressive general.

Despite the minimal impact of Evangelicals in government employment to
date, Pe14, a leader of an Evangelical seminary in Lima, remained confident of
better things to come:

> One of the characteristics of the present government is that there are Evangelicals
> in high positions in just about every area of public life. There's no dramatic
> evidence that they are sweeping the house clean, or anything like that. They don't
> have power, they are in servant positions, they tend to be used as dogsbodies. But
> they are all over the place, in every kind of institution, and they will make a
> difference eventually.

Promoting Civic Oversight

*Evangelical activities aimed at engaging local
communities for better governance*

The example of this most frequently mentioned by Evangelical leaders was participation in fora known as the Concertation Tables for the fight against poverty. Pe2, a leader of CONEP and a former Senator, described these as:

> a coming together of government, political parties and civil society to reach agreements they can all fight for, on development plans and on how to use part of the budget for the benefit of the poor. One of the roles of that Table is promoting citizen vigilance, specifically the use of resources for fighting poverty. The Catholic Church and the Evangelical church participate as part of the civil society - CONEP represents the Evangelicals within that context.

Pe27, a senior leader of the Presbyterian Church, also mentioned the Concertation Tables, describing them as 'very influential bodies in which Evangelicals play a part'. According to Pe15, a Lutheran leader in the Institute of Communication Studies (an NGO advocating for human rights), 'both the Catholic Church and the Evangelical church have very significant participation in the Concertation Tables in several areas, even in the National Committee. There is an impressive number of 33 Evangelicals who are leaders of those groups.'

Three informants gave local perspectives on the role of Evangelicals in the Concertation Tables. Pe26 in Andahuaylas said: 'Another thing the church does to fight against corruption is asking the authorities to explain in the community meeting how much money was spent on every building.' According to Pe3, a leader of a Christian NGO in Huanuco, Evangelical churches need some persuading to get involved: 'It's a process to get that sort of culture started. Paz y Esperanza is pushing to get people involved in fora like the Concertation Table.' From his experience in Moyobamba, Graham Gordon was sceptical about the extent of Evangelical influence in the Concertation Tables:

> From what I've seen at local level in Moyobamba, the role is very limited. People are involved much more as church leaders instead of as a church – the church may not know what they're doing. And the church leaders in these meetings usually won't have a particularly active role. They go, they sign in, they won't necessarily say much, and certainly they won't get involved in many follow up actions.

A different way in which Evangelicals have advocated for change as part of civil society is through exercising a 'prophetic voice' at national level. Two informants gave examples of this. Pe12, a leader of Paz y Esperanza, recalled that:

> Leaders of several different Evangelical organisations came together around an organisation called Evangelicals for Democracy to fight against Fujimori's

claimed right to be re-elected a second time, around 1998-2000. Fujimori's government had long stopped being a democratic government, and democracy was recognised as a value that is compatible with Christianity. In recent years CONEP has had a very critical posture towards the government, and published some statements that had to do with specific political acts or stands by the government.

Evangelical leaders think that neither the Evangelical nor the Catholic Church has a strong reputation on advocacy for better governance

Notwithstanding the above examples of Evangelical involvement in civil society for better governance, the consensus among most informants was that Evangelicals tend to be weak in this area. Pe8, a Pentecostal pastor and author in Lima, said: 'Not many Evangelical churches are trying to fight corruption.' Recalling the Evangelical role during Fujimori's rule, he added: 'When Siura was defending violations of human rights, he was an elder of a Peruvian Evangelical church in Arequipa, but his church never said anything.'

In the opinion of Pe11, a senior leader of the Pentecostal Church of Peru, the worst problem of Evangelicals in Peru is that 'we've made the gospel a domestic issue – church and home. There's no social involvement. The meaning of the gospel has to be replanted, an Evangelicalism that has an effect in the circle of influence that each Evangelical Christian has.' Pe27, a senior leader of the Presbyterian Church, described the reaction of the Mayor of Rebak District, in Lima, to a proposal from his church for supporting good governance:

> We wanted to work on human rights, good citizenship and environmentalism, from a biblical perspective as well as a legal perspective. The Mayor thought that was very good. He said, 'You are the first pastor, the first church, that has come to me with something of great importance for the district. The fraternity of pastors has also come here, but they only came to ask for exemption from taxes, or to request permission for a public crusades.'

A variety of informants gave local perspectives on this from Cusco and Huanuco. In the experience of Pe7, an IEP Pastor in Cusco, 'involvement with civil society and the government' varies across Evangelical denominations: 'The Pentecostals don't want to know anything about politics or anything to do with politics. The Baptist line is a bit in that direction. But on the other side the IEP and the Presbyterians tend to be more engaged.' Pe3, Pe4 and Pe5 are all Evangelical pastors who have been involved with Paz y Esperanza in the Andean town of Huanuco. They described their experiences of trying to mobilise Evangelical churches to fight corruption. Pe5, a pastor with the Christian and Missionary Alliance, said: 'They don't always agree to participate. There are some Christians saying 'I denounce this', but then the church says 'We didn't send him, it's just him'. Pe4, a pastor with the Assemblies of God, said: 'If there are cases of churches that are fighting corruption, they are few and isolated - though compared to the past there is

progress with several leaders, who are participating in public spaces.'
According to Pe3:

> The churches' focus is 'Corruption is wrong, let's be sure we're not corrupt', not
> 'Let's fight the existing corruption'. They have not taken a prophetic role in
> denouncing acts of corruption. What's required is a culture of citizen vigilance,
> but it's not on the churches' agenda. If there are cases of fighting public
> corruption they are very few and isolated, and there isn't the context of fighting
> together as a larger church. As Evangelicals we say 'We're marginalised, they
> don't invite us'. But the truth is self-exclusion: the church receives an invitation
> and it won't go.

Pe10, a leader of Paz y Esperanza, reflected:

> How could Christianity influence the country against corruption? I think it's a
> difficult question because the question is not on the agenda of the church.
> Evangelicals don't say anything about corruption (except for small groups like
> Paz y Esperanza). It's a private religion. We don't have a lot of examples of
> Christians fighting against political issues, just a few concentrated in some small
> towns and cities.

Although Pe12, a leader of Paz y Esperanza, had earlier mentioned the
lobbying activities of Evangelicals for Democracy, he clearly saw this as an
exception to the normal pattern:

> The government of Fujimori was the most corrupt that Peru has ever had, but
> many of the Evangelical churches either remained silent, or applauded. Many
> Evangelicals do not connect with other people. They don't participate, so their
> presence isn't felt in the community. There are very few in the churches who have
> directed their voices outside the church, to society and to the state. With that
> minimal voice, not only have they not fought against corruption, but by the
> passiveness they've allowed the corruption to continue. So I wouldn't say that the
> church has had a prominent role. Rather, it's been very permissive.

Pe15, a Lutheran leader in the Institute of Communication Studies (an NGO
advocating for human rights), summed up the Evangelical detachment from the
fight against corruption:

> The great problem now regarding the church and corruption isn't that there are no
> mechanisms or that the church is not being asked for their voice. The problem
> now is that Christians don't use the mechanisms that are in place to contribute to
> society - so the fight against corruption will be more difficult and much slower.

In the experience of Graham Gordon in Moyobamba, the Evangelical
churches' social involvement there is quite passive:

Most of the churches will complain internally about corrupt governments, but you see very few examples of a church getting involved as an institution in trying to combat corruption. In Moyobamba, for example, even though the Presbyterian church has its own TV and radio station you won't have any programs that have any political content, or programs about what's going on in society, or denouncing misuse of public funds, or projects that aren't being finished. And for local development planning, when civil society, the councillors and the Mayor come together and decide how they're going to spend the money for next year, the church is invited, but it usually doesn't turn up ... You have a few cases where one of the local vigilantes have captured a person who has robbed or killed and brought them to the court in Moyobamba, and in those situations they ask the Catholic and the Evangelical church to be present just as observers, to show that the people from the villages have behaved in a correct way. So in many of the towns people see the churches' role as trying to guarantee basic rights, not necessarily particularly vocal, but being the conscience of the town.

These Evangelical leaders' assessments of Evangelical weakness in advocacy for better governance were endorsed by two non-Evangelical informants. Pe29, a leader of Proethica (the national office of TI in Peru): 'the Evangelical Churches have no participation in relation to addressing corruption. Most Evangelicals don't participate in the political debate.' Pe28, a Catholic economist working for the Episcopal Commission for Social Action, gave a similar view:

> Some Evangelical churches are not working in social action, but only on the plane of spirituality, not linked with the normal world of the people. In this case there is not really legitimacy for fighting corruption because there is not really a message of transformation; the message of the church is only about spirituality.

A number of Evangelical leaders in Zambia and the Philippines, and to a lesser extent in Kenya, had praised the lead given by the Catholic Church in advocacy against corruption. In Peru, however, Evangelical leaders tended to be critical of the Catholic Church, particularly because of its close relationship with the state. Pe2, a leader of CONEP and a former Senator, said: 'In Peru the Catholic Church is perceived as receiving many favours from the state and that damages the integrity of the Church.' Pe11, a senior leader of the Pentecostal Church of Peru, said: 'The Catholic Church manipulates the government. There's a certain amount of priests in Peru who receive a salary from the state'. Pe14, a leader of an Evangelical seminary in Lima, said: 'The Roman Catholic hierarchy are in league with the state. They've got this famous concordat between the Vatican and the Peruvian State, so that Bishops get a salary from the state'.

Pe9, a leader of the Evangelical student organisation in Peru, said: 'The Catholic hierarchy is very committed to government, the Catholic community doesn't live its religious faith, it's very traditional'. According to Pe10, a leader of Paz y Esperanza, 'the Catholic bishops say they're against corruption, but instead of trying to relate faith to political ethics, I think there's a failure. It's a private religion for both Catholics and Evangelicals.' Pe31, a leader of the Bible Society and a former Senator, said: 'I have seen corruption in the churches: the Roman Catholics have properties all over the country, and they receive money from the state'. Pe15, a Lutheran leader in the Institute of Communication Studies (an NGO advocating for human rights), said:

> At independence the church was one of the largest landowners, so we see that the church, except for a few isolated voices, has been right in the middle of acts of corruption and injustice, to avoid losing its privilege. Maybe there's a section of the Catholic Church that fights against corruption, but it's really part of the system that answers to a clientele.

Pe30, a Catholic law lecturer in Lima, also felt the Catholic Church, as an institution, has failed to act to fight corruption:

> In the wider landscape of corruption – in violations of human rights - there were Catholic priests and nuns who were killed or threatened, either by the Shining Path or by the army. But there hasn't been a group, either Catholic or Evangelical, that has had a specific goal to fight corruption. It's been through the involvement of individuals in civil sector organisations - as citizens, not as a church.

Pe28, a Catholic economist working for the Episcopal Commission for Social Action, thought there was some interest in addressing this failure:

> The message of the church is only about spirituality, it does not have a message to eliminate bad social practices. This problem exists in both the Catholic Church and in Evangelical churches. The conceptual approach for the church fighting corruption is very new in Peru. There is not very much background or reflection about this, though some organisations are interested. For example there is a proposal in the network of the Bishops' Conferences of Latin America to research about corruption. What is the situation about corruption in Latin America? How is it possible to involve the church with the civil society in order to fight corruption?

Pe13, a leader in APRODEH (the Association for Human Rights), distinguished between the roles played by different levels of the Catholic Church:

> We know that we will always have Catholic priests, nuns, pastoral agents working in the field because they are in close relation with people and their needs, so they have a more social approach; and the Episcopal Conference has had a clear position of questioning and condemning corruption, for example when Montesinos paid various amounts of money to the media, to Congressmen, to judges, to the Attorney General. But there are very conservative bishops in the Catholic Church, particularly Cardinal Cipriani from Opus Dei, and other bishops in Ayucucho and Apurimac, who didn't give assistance to victims of human rights violations, or play a proactive role to stop human rights abuses. More and more

bishops have closed human rights offices in several regions of the country and
that has given us concern about the future.

The unanimous perspective of four government officers in the Andean town
of Andahuaylas was that none of the churches, either Catholic or Evangelical,
are active in fighting corruption. Pe24, Mayor of Andahuaylas said: 'The
churches are very passive people, they are not doing much against corruption.'
Pe22, the Provincial Governor, said: 'The churches don't have much interest in
fighting corruption. I don't receive any help from them and they don't speak
much about corruption. They talk mostly about how to get more believers for
the church.' Pe23, the Commissioner for the Ombudsman for Citizens' Rights,
said: 'We invite every institution which exists here in Andahuaylas, but we
couldn't yet see the church fighting against corruption.' Pe21, a lawyer
working in the government anti-corruption office in Andahuaylas, said: 'I can't
see much participation of the church in a practical way against corruption. The
church teaches mostly theological things, rather than social things. They are
more concentrated on having more adults for the church rather than talking
about corruption.'

Against this background of perceived failure of both the Catholic and the
Evangelical churches to promote participation and oversight by civil society
and communities, Pe33, a leader of CONEP, described how civic-minded
minorities in both churches come together across denominational lines:

> In the past few years we've had situations where Catholic leaders and Evangelical
> leaders have come together to dialogue and work together on common projects.
> On topics of justice, human rights, corruption, some Catholic priests have
> identified more with Evangelical pastors than with the Catholic Church itself; and
> some Evangelical pastors have identified more with the Catholics than with our
> own Evangelicals. And that's helping us understand that the construction of
> morality doesn't have to do with religion, but more with citizenship.

Theological hindrances to evangelical engagement in advocacy

One Evangelical leader suggested that what inhibits Evangelicals from
engaging local communities in pursuit of better governance is a lack of
awareness. According to Pe2, a leader of CONEP and a former Senator, 'what
is lacking in the church is the awareness that corruption causes poverty. As
Evangelical churches we have worked very little in public awareness, so
corruption is not seen as a big problem in the country, even by Evangelicals.'

However, a much more frequently mentioned explanation was that a
dualistic theology prevails in the Evangelical sector. Pe33, a leader of CONEP,
said: 'Dualistic theology is dominant in the majority of Evangelical churches.
That's why many Evangelicals feel rather discouraged about participating in
processes of expressing citizenship.' Pe8, a Pentecostal pastor and author in
Lima, said: 'From a theological perspective the Evangelical churches think it's
not part of the mission of the church to speak publicly about corruption; they
believe the only task of the church is to proclaim the gospel.' Pe11, a senior

leader of the Pentecostal Church of Peru, said: 'We haven't produced a theological-political discourse, so the two things work very separately – theology on one side, politics on the other.' According to Pe3, a leader of a Christian NGO in Huanuco, 'we don't see fighting corruption as part of the mission. We have more of a pietistic, internal focus and we see those issues as something that's outside and that doesn't relate to us.' Pe15, a Lutheran leader in the Institute of Communication Studies (an NGO advocating for human rights), said: 'Many Evangelicals do not get involved in society, because they have a fundamentalist religious outlook. The priority is conversion of souls and there isn't a holistic view of responsibility to human beings, only to their souls.'

Three Evangelical informants described an extension of the belief that involvement in society is merely pointless: it may even be seen as sinful. Pe27, a senior leader of the Presbyterian Church, described his experience in Elagustine, a district in Lima:

> The Mayor asked me to organise a meeting with the pastors. Out of a group of twenty-five pastors, only three came. On a second try the pastors said, 'No, because that's of the world'. That shows that the majority of the denominations would say that being in a relationship with the Mayor, or the government, is worldly, it is sin.

Pe20, an IEP pastor in Andhuaylas, said: 'Many pastors think that politics is like sin. Almost every believer thinks that politics means corruption. If a Christian becomes Mayor they still think he is going to do the same things as the one who is not a Christian.' And Pe33, a leader of CONEP, observed that 'we need to work theologically to overcome the idea of many pastors and leaders that the world is dirty.' Finally, Pe9, a leader of the Evangelical student movement in Peru, saw another belief as a hindrance to Evangelical involvement in advocacy in Peru: 'The neo-Pentecostal leaders justified Fujimori's actions because they saw him as sent by God: "We need to obey political authority without criticism, because that's the will of God".'

The two Evangelical leaders who talked about the origins of dualistic theology in Peruvian Evangelicalism both attributed it to the influence of American missionaries since the 1950s. According to Pe9, a leader of the Evangelical student organisation in Peru:

> The churches at the beginning of the twentieth century were involved socially and politically. But starting in the1950's there was a wave of American missionaries who were expelled from China after Mao's Cultural Revolution. As they arrived in Latin America after such a traumatic experience in China, they noticed that there were many guerrilla movements here, stemming from the Cuban revolution. So they came with the two aims of spreading the gospel and saving Latin America from the torture of communism. In that context they saw all socio-political things as connected to communism, and along with the gospel came an ideology that was opposed to anything that had to do with the socio-political reality of the

country. So the church wasn't allowed a prophetic message. A very individualistic gospel was shared. An understanding of theology that separates from reality was promoted: 'What happens now doesn't matter; everything on earth is going to be burned'.

Pe10, a leader of Paz y Esperanza, described the continuing influence of that theology:

> The earlier Methodist and Presbyterian missionaries were more concerned about society, but in the 1950s and 60s we received missionaries from the US who had a very divided mind, where Christianity has no relation with transformation of society. That view of Christianity has more influence among the Evangelicals in Peru. The idea that Christianity could change society remains in just a very small group in Peru - the Lutherans, Methodists and Presbyterians – but without any real influence in the country.

Some Evangelicals have recently started to campaign for Evangelical rights and sexual morality

The comments above suggest that mobilizing communities for better governance is not on the agenda of most Evangelicals. However, several informants described a new and different strand of Evangelicalism in Peru, which has become quite vocal over two issues: religious equality for Evangelicals, and sexual morality. According to Pe9, a leader of the Evangelical student organisation in Peru:

> The most conservative part of the church has formed a council called UNICEP, led by the neo-Pentecostal churches with very North American leanings. The only thing that this movement cares about is the rights of Evangelicals, not the rights of the poor, the marginalised, the victims of violence. The focus is on the right of Evangelicals to acquire power, 'religious equality' (to have the same power that the Catholic Church has). There's not a service attitude, rather a 'We need power' attitude – equality in power with those who have power in the country. But equality for those who live in extreme poverty is not considered, it's not part of the agenda.

Pe10, a leader of Paz y Esperanza, elaborated on the benefits that Evangelicals are seeking, then described their concerns about sexual morality:

> Now that we have a middle class church in Lima, Evangelicals are more aware about their own rights – religious freedoms, how to reduce taxes for Evangelical pastors or churches, how to get some benefits from the state. If the Catholic Church receives some land to build a church, Evangelicals want the same rights. Evangelicals want to protect their rights, but not the rights of others. There's no plan for the country for the coming years. Evangelicals want to replace the Catholics, and that's all ... The charismatic sector literally copies the agenda of the Moral Majority in the US: anti-abortion, anti-homosexual marriage, and a very conservative view about politics. So there is more and more presence of the

churches in the political area, but it's pro-life, Focus on the Family - not on poverty, corruption or human rights. The agenda is very narrow. This is the public presence of Evangelicals that we have in the country.

Pe33, a leader of CONEP, expressed similar views:

Evangelicals who participate as citizens do so with the thought that the benefits need to be for the church. We need to change that, saying that it's not only for the benefit of the church, but responsibility for social change ... There's great focus within Evangelical sectors on the campaign against abortion, against divorce, and against gay marriage. But there's not a campaign in the same way against corruption, against injustice. And when somebody does step in to try to develop something in those areas, they're seen as having communist, anti-systemic tendencies. There's an uneven understanding within the socio-political conscience of the church.

The comments of Pe11, a senior leader of the Pentecostal Church of Peru, illustrate the Evangelical sense of unfair treatment by the state: 'The Catholic Church manipulates the government and takes all the power. There isn't really freedom of the Press, everything is regulated by the Catholic Church. Some priests in Peru receive a salary from the state.' The Pentecostal Church had recently been called by the government to submit their requests. Four of their five requests concerned equal treatment for Evangelicals, including a specific proposal that the Evangelical Church should receive financial support from the state. This sat alongside their fifth proposal, which was that 'the Evangelical Church should be able to name a permanent Commission of Surveillance to follow up government projects, in order to prevent corruption' – with apparently no awareness of the difficulty that an institution financed by the state would face in criticising the state.

Compared with informants in the Philippines, Kenya and Zambia, those in Peru said relatively little about attempts by political leaders to co-opt the Evangelical sector. One notable exception was Fujimori and the neo-Pentecostal church. In the assessment of Pe12, a leader of Paz y Esperanza:

The US government supported Fujimori for a good part of his ten years, and American churches connected with the neo-Pentecostal church in Peru encouraged them to be aligned with Fujimori's government. So they lacked a critical eye and a critical voice to what happened.

Another exception, in the opinion of Pe7, an IEP pastor in Cusco, was the relationship between the Evangelical churches and a former Mayor of Cusco:

The churches consented to being passive about problems of political corruption. The Mayor was not a Christian but there were Christian people within the group elected around him. This closeness was an opportunity for the church to use many resources available to the city government. For a joint service, we had the city government's theatre at no charge. We would automatically be authorised for events. The Mayor was very close to the Evangelicals, very appreciative, and we had a good relationship. But evaluating this situation now, I feel that sometimes we didn't speak out about things, for example about some uses of money that weren't all that great. They were tolerated. The church was silent.

On the whole, however, informants said little about attempts by political leaders to co-opt the Evangelical sector. This may reflect their numerical weakness and the likely opposition of the (much more powerful) Catholic Church to political attempts to woo Evangelicals.

Initiatives to increase Evangelical engagement in society

Three informants mentioned recent initiatives that aim to increase Evangelical participation in society. Pe4, an Evangelical pastor in Huanuco, described a training programme on Evangelical leadership and public advocacy that he has been working on since 2004:

> The goal of the programme is that the churches become aware of their role as citizens - being active in accountability, recognising their role in advocacy and being active in their communities. Pastors have come from around the region and are participating. There's been some resistance to the topic, but the processes of change are beginning – several are starting to realise the importance of their participation.

Pe8, a Pentecostal pastor and author in Lima, described the 'School of Leaders' that he and Pe2 initiated in 2007:

> Over two years, part-time, it will train people in political and social issues from a biblical foundation and with practical examples on how to fight against poverty and corruption, and other social and political issues. The people on the School of Leaders are already linked to grassroots movements like the Mothers' Clubs, the Glass of Milk Committees. There are many evangelical women involved. We want to improve their participation, and to make them models of social and political involvement. It's another way for us to do politics, from below.

Pe14, a leader of an Evangelical seminary in Lima, described a new Masters course that the seminary plans to start in 2010:

> It's focused on Christian professionals, to give them a boost in their theology. The point of the degree will be to do an investigation into their profession and how they can help improve public life. There is demand for it right now; people are asking for it all the time.

Finally, Pe27, a senior leader of the Presbyterian Church, suggested a different force for change:

> Church members know, more and more, what their rights and their responsibilities are within society. But what is lacking is for the leadership to

really recognise, or feel, that change. When I visit the jungle or the mountains and talk to the members of the church, they say, 'Our pastors don't train us or encourage us to work in these things. They live in a reality apart from our lives'. So change is coming, though it is very, very slow, and it's coming from below.

Summary

The reputation of Evangelicals for honest behaviour

Evangelicals in Peru have a reputation for honest behaviour. This view was expressed by most Evangelical informants and by the only Catholic informant to give an opinion on the matter (Pe30, a Catholic law lecturer in Lima). The election of Evangelicals as Mayor in seven out of 19 districts in Andahuaylas, where Evangelicals comprise only one per cent of the population, is consistent with this favourable view of Evangelical behaviour. Several Evangelical leaders were candid about failures of Evangelicals to live up to their reputation, for example by misusing church or public resources, paying bribes, or growing and trafficking illegal drugs, but these admitted shortcomings did not negate the Evangelical reputation for honest behaviour. Suggested causes of corruption among Evangelicals included lack of accountability and the prosperity gospel.

Preaching about corruption

Evangelical leaders disagreed about the extent to which Evangelical preaching addresses corruption and the extent to which it is a useful resource for fighting corruption. Those who lead churches or theological institutions were more likely to say that Evangelical preaching addresses corruption, and to express optimism about the impact that preaching would eventually have on corruption, than those with experience as politicians or as leaders of NGOs. For example, Pe27, a senior leader of the Presbyterian Church said: 'the Evangelical presence has to be very consistent with the Word of God, so that new generations are prepared to really serve; and with the passage of time, those things can become social norms and be instituted as laws'. That perspective contrasts sharply with that of Pe33, a leader of CONEP: 'The problem in our churches is that we are primarily expert in individual formation ... The political system is corrupt. So we need to make not moral decisions but political decisions to eliminate a system that's corrupt'.

Reforming government by having Evangelicals inside government

The perceived failure of many Evangelical politicians to challenge corruption and human rights abuses under Fujimori's government had left some Evangelical leaders sceptical about the potential for Evangelical politicians to improve governance at national level. None of the Evangelical leaders interviewed reflected positively on the decision of Humberto Lay, a Pentecostal pastor, to campaign for the Presidency in 2006. They were more positive about the track record of Evangelical politicians in local politics, but no informant had been impressed by any controlling effect on corruption from the presence of Evangelical employees in government offices. A number of Evangelical leaders envisaged the possibility that Evangelicals might perform better in national politics in future. Their suggestions as to what have been the 'missing ingredients' to date tended to focus on the failings of the individuals, such as lack of understanding, commitment, training or experience, rather than on systemic problems, such as a lack of critical mass of reformers.

Promoting civic oversight

Most informants saw Evangelicals as uninterested in taking opportunities for civic participation, though there were notable exceptions such as CONEP's participation in the Concertation Tables and the advocacy work of Paz y Esperanza. Evangelical leaders feel they have inherited from the USA a dualistic theology which they think discourages socio-political involvement because it sees involvement in society as pointless, and possibly even sinful. However, several informants described a new and different strand of Evangelicalism in Peru, led by neo-Pentecostal churches with North American leanings, which is vocal regarding religious equality for Evangelicals and sexual morality, but not corruption. In contrast with Zambia, the Philippines and Kenya, Evangelical leaders in Peru did not think the Catholic Church has played a positive role in challenging corrupt behaviour by the state.

Comparisons Across the Four Countries

Using Church-Sect Theory to Understand Evangelicalism and Corruption

One of the most important things a research supervisor can do is to point you in the right direction at critical moments, and Peter Clarke did just that for me as I was trying to understand why the relationship between Evangelicalism and corruption varies so much between countries. He suggested that these differences can best be understood through the lens of church-sect theory, with Evangelicals reflecting the church type in Kenya and Zambia and the sect type in the Philippines and Peru.

The distinction between 'church' and 'sect' was first described a century ago by the German Protestant theologian Ernst Troeltsch:

> The church is an institution which has been endowed with grace and salvation as the result of the work of Redemption; it is then able to receive the masses, and to adjust itself to the world, because, to a certain extent, it can afford to ignore the need for subjective holiness [1] for the sake of the objective treasures of grace and of redemption.

> The sect is a voluntary society, composed of strict and definite Christian believers bound to each other by the fact that all have experienced "the new birth". These "believers" live apart from the world, are limited to small groups, emphasize the law instead of grace, and in varying degrees within their own circle set up the Christian order, based on love; all this is done in preparation for and expectation of the coming kingdom of God. [2]

The American sociologist Benton Johnson developed this theory by proposing that 'church' and 'sect' should be used simply as names applied to end-points of a single axis of variation formed by the degree of tension between a religious group and its socio-cultural environment, with tension being highest at the 'sect' end of the axis.[3]

The British sociologist Bryan Wilson argued that sects can be usefully differentiated on the basis of their responses to the world as they answer the

---

[1] In contemporary English we would probably translate 'subjective holiness' as 'personal holiness'.

[2] Ernst Troeltsch *The Social Teaching of the Christian Churches* (London: Allen & Unwin 1912), 993.

[3] Benton Johnson 'On Church and Sect' *American Sociological Review* 28 (1963), 539-549.

question 'What shall we do to be saved?'[4] Most of the different types of response which he described can be identified among the comments of informants in the Philippines and Peru, so it is useful to have a list of Wilson's types and his brief descriptions of them:

- Conversionist: 'Only by acquiring a new conception of himself, by being born again, will a man be saved ... Only when men have had such an experience of salvation can society hope for betterment ... Social reformers or revolutionaries seeking to improve social conditions ... are irrelevant.' Wilson identified this type of response as being typical of evangelical Protestantism.

- Reformist: The world is a place 'in which there is evil, but evil which might in some of its manifestations be overcome by reform in accordance with the dictates of conscience' ... Reformist sects 'see salvation as very largely a matter of transforming social organisation'.[5]

- Manipulationist: 'Seek salvation in the world, but essentially by the employment of means not generally known in the world.' This might involve, for example, pursuing status or wealth through supernatural means.

- Introversionist: 'The world must be abandoned. Those who retreat hope to preserve and cultivate their own holiness.'

- Revolutionist: 'The world is evil, and the only prospect of salvation is the overturning of the world by supernatural action.'

As you will see from what follows, I found that the framework of church and sect, and Wilson's typology of sects, provide a useful basis for interpreting the very different ways that Evangelicals relate to corruption in the different case-study countries.

The Reputation of Evangelicals for Honest Behaviour

The reputation of Evangelicals for honest behaviour is very variable across the four case-study countries. They have a good reputation for honesty where they are a minority religious group, but not where they are the majority. This pattern is consistent with Troeltsch's theory of church and sect types of Christian movement. Evangelicals in Kenya, where at least half the population can be considered Evangelical, and in Zambia, where Evangelicals also outnumber Catholics, fit the description of movements that 'receive the masses', tend to 'ignore the need for subjective holiness', and are in a low state of tension with their socio-cultural environment. For all these reasons, they fit Troeltsch's church-type. Conversely, Evangelicals in the Philippines and Peru, the two mainly Catholic case-study countries, can be described as 'strict and definite

---

[4]Bryan Wilson *Religious Sects: A sociological study* (London: Weidenfeld & Nicolson 1970), 37-40.
[5] Wilson *Religious Sects*, 46.

Christian believers' who are 'limited to small groups', who expect high standards of rectitude in social behaviour and are in a high state of tension with their socio-cultural environment; they therefore fit the sect-type.

How Does this Fit with the Protestant Advantage in Controlling Corruption?

At first sight, the conclusion that Evangelical Protestants have a poor reputation for honest behaviour in countries where they are the majority appears to contradict the observation that, other things being equal, countries with more Protestants have lower levels of corruption.[6] In fact there is no contradiction if one recognises that countries with an Evangelical Protestant majority, compromised though it may be, are better able to control corruption than countries with a Catholic, Islamic, Hindu, Buddhist or any other religious majority. Church-sect theory implies that all religious majorities tend to be compromised; Treisman's findings imply that countries with a lot of compromised Evangelicals are able to control corruption more effectively than countries with a lot of compromised Catholics or compromised Muslims.

Does Church-Sect Theory Explain the Differences Between Martin and Gifford?

You may recall from Chapter 4 the sharply contrasting characterisations of Evangelicals that different sociologists have produced. David Martin has characterized them in positive terms, as people who exert a political impact through 'the adoption of economic and work disciplines' and 'a concern for broad moral principles'.[7] Paul Gifford, however, has described the role of churches, including Evangelical churches, in sub-Saharan Africa in very different, and negative, terms: 'there seems little significant difference between the exercise of leadership in the churches and in national life generally; indeed, in some places it may sometimes be more autocratic and self-seeking'.[8] Having seen the extent to which my own findings were consistent with church-sect theory, I wondered to what extent it might account for the differences between Martin and Gifford. After looking in detail at their various comments, I concluded that many of them can.

Gifford has written mainly about churches in Anglophone Africa, in countries where Evangelicals tend to be a majority and hence reflect the 'church' type, barely distinguishable from their surrounding culture. In these countries Catholics are in the minority, and Gifford tends to be less critical of them than of Evangelicals. The opposite is true for many of David Martin's judgements, which are often based on observations from Latin America. In that

---

[6] Treisman 'The Causes of Corruption'.
[7] Martin 'The Evangelical Upsurge', 39.
[8] Gifford *African Christianity*, 343.

context Evangelicals are heavily outnumbered by Catholics, and hence reflect the 'sect' type, keen to distance themselves from the prevailing culture,

However, not all of their differences can be accounted for on the basis of church-sect theory. When David Martin writes about Evangelicals in Africa he does so in remarkably positive terms. In South Africa 'Pentecostals have picked up the older Methodist stress on respectability'.[9] In Nigeria 'born again people and institutions are considered more reliable and trustworthy ... Most born-again Christians do not bribe officials or even tolerate such behaviour'.[10] In Kenya, 'Pentecostals adopt a helpful discipline which bolsters the integrity and economy of the family'.[11] In Zimbabwe 'the church encourages accumulation and the virtues of responsibility, such as ... hard work and trustworthiness'.[12]

It is possible that Martin and Gifford portray African Evangelicals so differently because they are writing about different groups. The historian David Maxwell has commented that:

> Gifford's African Christianity is predominantly the faith of the clerical elite ... If he had been able to move beyond the urban mega-churches to townships and rural locations, Gifford might have been reassured that the faith gospel has a different meaning. Here Pentecostals seek security rather than prosperity.[13]

Another possible interpretation is that Martin is inclined to describe the more positive aspects of Evangelicals in Africa, and Gifford is more inclined to report the negative. I have to say that my informants' sober assessment of the recent history of Evangelicalism in Kenya and Zambia is more in tune with Gifford than with Martin.

Perceived Causes of Corruption within Evangelical Churches

Causes of corruption in Evangelical churches that were mentioned by informants in at least two countries were co-option by the state, poverty (or fear of poverty), the prosperity gospel, lack of local accountability from leaders, and access to western funds with little accountability for their use. The first of these (co-option by the state) fits with the church-sect interpretation of the role played by Evangelicals. It was mentioned only in Kenya and Zambia, where Evangelicals are numerous and correspond to the church type. Although all four case-study countries follow democratic electoral processes, the numerical dominance of the Evangelical sector in Kenya and Zambia makes it a natural

---

[9] David Martin: *Pentecostalism: The world their parish* (Oxford: Blackwell 2002), 137.

[10] Martin *Pentecostalism*, 140.

[11] Martin *Pentecostalism*, 144.

[12] Martin *Pentecostalism*, 147.

[13] David Maxwell 'In Defence of African Creativity' *Journal of Religion in Africa* 30/4 (2000), 474-5.

target for co-option by political leaders in those countries. Evangelicals in the Philippines and Peru are probably a more risky target for co-option by political leaders, since courting the Evangelical minority may offend the Catholic majority.

The prosperity gospel, lack of local accountability from leaders, and access to western funds with little accountability for their use, were all suggested as causes of corruption in Evangelical churches by informants in Kenya, Zambia and Peru, indicating that they are relevant across a range of income levels, and regardless of whether Evangelicals are the majority religious group. The prosperity gospel, in which church members are taught that God will bless them with riches if they first give their money to the pastor, is a clear example of a 'manipulationist' response to the world.[14] In Zambia the problem of weak local accountability from leaders was reinforced by the teaching from the pulpit, particularly in Pentecostal churches, that congregations should 'touch not God's anointed' (in other words, that they should not seek to hold their leaders accountable for how church resources are used). Finally, two other causes of corruption in churches were suggested only by informants in Kenya: tribalism, and western Christians who have modelled, and continue to model, a lifestyle that is affluent by Kenyan standards.

Preaching about Corruption

Although most Evangelicals in the Philippines and Peru agreed that Evangelicals in their country have a good reputation for honesty, they were divided in the extent to which they thought that preaching Evangelical faith could reduce corruption in the country. Some think that a conversionist approach is an effective strategy for fighting corruption. Others are reformists, who see changing political structures as a more effective approach.

The conversionist approach is the very foundation of FOCIG in the Philippines, which has a substantial programme seeking to convert national government officials to Evangelical faith, then teach them to provide excellent public service. Filipino Evangelical opinion about this strategy ranged from describing it as 'the best contribution of the Evangelical community to eradicating corruption' (informant Ph25, clearly another conversionist) to the reformist perspective of informant Ph13: 'you can hardly transform a nation by making everyone goody two shoes. You have to redeem structures that have been used for evil purposes - government fund management, for instance - and Evangelicalism hardly addresses those issues.'

Likewise in Peru, Evangelical opinion about the power of preaching to reduce corruption varied from conversionist views such as 'the Evangelical presence has to be very consistent with the Word of God, so that new generations are prepared to really serve; and with the passage of time, those things can become social norms and be instituted as laws' (informant Pe27, a

---

[14] Wilson *Religious Sects*, 39.

senior leader of the Presbyterian Church) to reformist perspectives such as 'I don't think that when Peru is Evangelical it'll be paradise ... The political system is corrupt. So we need to make not moral decisions but political decisions to eliminate a system that's corrupt' (informant Pe33, a leader of CONEP).

Evangelicals in countries where they are a majority and lack a reputation for honesty, and hence are constrained in preaching virtue, may nonetheless think that conversionism would be an effective strategy for fighting corruption, if only they could get their own house in order. In Kenya corruption in the Evangelical sector is widely acknowledged by Evangelical leaders, yet it co-exists with a conversionist belief in the power of preaching to change the nation. The following words of the Deputy Director of the Kenya Anti-Corruption Commission reflect a conversionist view that was common among Kenyan Evangelical informants: 'Scripture is the best basis for fighting corruption. The church has a fundamental role. At the end of the day it is men and women who must change their hearts and minds in order to defeat corruption.' However, church-sect theory implies that it would be difficult to translate this rhetoric into reality, because majority Christian movements are inclined to ignore the need for personal holiness.

Only in Zambia was Evangelical opinion noticeably downbeat regarding the potential of preaching to fight corruption, and there were no obvious initiatives in place to address the Evangelical sector's weak reputation for honesty.[15]

Reforming Government by Having Evangelicals Inside Government

In none of the four case-study countries was there great optimism among Evangelical informants about the prospects for reducing corruption through electing an Evangelical as President – though in both the Philippines and Peru an Evangelical pastor has recently campaigned for the post: Humberto Lay in Peru in 2006, and Eddie Villaneuva in the Philippines in 2004. Most Evangelical informants in these two countries regretted these Evangelical candidates' decisions to campaign.

Kenya and Zambia have both had the unfortunate experience of being ruled by Evangelical Presidents (Moi and Chiluba, respectively) who are widely perceived as corrupt. Although some informants in these countries resolved this apparent contradiction by interpreting the former Presidents' professed Evangelical faith as insincere, a greater number thought the professed faith was genuine. Informant Z8, an Evangelical and a recent member of the Zambian Cabinet, gave two different interpretations of the failure of Evangelical faith to

---

[15] This mirrors some comparisons drawn by Gifford a decade previously: 'If in Ghana and particularly Uganda there are signs of hope amid the grinding poverty ... in Zambia and Cameroon, where the elites seem to have no idea how to arrest the steep decline (indeed no idea except enriching themselves), one can sense growing despair (*African Christianity*, 324).

influence Presidential behaviour. According to the first interpretation, the discordance between faith and behaviour results from a lack of preparation for the role. The solution, therefore, is adequate personal development so that the Evangelical President can 'be strong enough to think for himself, to connect his values and Christian faith to the everyday life of government' (informant Z8).

The second interpretation sees the problem as structural, arising from the limited power of the President in a democracy: 'You don't run government alone as President. It's a consensus issue, and if a Christian President is going to be a democrat, the decision that wins the vote may not necessarily be Christian, or even in the interests of the nation' (informant Z8). On this interpretation, no amount of personal preparation for the President will suffice. Either the President must have a critical mass of likeminded colleagues, or he must rule as a benevolent dictator. This solution was suggested by only two informants across the four case-study countries, and both of them were Kenyan Evangelicals. The anti-corruption author Michael Johnston has categorised Kenya under Moi as an Official Moghul society, describing Moi's rule as securing 'monopoly political power in a setting of extremely weak state institutions ... while weakening legal checks and countervailing political forces'. This is the type of society in which Johnston envisaged benevolent dictatorship as an appropriate strategy for fighting corruption:

> Could new leaders with an anti-corruption agenda use their unchecked power, along with a sharp tightening of law enforcement and monitoring of business excesses, to 'flip' an Official Moghul society into a new, low-corruption situation? Imagine such a leadership refusing to get involved in corruption, cracking down on former protégés, and using its power and resources to support legitimate economic alternatives.[16]

A number of informants thought that Evangelicals inside government stand a better chance of reducing corruption at local than at national level (though, of course, this would limit its impact on a national scale). Such optimism was confined to the Philippines and Peru, where Evangelicals have quite limited experience of being in government, and of the difficulties of changing a corrupt system from within. Even within this limited experience, there had been problems regarding the lack of training of Evangelicals for public service and Evangelical constituents' expectations of preferential treatment from their Evangelical representatives (informant Pe32, Graham Gordon).

Promoting Civic Oversight of the State

Evangelicals in all four case-study countries saw themselves as weak in reducing corruption by this route, for reasons that include Evangelical theologies of dualism (the belief that Christians should only be concerned

---

[16] Johnston *Syndromes of Corruption*, 214.

about spiritual, not physical, matters) and submission to the state, and an emphasis on personal responsibility for poverty rather than the contribution of social or political factors.

In all four countries except Peru the Catholic Church was seen to be stronger in speaking out against corruption. Representative comments from Evangelical leaders include: 'the Catholic Church has been more resolute, more determined, than the Evangelical churches in regard to pursuing good governance' (informant Ph18, a former President of the Senate in the Philippines); 'the Catholics raise issues that are pertinent to the fight against corruption, and engage the public and the government, and lobby through parliament ...We do not engage as Protestants at a level where you can challenge the structures (informant Z3, a United Church of Zambia pastor); 'the Catholic Church has always beaten Evangelicals in terms of raising the flag whenever there is corruption and wherever the government is not doing its work' (K16, a leader of Christians for a Just Society); and 'The Catholics are better organized because it is the Bishops' Conference which issues statements, not just one Bishop. The Protestants are so divided. There are those who belong to NCCK, the Pentecostals and EAK - they all hold different positions' (David Gitari, a retired Anglican bishop).

Only in Peru were Evangelicals critical of the Catholic Church's current role: informant Pe10, a leader of Paz y Esperanza, said: 'the Catholic bishops say they're against corruption, but instead of trying to relate faith to political ethics, I think there's a failure.' This perspective was endorsed by informant Pe28, a Catholic who works for the Episcopal Commission for Social Action: 'The message of the church is only about spirituality, it does not have a message to eliminate bad social practices. This problem exists in both the Catholic Church and in Evangelical churches.'

Given the Catholic Church's role in Spain's colonisation of the Philippines, it may seem surprising that Evangelical informants there tended to see the Catholic Church as ahead of them in speaking out against corruption. Melba Maggay attributed this reform of the Catholic role to the influence of Americans:

> After we threw out the Spaniards and started Filipinising, it was under pressure, particularly when the American Protestants came in the 1900s. And they started having American Catholic missionaries also - before, they used to get just Spanish and Belgian priests. It forced the Catholic Church to purify their ranks, to re-think their identity as a church. It's only in the last 25 years or so that the church has changed.

Peru is probably more typical of former Spanish colonies than the Philippines, because only in the Philippines has the close relationship between Catholic Church and state been interrupted by nearly 50 years of American rule in the twentieth century. In Kenya and Zambia, of course, the Catholic Church has never had a close relationship to the state.

In Kenya and Zambia, the explanations given for Evangelical weakness in promoting civic oversight of the state emphasised material considerations that would apply to any group, regardless of their beliefs: co-option by the state and fear of the state. Theological explanations, such as dualism or the belief that Christians should submit to the authorities, were less frequently mentioned. Conversely, informants in both the Philippines and Peru gave mainly theological explanations for Evangelical weakness in promoting civic oversight of the state. In both countries, the minority of Evangelicals who are more engaged with civil society attribute this weakness to dualistic theology, to a belief that concern for social justice implies sympathy with Communism, and to the idea that involvement in public life leads inevitably to sin, because the world is seen as 'dirty'.

Dualistic theology exemplifies an introversionist response to the world, according to which 'the world must be abandoned. Those who retreat hope to preserve and cultivate their own holiness'.[17] A good example of this in Peru was offered by informant Pe3:

> The churches' focus is 'Corruption is wrong, let's be sure we're not corrupt', not 'Let's fight the existing corruption'. They have not taken a prophetic role in denouncing acts of corruption. What's required is a culture of citizen vigilance, but it's not on the churches' agenda.

Those who reject involvement in public life as 'dirty' can be seen as revolutionists, for whom 'the world is evil, and the only prospect of salvation is the overturning of the world by supernatural action'.[18] An example of this was given by informant Pe15:

> Unfortunately the main topics of preaching often have nothing to do with the realities of society and when they do get to talk about corruption they use it to proof-text that we are getting towards the end times, that Jesus is about to appear and we'll all head off.

Informants in both the Philippines and Peru saw these ideas as emanating mainly from the USA (and also, more recently, from Chinese Evangelicals in the Philippines). Although some Evangelical leaders in both the Philippines and Peru have been working for a generation to develop a different theology that supports social and political involvement, they remain a minority in Evangelical circles in those countries.

---

[17] Wilson *Religious Sects*, 39.
[18] Wilson *Religious Sects*, 38.

Satisfying Elite Interests

In interviews with 101 informants there was almost no mention at all of any strategy based on satisfying elite interests, as proposed by authors such as Michael Johnston and Douglass North. The sole exception was Karobia who, as a leader of the Kenyan NGO 'Christians for a Just Society', had spent over a decade trying to galvanize Evangelical churches to oppose corruption. He alone had reached the point of saying:

> In South Korea they have corruption, but they organized it in a certain way. You're stealing, but you have a vision for multiplying jobs, growing the economy, you don't finish off the enterprise ... Our form of corruption in sub-Saharan Africa isn't visionary corruption ...Whether it's a public company or a parastatal, we just run it down, finish it off. We cannibalise, get the monies and take them abroad. So one of the solutions that is being put to the government is to say: 'Keep the money, but invest it here. Don't invest it in the Channel Islands or Switzerland. Invest here.'

Even if satisfying elite interests in this way may help to control corruption, it is hard to see this strategy as the natural territory of the church. Indeed both of the mechanisms that may explain Evangelicalism's controlling effect on corruption (encouraging people to be good, or facilitating challenges to the state) would be undermined if Evangelicals adopted this approach.

Conclusion

Summary of the Book

This book began with two questions. Why is economic inequality greatest in Christian, and especially Protestant, developing countries? And can the church reduce those economic inequalities?

Having investigated the first question, it turns out that, although Christianity is associated with the main influences on economic inequality, it is not a significant cause of inequality in itself. Economic inequality is greatest in countries that export raw products and where governments are large and corrupt. Protestant and Catholic developing countries are raw product exporters. They have ended up that way because their pre-colonial societies were sparsely populated and relatively unsophisticated in terms of technology, political organisation and religion; they were therefore much more likely to be used for raw product production and to convert to Christianity than the densely populated and sophisticated societies of Asia. Many Protestant developing countries have the additional problem of having large and corrupt governments. These large governments are probably a legacy of colonial attempts to establish welfare states when they were under British rule post 1945. Unfortunately, they do not control corruption sufficiently to ensure that state resources benefit the majority rather than ruling elites.

In the light of these findings, I tightened up my second question from the rather general 'Can the church reduce economic inequalities?' to focus on the church and corruption. Although countries with more Protestants tend to have slightly less corruption, this effect is stronger in high income countries with a long Protestant history than in low- or middle-income countries where Protestantism is more recent. Other writers have suggested that Protestants may oppose corruption through preaching, through working within state institutions, or through promoting civic oversight of the state. Key informants in the four countries studied here did not regard Evangelicals as particularly effective in opposing corruption through any of these suggested mechanisms, but for reasons that differed across the four countries. Evangelicals in two mainly Protestant countries (Kenya and Zambia) are seen as having lost their moral authority through being compromised by the state. Evangelicals in the two mainly Catholic countries (the Philippines and Peru) have a reputation for honest behaviour, but are seen as too detached from society to have much impact on corruption. In none of these countries have Evangelicals, by and large, succeeded in being 'in the world' without becoming 'of the world'.

Interpreting the Pessimism of the Evangelical Leaders

How should one interpret the generally pessimistic views of Evangelical leaders, particularly in Kenya and Zambia, regarding the effectiveness of Evangelicals in opposing corruption through any of the suggested mechanisms? Preaching to promote honest behaviour was the only anti-corruption strategy that Evangelical leaders saw as a current area of strength. This was limited to the Philippines and Peru, where Evangelicals have a reputation for honest behaviour, and even there a number of Evangelical leaders did not agree that preaching to promote honest behaviour is an effective strategy for opposing corruption.

At least three possibilities need to be considered. The first is that Evangelicals in low- and middle-income countries today may be failing to have the same effect on corruption that Evangelical Protestants in previous generations, in other parts of the world, produced.[1] Christians in low- and middle-income countries today may face novel threats to their integrity, such as access to resources that are donated by well-meaning Christians in high-income countries, but without adequate accountability systems in place. This could undermine their moral authority and make it harder for them to challenge corruption.

A second possibility is that Evangelical efforts to oppose corruption <u>are</u> having a positive effect in low- and middle-income countries, but the effect is too slow for informants who are in the thick of things to discern it. Real change in the relationship between rulers and citizens probably takes place over a generation or two, not just a few years,[2] so without decades of experience and a good memory it is probably difficult to perceive real change. There are indications that many informants lacked this long-term perspective, omitting to mention even quite recent Evangelical contributions. For example, it was striking how few Evangelical informants mentioned the role of the Evangelical church leaders Henry Okullu, Alexander Muge, David Gitari, and Timothy Njoya in opposing the one-party system and queue-voting during the Moi era in Kenya. The Evangelical informants may also have been too critical of themselves and other Evangelicals, and thereby under-estimated the impact of Evangelical contributions; many of them were quite forthcoming with examples of corruption among Evangelicals, which suggests that such a tendency towards self-criticism exists. Perhaps I was asking too much in expecting my key informants to be able to assess the effectiveness of Evangelicals in opposing corruption. On this interpretation, all that is required is patience; given long enough, the positive effect of Evangelical efforts to oppose corruption will become apparent.

A third possible interpretation is that Protestantism reduces corruption through <u>unintentional</u> mechanisms, rather than through deliberate efforts to

---

[1] Treisman 'The Causes of Corruption'.
[2] North, Wallis and Weingast 'A Conceptual Framework', 26.

oppose corruption. This could occur if Protestantism displaces other religions which, because they are more hierarchical and more centrally controlled, tend to discourage challenges to abuse of authority. On this interpretation, it does not matter much if active Evangelical efforts to oppose corruption are weak, because the mere fact that people belong to Evangelical churches (which are 'so fragmented that they cannot hope to operate in concert to establish some kind of ideological monopoly')[3] rather than to more authoritarian religions, helps to create an environment where abuses of authority are more readily challenged. This interpretation has similarities with explanations that have been proposed by others for the (unintentional) impact of early Christianity on revitalizing the Roman Empire,[4] and the role of Protestantism in facilitating the rise of modern science[5] and the spirit of capitalism.[6] Regarding Protestantism and democracy, Paul Freston writes:

> Of all the major religions, Protestant Christianity has the longest historical links with processes of democratization. John Witte speaks of three waves of Christian democratizing impulses which accompanied, or even anticipated, Samuel Huntington's 'three waves' of democratization. The first of Witte's waves was Protestant, in the Northern Europe and North America of the seventeenth and eighteenth centuries. Of course, this first wave was largely an unintended result of the fracturing of the religious field and the experience of wars of religion, rather than the intended result of most Protestant leaders' convictions regarding democracy.[7]

This 'unintended consequences' interpretation therefore has a good pedigree. If it is correct, it could be argued that all that Evangelicals need to do to help oppose corruption is to propagate Evangelicalism, thereby displacing more authoritarian religions.

Although it is not clear which of these three interpretations is correct, the approach most likely to ensure that Evangelicals help to reduce corruption is one that seeks to maximize their moral authority while also being actively

---

[3] Martin 'The Evangelical Upsurge', 39.

[4] Rodney Stark *The Rise of Christianity* (Princeton: Princeton University Press 1996). Stark's thesis is that 'central doctrines of Christianity prompted and sustained attractive, liberating, and effective social relations and organizations' thereby permitting 'Christianity to be among the most sweeping and successful revitalization movements in history' (p. 211).

[5] Robert Merton *Science, Technology and Society in Seventeenth Century England* (Atlantic Highlands, NJ: Humanities Press 1938). Merton argued that there was a relationship between Puritan thought and the rise of modern science: 'The Puritan ethic, as an ideal-typical expression of the value-attitudes basic to ascetic Protestantism generally, so canalized the interests of seventeenth century Englishmen as to constitute one important element in the enhanced cultivation of science' (pp. 574-5).

[6] Max Weber *The Protestant Ethic and the Spirit of Capitalism* tr Talcott Parsons (London: Allen & Unwin 1930).

[7] Freston *Evangelical Christianity and Democracy*, 2.

engaged with society. Any strategy which assumes that the third ('unintended consequences') interpretation is correct is unacceptably high-risk. It may be wrong, and relying on it runs the risk of failing to address the lack of moral authority of Evangelicals in countries where they are a majority, and failing to harness their potential contribution to opposing corruption in countries where they do have moral authority.

Why Bother Fighting Corruption When it is so Difficult?

Make no mistake, fighting corruption is a difficult, sometimes dangerous, business. Three of my Evangelical informants (Jovita Salonga, former President of the Philippine Senate; David Gitari, former Anglican Archbishop of Kenya; and Z11, a Zambian bishop) are survivors of assassination attempts. Others have received death threats or had their offices burned down. It would be a lot easier just to turn a blind eye to corruption and focus instead on development projects that do not threaten corrupt elites, and that is what many Christians do. In a paper submitted to the Lausanne Congress in Cape Town, the Argentinian lawyer Roberto Laver gave the following assessment:

> Surprisingly, corruption is receiving far more attention from 'secular' organizations than religious ones. While faith leaders and organizations are increasingly engaged across much of the development agenda, particularly in the areas of HIV/AIDS and education, they are generally less active in the governance and anti-corruption arena ... The evangelical church is not yet paying enough attention to the challenge; it needs to better understand how fighting corruption is a matter of its biblical mandate to pursue social justice.[8]

There are exceptions to this general picture, such as Tearfund UK's campaign on governance and corruption, but my experience is that Roberto is right: Christians are much more involved in development projects than in fighting corruption.

There are two powerful reasons why this needs to change. The first is that it is profoundly inconsistent for Christians to turn a blind eye to the injustice of corruption. The evangelical statesman John Stott has expressed this well:

> We cannot evade our political responsibility to share in changing the structures that inhibit development. Christians cannot regard with equanimity the injustices that spoil God's world and demean his creatures. Injustice must bring pain to the God whose justice flared brightly at the cross; it should bring pain to God's people too.[9]

---

[8] Roberto Laver '"Good news" in the fight against corruption'. *Review of Faith and International Affairs* 8/4 (2010), 49-57.
[9] John Stott *The Cross of Christ* (Leicester: Inter-Varsity Press 2006).

The second reason why Christians need to get serious about fighting corruption concerns a combination of features that characterize many African countries: they have a lot of natural resources, a lot of corruption - and a lot of Christians. If African Christians could make an impact on corruption, Africa's natural resource wealth could transform the continent. But unless this happens, Africa will be impoverished by its natural resource wealth, and African Christians will be either impotent onlookers or co-opted accomplices.

The economist Paul Collier points out that natural resources can be a blessing or a curse to a nation, depending on how it is governed: 'what matters is the quality of governance relative to the value of the natural assets'.[10] He estimates that corruption may halve the proportion of the value of natural assets that reaches the national treasury. And that means half of a staggeringly large amount of money. In 2008 exports of oil, gas and minerals from Africa were worth $393 billion, which is roughly nine times the $44 billion that Africa received that year in international aid.[11] Using Collier's estimate that half of the proceeds may be lost to corruption, it cost Africa something like $200 billion in 2008.

Even $200 billion is a small amount compared to the sums that will soon be changing hands under the table. The business of selling off Africa's natural assets has barely started. Collier estimates that the true asset wealth of Africa is around five times what it has found to date. Chinese companies are busy digging, drilling and building the roads that can take Africa's resources to China. When extraction is in full swing, Africa stands to lose about $1,000 billion each year through corruption.

But the real killer in all this is not the immediate financial loss to the treasury of stolen revenues from natural assets. It is the way that natural assets offer both the opportunity and the incentive to undermine good governance. Unless strong checks and balances are already in place, the incumbent ruler of a resource-rich country can use the proceeds from selling those resources to bribe or bully their way to victory in any elections. And, of course, continued control over those resources provides a powerful incentive to do so. Collier analysed this and concluded that 'resource revenues appear to corrupt democratic politics, turning it from being an improvement on autocracy to being even worse'.[12] That is the enormous challenge that faces Christians in Africa.

What can Christians in Northern Countries Do to Help?

The first thing to say is that Christians in northern countries need to be sensitive to possible southern resentment towards them. For example, K18, a

---

[10] Paul Collier *The Plundered Planet: How to reconcile prosperity with nature* (London: Allen Lane 2010), 60.

[11] World Trade Organisation 'International Trade Statistics' 2009, 42.

[12] Collier *The Plundered Planet*, 53.

leader of the Fellowship of Christian Unions in Kenya said 'there are rich people in Kenya oppressing poor people, on pretty much the same scale as the rich countries oppress the poor countries. So the situation in the worst of the countries is actually a miniature representation of the globe'; and Z20, a leader in a Zambian Christian NGO, said 'there's a perception by most of our educated people that because of what we went through – colonization and things like that – we are much better than the North and there's very little we can learn from them'. These comments are very broad generalizations, but they indicate the strength of feeling that may exist.

Second, northern Christians need to recognize that even those who lose out as a result of corruption may not see it as wrong. This was communicated by several informants in Zambia. Father Peter Henriot suggested that 'it is expected that those who have a bit of authority have a right to claim something for themselves, even outside the laid-down rules'; Z10, an Evangelical bishop, thought that people don't see corruption as 'a vice within society'; and Z12, a senior member of staff at the Zambia Anti-Corruption Commission, felt that 'the biggest challenge in fighting corruption is to get the public to believe that it is an evil and that it's detrimental to their welfare'. There is an important role here for initiatives that raise public awareness in low- and middle-income countries of the harm that corruption causes them.

Third, northern Christians need to understand how the context in southern countries affects Christians there. They should not assume that Evangelicals, regardless of their context, always tend to be honest people with the moral authority to fight corruption. Northern Christians should be aware that corruption within the Evangelical sector is more likely in countries that are poor (because poverty and corruption go hand in hand) and where Evangelicals form a majority (because all religious groups, including Evangelicals, tend to become compromised when they are a majority in society). In such contexts, it may be difficult for Evangelicals to play an effective role in challenging corruption until they have recovered some of their moral authority through addressing corruption within their own ranks. Given the Evangelical emphasis on the authority of the Bible, initiatives that use the Bible as the basis for challenging corrupt practices in the church (an approach that was being taken by the Evangelical Alliance of Kenya in 2007) may be fruitful. Conversely, in middle-income countries where Evangelicals form a minority, dualistic theology is more likely to be a problem than corruption within the church; the priority in such countries is to support a Biblically-based theology that connects Christian faith with social and political realities, so that more Evangelicals adopt a reformist, or at least a conversionist, approach to the world[13] and become more active citizens.

Fourth, in situations where Evangelicals do have sufficient moral authority and are engaged with society, northern Christians should support diverse strategies for opposing corruption, because it remains unclear why Evangelical

---

[13] See page 188 for a discussion of reformist and conversionist approaches to the world.

Protestantism is associated with less corruption. Converting senior generals, encouraging Evangelicals to act as reformers within government, and urging Evangelicals to be active citizens who hold their government to account are probably all worthwhile contributions, and there are probably synergies between them. In the Philippines for example, Ph24, Director of a secular anti-corruption NGO, saw as particularly promising an approach that combines support for reform-minded leaders, such as the Evangelicals that FOCIG aims to produce, with surveillance that keeps them accountable:

> What generally works is partnering with like-minded government officials, those that are already oriented towards reform ... The reforms that we've tried out to date have always depended on the political will of the person dealing with it. What we want to do is to identify second tier leaders, the Under-Secretaries, and help them stay the course and not give up, because I can imagine to be in that position as a reformer, to be ostracised and persecuted because of what you're trying to do, is a tough thing to experience alone. And while one of the things we do in TAN is criticise government where we see fit, we also realise the flipside of that coin is to identify the areas of good, and support that.

An expansion of this sort of initiative could yield dividends, and Evangelicals could play a useful role, provided they are both honest and engaged with society. At the time of writing I am setting up a UK-based charity called 'Faith in Government' to support initiatives such as FOCIG. Its purpose is 'to help Christian leaders in the public and private sectors in low- and middle-income countries to promote the sound administration and development of the law, according to the tenets of their faith'. A complementary approach, based on encouraging Evangelicals to be active citizens who hold their government to account, is being supported by Tearfund UK.

Fifth, organizations need to handle north-south partnerships involving money in ways that minimise the risk of corruption, while remaining alert to the risk of paternalism. Evangelical informants suggested three practical steps that would help in this area:

- Donor organisations should check the credentials of potential recipients of funding. This might seem obvious, but informants such as Z17, a Pentecostal pastor, thought it was often lacking: 'our brothers from abroad don't really look at who they're giving things to, their Christian character ... They don't even get a referee from somewhere to say "This person is fit to run such an organisation and to receive funding".'
- There may often be situations where financial donors need to work with southern partners to establish adequate mechanisms for ensuring financial accountability in the partnership. As Z8, a former Vice President of Zambia, said:

> Money comes in huge quantities to these church organisation or individuals and they do not have the capacity to manage those resources in a manner that is

internationally acceptable. It's no fault of their own, but they just don't have the system.

- Northern donors should ensure that the core costs of southern partners are adequately covered in a mutually-agreed way, to avoid a situation where southern partners feel they have to resource their core costs by diverting funds ear-marked for programme beneficiaries (this scenario was suggested by two Evangelical informants, Z19 and Pe29).

Finally, it is important to plan for the long haul and not to be discouraged if progress appears slow. Douglass North notes that transitions from Limited to Open Access Orders, on the infrequent occasions in history when they have occurred, have taken place over something of the order of fifty years. To academics, this is 'a period of time that is quite short by historical standards',[14] but from the perspective of those who are trying to promote reform it is a painfully long time. The potential for discouragement was evident in some of the key informant interviews, for example with Niels Riconalla in the Philippines: 'I have been with this government for the last 22 years and it's very frustrating to see very little progress.' Perseverance is essential for anyone who wants to fight corruption.

Final remarks

This book explains why economic inequality is greatest in Christian, and especially Protestant, developing countries. The most effective way in which Protestants could help to reduce inequality and poverty is through opposing corruption, so that public resources are used for public benefit. It is painfully apparent from the country case studies described here that little of that potential has yet been realised in low- and middle-income countries. If Protestants in those countries can maintain, or recover, their moral authority while also engaging with society, learning to be in the world but not of the world, they will have an impact on corruption, and hence on inequality and poverty.

If you are reading this final paragraph you have probably read most of the book. I hope you are now convinced that Christians can, and must, make a difference to corruption. If you want to join a group of like-minded Christians, I would love to hear from you. We have formed an NGO called 'Faith in Government' to 'help Christian leaders in the public and private sectors in low- and middle-income countries promote the sound administration and development of the law, according to the tenets of their faith'. To find out more, please contact me at mallaby@ocms.ac.uk

---

[14] North, Wallis and Weingast 'A Conceptual Framework', 26.

Appendices

Appendix A: Country data used in Chapter 2

77 never-Communist countries (overleaf)

Country	Prevailing religion, 2000	Prevailing religion, 1600	Gini coefficient of distribution of consumption, c.2000	Gross national income per capita, 2000 (US$)	People per square km, 1600	Mining exports as % of total exports, 2000	Food and agricultural raw material exports, as % of total exports, 2000	Gini coefficient of land ownership	Index of control of corruption, 2000	Government revenue as % of GDP, 2000	Domestic credit provided by the banking sector as % of GDP, 2000
Austria	Old Catholic	Catholic	0.21	26010	29	3	7	0.59	1.95	35	102
Belgium	Old Catholic	Catholic	0.19	24900	55	3	12	0.56	1.38	43	78
France	Old Catholic	Catholic	0.24	24470	33	2	12	0.58	1.48	38.9	85
Ireland	Old Catholic	Catholic	0.24	22990	11	0	8	0.44	1.57	30.6	106
Italy	Old Catholic	Catholic	0.31	20160	37	1	7	0.73	0.91	38.5	76
Luxembourg	Old Catholic	Catholic	0.22	43560	55	5	8	0.48	2.07	39.8	102
Portugal	Old Catholic	Catholic	0.32	10940	22	2	10	0.74	1.44	31.1	131
Spain	Old Catholic	Catholic	0.27	15320	14	2	15	0.77	1.69	26.9	98
Germany	Old mixed Christian	Catholic	0.21	25510	29	2	5	0.63	1.74	26.3	119
Greece	Old mixed Christian	Catholic	0.36	11290	9	7	31	0.58	0.82	21.9	51
Netherlands	Old mixed Christian	Catholic	0.22	25200	39	2	18	0.57	2.36	41.1	134
Switzerland	Old mixed Christian	Catholic	0.24	40110	25	6	4	0.50	2.24	22.3	161
Canada	Old mixed Christian extension	Local	0.26	21810	0.04	5	12	0.64	2.32	20.1	97
Denmark	Old Protestant	Catholic	0.20	31460	17	1	23	0.51	2.38	31.5	135
Finland	Old Protestant	Catholic	0.18	24920	0.4	3	8	0.27	2.56	27.8	54
Norway	Old Protestant	Catholic	0.20	35660	5	6	7	0.18	2.13	34.5	76
Sweden	Old Protestant	Catholic	0.18	28650	2	3	7	0.32	2.50	35.1	43
United Kingdom	Old Protestant	Catholic	0.27	24920	31	2	5	0.66	2.19	34.6	132
Australia	Old Protestant extension	Local	0.25	20060	0.03	23	27	0.88	2.07	21.9	84
New Zealand	Old Protestant extension	Local	0.30	13680	0.01	6	60	0.75	2.38	29	112
United States	Old Protestant extension	Local	0.31	34400	0.1	2	9	0.76	1.79	20.1	171
India	Hindu-Buddhist	Hindu-Buddhist	0.33	450	30	19	15	0.64	-0.25	9.6	29
Japan	Hindu-Buddhist	Hindu-Buddhist	0.18	35140	54	1	0	0.59	1.39	20.7	223
Nepal	Hindu-Buddhist	Local	0.36	220	19	2	21	0.45	-0.56	8.7	31
Sri Lanka	Hindu-Buddhist	Hindu-Buddhist	0.38	810	27	0	23	0.58	-0.09	14.5	29
Thailand	Hindu-Buddhist	Hindu-Buddhist	0.40	1990	5	1	17	0.47	-0.30	14.1	108

Country	Prevailing religion, 2000	Prevailing religion, 1500	Gini coefficient of distribution of consumption, c.2000	Gross national income per capita, 2000 (US$)	People per square km, 1500	Mining exports, excluding gems, as % of total exports, 2000	Food and agricultural raw material exports, as % of total exports, 2000	Gini coefficient of land ownership	Index of control of corruption, 2000	Government revenue as % of GDP, 2000	Domestic credit provided by the banking sector as % of GDP, 2000
Algeria	Islamic	Islamic	0.35	1570	3	0	0	0.72	-0.62	27.6	6
Bangladesh	Islamic	Islamic	0.31	390	26	0	8	0.62	-0.60	7	25
Egypt	Islamic	Islamic	0.34	1460	153	4	14	0.65	-0.17	16.6	59
Indonesia	Islamic	Multi-faith	0.34	590	6	5	13	0.46	-1.00	16.5	20
Iran	Islamic	Islamic	0.43	1670	6	1	3	0.55	-0.59	9.2	28
Jordan	Islamic	Islamic	0.39	1810	32	15	16	0.78	0.15	19.8	78
Morocco	Islamic	Islamic	0.38	1220	4	9	23	0.62	0.37	25	57
Pakistan	Islamic	Multi-faith	0.27	480	78	0	14	0.57	-0.80	12.1	23
Senegal	Islamic	Local	0.40	450	5	5	61	0.5	-0.38	18.1	20
Tunisia	Islamic	Islamic	0.40	2080	9	2	10	0.70	0.70	26	66
Turkey	Islamic	Islamic	0.37	2980	13	3	14	0.61	-0.28	22	25
Israel	Jewish	Islamic	0.35	17060	15	1	4	no data	1.27	37.7	83
Burkina Faso	Multi-faith	Local	0.38	250	5	2	74	0.42	-0.68	13.5	12
Cameroon	Multi-faith	Local	0.45	640	2	6	32	0.45	-1.05	12.8	8
Cote d'Ivoire	Multi-faith	Local	0.45	650	5	1	64	0.42	-0.60	20.1	15
Korea, Rep.	Multi-faith	Local	0.25	9790	20	1	3	0.34	0.37	17.3	91
Madagascar	Multi-faith	Local	0.46	240	1	4	39	0.58	-0.76	11.3	9
Malaysia	Multi-faith	Islamic	0.42	3430	2	1	9	0.64	0.28	18.9	178
Sierra Leone	Multi-faith	Local	0.63	140	7	70	0.79	0.46	-0.79	6.8	2
Singapore	Multi-faith	Multi-faith	0.35	23030	4	1	2	no data	2.51	15.5	109
Argentina	New Catholic	Local	0.44	7470	0.2	3	46	0.83	-0.34	12.9	24
Bolivia	New Catholic	Local	0.53	1000	1	25	33	0.65	-0.65	14.2	59
Brazil	New Catholic	Local	0.52	3590	0.1	11	28	0.85	0.04	20.6	33
Chile	New Catholic	Local	0.44	4850	2	45	35	0.63	1.56	19	71
Colombia	New Catholic	Local	0.47	2060	1	1	24	0.80	-0.40	10.8	27
Costa Rica	New Catholic	Local	0.39	3700	2	1	33	0.83	1.05	18.8	24
Dominican Republic	New Catholic	Local	0.40	2170	2	2	43	0.79	-0.30	15.2	35
Ecuador	New Catholic	Local	0.44	1340	3	0	41	0.82	-0.96	13.9	33
El Salvador	New Catholic	Local	0.43	2000	2	2	42	0.81	-0.16	13.2	45
Guatemala	New Catholic	Local	0.49	1740	2	2	60	0.79	-0.64	10.2	20
Mexico	New Catholic	Local	0.52	5110	3	1	6	0.77	-0.36	12.3	18
Panama	New Catholic	Local	0.55	3740	2	2	75	0.52	-0.33	18.2	102
Paraguay	New Catholic	Local	0.48	1460	1	0	80	0.93	-1.01	21.2	30
Peru	New Catholic	Local	0.48	2050	2	39	33	0.86	-0.07	13.3	26
Philippines	New Catholic	Local	0.46	1040	2	2	6	0.55	-0.46	13.9	44
Uruguay	New Catholic	Local	0.36	6150	0.01	0	56	0.79	0.76	24.9	51
Venezuela	New Catholic	Local	0.35	4100	1	3	1	0.88	-0.61	12.9	12

Country	Prevailing religion, 2000	Prevailing religion, 1500	Gini coefficient of distribution of consumption, c.2000	Gross national income per capita, 2000 (US$)	People per square km, 1600	Mining exports, excluding gems, as % of total exports, 2000	Food and agricultural raw material exports, as % of total exports, 2000	Gini coefficient of land ownership	Index of control of corruption, 2000	Government revenue as % of GDP, 2000	Domestic credit provided by the banking sector as % of GDP, 2000
Lesotho	New mixed Christian	Local	0.63	630	1	1	8	0.49	0.32	34.4	14
Trinidad & Tobago	New mixed Christian	Local	0.39	5230	2	0	6	no data	0.38	24.2	43
Uganda	New mixed Christian	Local	0.47	260	9	5	82	0.59	-0.86	10.3	7
Botswana	New Protestant	Local	0.63	2870	0.2	89	3	0.6	1.02	45.3	14
Central African Republic	New Protestant	Local	0.61	270	2	34	18	0.37	-1.02	8.1	5
Ghana	New Protestant	Local	0.41	330	5	56	58	0.54	-0.34	18.1	14
Jamaica	New Protestant	Local	0.42	2940	2	4	23	0.80	-0.17	23.3	29
Kenya	New Protestant	Local	0.44	430	4	3	68	0.59	-1.04	21.2	28
Namibia	New Protestant	Local	0.71	1870	0.2	47	27	0.36	1.13	29.5	46
Papua New Guinea	New Protestant	Local	0.50	650	2	51	17	no data	-0.85	18.4	18
South Africa	New Protestant	Local	0.58	3050	1	17	12	0.80	0.57	25.9	134
Swaziland	New Protestant	Local	0.53	1370	1	0	44	0.40	-0.13	27.5	14
Zambia	New Protestant	Local	0.53	290	1	49	13	0.76	-0.82	16.7	9
Zimbabwe	New Protestant	Local	0.57	460	1	12	60	0.70	-0.87	26.1	25

32 ever-Communist countries

Country	Gini coefficient of distribution of consumption, c.2000	Gross national income per capita, 2000 (US$)	Mining exports as % of total exports, 2000	Food and agricultural raw material exports, as % of total exports, 2000	Gini coefficient of land ownership	Index of control of corruption, 2000	Government revenue as % of GDP, 2000	Domestic credit provided by the banking sector as % of GDP, 2000
Albania	0.31	1180	4	13	0.84	-0.61	21.6	48.1
Armenia	0.26	660	22	19	no data	-0.74	17.7	11.5
Azerbaijan	0.36	610	2	5	no data	-1.06	17.6	9.6
Belorussia	0.30	1380	1	11	no data	-0.05	28.7	19.2
Benin	0.36	340	0	87	no data	0.00	15.5	8.5
Bosnia-Herzegovina	0.25	1290	no data	no data	no data	-0.48	40.2	40.8
Bulgaria	0.28	1600	13	13	no data	-0.13	33.7	17.8
Cambodia	0.40	280	no data	3	no data	-0.72	10.3	6.4
China	0.45	930	3	6	no data	-0.34	7.1	119.7
Croatia	0.29	4500	3	14	no data	0.04	41.7	47.2
Czech Republic	0.18	5690	2	6	0.92	0.40	30.5	49.4
Estonia	0.32	4070	6	17	0.79	0.78	32.2	35.4
Ethiopia	0.30	130	1	90	0.47	0.06	15.2	50.7
Georgia	0.38	700	no data	3	no data	-0.71	10.4	21.5
Guinea	0.39	400	63	6	no data	-0.41	12.0	8.6
Hungary	0.24	4600	2	8	no data	0.78	39.0	53.5
Kazakhstan	0.30	1270	18	8	no data	-0.85	11.3	12.3
Kyrgyzstan	0.29	280	45	30	no data	0.04	14.2	12.2
Latvia	0.34	3240	6	35	0.58	0.04	26.1	23.3
Lithuania	0.29	3180	2	17	no data	0.29	25.9	15.2
Moldavia	0.36	370	1	65	no data	-0.84	24.5	25.2
Mongolia	0.30	400	no data	28	no data	-0.21	37.9	10.8
Nicaragua	0.40	750	4	90	0.72	-0.88	18.4	95.7
Poland	0.31	4540	5	10	0.69	0.49	31.6	32.7
Romania	0.28	1700	7	8	no data	-0.45	25.8	14.0
Russia	0.32	1710	9	4	no data	-1.02	31.7	24.7
Slovak Rep.	0.19	3870	3	6	no data	0.27	35.2	56.4
Slovenia	0.28	10760	4	6	0.62	1.10	40.2	44.2
Tajikistan	0.32	180	no data	13	no data	-1.05	10.6	17.9
Ukraine	0.34	700	no data	2	no data	-0.96	26.8	23.8
Yemen	0.33	410	0	5	no data	-0.67	23.9	5.2
Serbia & Montenegro	0.28	1250	16	23	0.54	-1.05	35.8	60.6

Appendix B: Sources of Statistical Data

AD 1500 population estimates
McEvedy C and Jones R
   1978: *Atlas of World Population History* New York: Penguin
GNI per capita in AD 2000, GDP in AD1970, 'government revenue as % of GDP', and
Domestic Credit
World Bank
   2007c: 'World Development Indicators' Available at
   http://publications.worldbank.org/WDI/ Accessed 20.8.07
Export data
United Nations COMTRADE Database
   2006: Available at http://unstats.un.org/unsd/cr/registry/regcs Accessed on 1.11.06,
   using the Standard International Trade Classification revision 3.
Gini coefficient of land ownership
Table A2 in World Bank
   2005: *Equity and Development: World Development Report 2006* Oxford: Oxford
   University Press
Taylor CL and Jodice DA
   1983: *World Handbook of Political and Social Indicators* 3rd edn New Haven CT:
   Yale University Press
Index of control of corruption
Kaufmann D, Kraay A and Mastruzzi M
   2004: 'Governance Matters III: Governance indicators for 1996-2002' *World Bank
   Economic Review* 18/2:253-87
Distribution of consumption and incomes
Table A2 in World Bank
   2005: *Equity and Development: World Development Report 2006* Oxford: Oxford
   University Press
World Institute for Development Economics Research
   2005: 'World Income Inequality Database version 2a' Available at
   http://www.wider.unu.edu/research/Database/en_GB/database/ Accessed 3.6.07
Prevailing religion
Barrett DB, Kurian GT, Johnson TM eds
   2001: *World Christian Encyclopedia* 2nd edn Oxford: Oxford University Press

Appendix C: Key Informants

Table C.1 Key informants in the Philippines

Code	Occupation (and name where consent obtained)	Age group (years)	Gen-der	Religious affiliation	Date and location of interview (all in or near Manila)
Ph1	Melba Maggay, Director of the Institute for the Study of Asian Church and Culture (ISACC)	>60	F	Evangelical	1st March 2007, her office
Ph2	Niels Riconalla, Chairman of the Fellowship of Christians in Government (FOCIG)	45-60	M	Evangelical	2nd March 2007, a restaurant
Ph3	Theologian	>60	M	Evangelical	3rd March 2007, his house
Ph4	Author	>60	F	Evangelical	3rd March 2007, her house
Ph5	Member of staff of a Christian anti-corruption NGO	30-44	F	Evangelical	5th March 2007, her office
Ph6	Mission mobiliser and author	45-60	M	Evangelical	5th March 2007, a restaurant
Ph7	Theologian	>60	M	Evangelical	5th March 2007, Asian Theological Seminary
Ph8	A member of staff of the National Council of Churches in the Philippines	30-44	M	Liberal Protestant (NCCP)	6th March 2007, his office
Ph9	Member of staff of the Alliance of Christian Development Agencies (ACDA)	30-44	F	Evangelical	7th March 2007, her office
Ph10	A General in the Armed Forces of the Philippines	45-60	M	Evangelical	7th March 2007, FOCIG office
Ph11	Lecturer in politics	30-44	F	Evangelical	8th March 2007, her office
Ph12	Attorney	45-60	M	Evangelical	8th March 2007, an office
Ph13	A senior Evangelical church leader	45-60	M	Evangelical	8th March 2007, his office
Ph14	An Evangelical bishop	45-60	M	Evangelical	8th March 2007, his office
Ph15	An attorney who works for COMELEC	45-60	M	Evangelical	8th March 2007, a restaurant
Ph16	A leader of the Christian Reformed World Relief Committee (CRWRC)	45-60	M	Evangelical	9th March 2007, his office
Ph17	Professor of history	45-60	M	Evangelical	9th March 2007, his office

Code	Occupation (and name where consent obtained)	Age group (years)	Gen der	Religious affiliation	Date and location of interview (all in or near Manila)
Ph18	Jovita Salonga, former President of the Senate	>60	M	Evangelical	10th March 2007, his house
Ph19	Member of staff of a secular anti-corruption NGO	<30	F	Evangelical	13th March 2007, a restaurant
Ph20	Dolores Español , Chairperson of Transparency International (TI) in the Philippines	45-60	F	Evangelical	13th March 2007, her office at TI
Ph21	A spokesperson for the Catholic Bishops Conference of the Philippines (CBCP)	45-60	M	Catholic	13th March 2007, his office at CBCP
Ph22	A leader in the National Council of Churches in the Philippines	45-60	M	Liberal Protestant (Anglican)	14th March 2007, a restaurant
Ph23	Robert Nacianceno, the General Manager of Metro-Manila Development Authority (MMDA)	45-60	M	Evangelical	15th March 2007, his office at MMDA
Ph24	Director of a secular anti-corruption NGO	30-44	M	Catholic	16th March 2007, a restaurant
Ph25	BJ Sebastian, an Evangelical businessman	45-60	M	Evangelical	16th March 2007, a restaurant
Ph26	A General in the Armed Forces of the Philippines	45-60	M	Evangelical	10th July 2008, a restaurant

Table C.2 Key informants in Kenya

Code	Occupation (and name where consent obtained)	Age group (years)	Gen- der	Religious affiliation	Date and location of interview (all in or near Nairobi)
K1	Programme Officer for Transparency International in Kenya	30-44	M	Evangelical (denomination not recorded)	4th June 2007, his office
K2	Bishop	>60	M	Evangelical (Anglican)	5th June 2007, his office
K3	A leader of the National Council of Churches of Kenya	45-60	M	Evangelical (Quaker)	5th June 2007, ACK guest house
K4	Dr Arbogast Akidiva, Principal Officer for Education at Kenya Anti-Corruption Commission	45-60	M	Evangelical (denomination not recorded)	6th June 2007, during KACC-EAK conference
K5	A leader of the Evangelical Alliance of Kenya	45-60	M	Evangelical (independent)	7th June 2007, during KACC-EAK conference

Code	Occupation (and name where consent obtained)	Age group (years)	Gen-der	Religious affiliation	Date and location of interview (all in or near Nairobi)
K6	Dr Smokin Wanjala, Deputy Director of KACC	45-60	M	Evangelical (denomination not recorded)	7th June 2007, during KACC-EAK conference
K7	Symonds Akivaga, Senior Lecturer in Education at the University of Nairobi. Author of two books on corruption in Kenya	45-60	M	No current religious affiliation	7th June 2007, Fairview Hotel
K8	Bishop	45-60	M	Evangelical (Anglican)	8th June 2007, his office
K9	Diocesan secretary	>60	M	Evangelical (Anglican)	8th June 2007, ACK guest house
K10	David Gitari, retired archbishop	>60	M	Evangelical (Anglican)	9th June 2007, his home
K11	Senior leader of the Catholic Church in Kenya	45-60	M	Catholic	11th June 2007, his office
K12	Lecturer in Law	30-44	M	Catholic	11th June 2007, his office
K13	Senior leader of the African Independent Pentecostal Church of Africa	45-60	M	Evangelical (African Independent Pentecostal Church of Africa)	11th June 2007, his office
K14	Member of staff of the Evangelical Alliance of Kenya	30-44	M	Evangelical (independent)	12th June 2007, ACK guest house
K15	Karobia, a leader of Christians for a Just Society (CFJS)	30-44	M	Evangelical (Baptist)	12th June 2007, a restaurant in Nairobi
K16	A leader of Christians for a Just Society (CFJS)	30-44	M	Evangelical (denomination not recorded)	12th June 2007, a restaurant in Nairobi
K17	A leader of the Ecumenical Centre for Justice and Peace	45-60	M	Evangelical (Anglican)	13th June 2007, his office
K18	A leader of the Fellowship of Christian Unions (FOCUS)	30-44	M	Evangelical (denomination not recorded)	13th June 2007, his office
K19	An Evangelical lawyer, experienced in working with churches	30-44	M	Evangelical (denomination not recorded)	13th June 2007, ACK guest house

Table C.3 Key informants in Zambia

Code	Occupation (and name where consent obtained)	Age group (years)	Gen-der	Religious affiliation	Date and location of interview
Z1	Lawyer	30-44	F	Evangelical (Pentecostal)	14th June 2007, my guest-house in Lusaka
Z2	A leader in Transparency International in Zambia	30-44	M	No religious affiliation	15th June 2007, his office in Lusaka
Z3	UCZ Pastor	30-44	F	Evangelical (United Church of Zambia)	15th June 2007, Hotel Inter-Continental in Lusaka
Z4	Retired military officer	>60	M	Evangelical (Pentecostal)	16th June 2007, my guest-house in Lusaka
Z5	Senior leader in the United Church of Zambia	45-60	M	Evangelical (United Church of Zambia)	18th June 2007, his office in Lusaka
Z6	Newspaper journalist	30-44	M	Evangelical (Pentecostal)	18th June 2007, his office in Lusaka
Z7	Director of a Zambian anti-corruption NGO	45-60	M	Evangelical (Methodist)	19th June 2007, my guest-house in Lusaka
Z8	Former Vice President of Zambia	45-60	M	Evangelical (Pentecostal)	19th June 2007, his home in Lusaka
Z9	Dyness Kasungami, Human Development Advisor for DFID	30-44	F	Evangelical (United Church of Zambia)	19th June 2007, her office in Lusaka
Z10	Bishop	30-44	M	Evangelical (Pentecostal)	20th June 2007, his office in Lusaka
Z11	Bishop	45-60	M	Evangelical (Pentecostal)	20th June 2007, his office in Lusaka
Z12	Senior member of staff at the Zambia Anti-Corruption Commission	45-60	M	Evangelical (Baptist)	20th June 2007, his office in Lusaka
Z13	University Chaplain	30-44	F	Evangelical (United Church of Zambia)	21st June 2007, her office in Lusaka
Z14	Member of staff in the Auditor-General's office	30-44	F	Catholic	21st June 2007, her office in Lusaka

Code	Occupation (and name where consent obtained)	Age group (years)	Gen-der	Religious affiliation	Date and location of interview
Z15	Member of staff in the Auditor-General's office	45-60	M	Evangelical (Seventh Day Adventist)	21st June 2007, his office in Lusaka
Z16	UCZ Pastor	30-44	F	Evangelical (United Church of Zambia)	22nd June 2007, her house in Ndola
Z17	Pentecostal pastor	30-44	M	Evangelical (Pentecostal)	22nd June 2007, an office in Ndola
Z18	Pentecostal pastor	30-44	M	Evangelical (Pentecostal)	22nd June 2007, an office in Ndola
Z19	Anglican church leader	30-44	M	Anglo-Catholic	22nd June 2007, his office in Ndola
Z20	A leader in a Zambian Christian NGO	45-60	M	Evangelical (Pentecostal)	24th June 2007, my guest-house in Ndola
Z21	A leader in the Council of Churches of Zambia	45-60	F	Evangelical (denomination not recorded)	25th June 2007, her office in Lusaka
Z22	A leader in the Zambian Episcopal Conference	45-60	M	Catholic	25th June 2007, his office in Lusaka
Z23	Father Peter Henriot, Director of the Jesuit Centre for Theological Reflection	>60	M	Catholic	20th June 2007, his office in Lusaka

Table C.4 Key informants in Peru

Code	Occupation (and name where consent obtained)	Age group (years)	Gen-der	Religious affiliation	Date and location of interview
Pe1	Doctor, and former Councillor in a small city	45-60	M	Evangelical Presbyterian and Reformed Church of Peru	23rd April 2008, a conference centre in Lima
Pe2	A leader of the National Evangelical Council (CONEP) and a former Senator	>60	M	Peruvian Evangelical Church	23rd April 2008, a conference centre in Lima
Pe3	A leader of an Evangelical NGO in Huanuco, and an Evangelical pastor	30-44	M	Peruvian Evangelical Church	24th April 2008, a conference centre in Lima
Pe4	Evangelical pastor in Huanuco	30-44	M	Evangelical (Assemblies of God)	24th April 2008, a conference centre in Lima

Code	Occupation (and name where consent obtained)	Age group (years)	Gen- der	Religious affiliation	Date and location of interview
Pe5	Evangelical pastor in Huanuco	45-60	M	Evangelical (Christian and Missionary Alliance Church)	24th April 2008, a conference centre in Lima
Pe6	A leader in a large Evangelical INGO	45-60	M	Evangelical (denominatio n not recorded)	24th April 2008, a conference centre in Lima
Pe7	Evangelical pastor in Cusco	45-60	M	Peruvian Evangelical Church	26th April 2008, a conference centre in Lima
Pe8	Pentecostal pastor and author in Lima	45-60	M	Evangelical- Pentecostal (Mt. Sinai Church of God)	28th April 2008, CONEP office in Lima
Pe9	A leader of the Evangelical student movement in Peru (AGEUP)	30-44	M	Peruvian Evangelical Church	29th April 2008, his office in Lima
Pe10	A leader of Paz y Esperanza (an Evangelical NGO)	45-60	M	Evangelical (Christian and Missionary Alliance Church)	29th April 2008, his office in Lima
Pe11	A leader of the Pentecostal Church of Peru	30-44	M	Evangelical (Pentecostal Church of Peru)	29th April 2008, his office in Lima
Pe12	A leader of Paz y Esperanza (an Evangelical NGO)	30-44	M	Evangelical (denominatio n not recorded)	29th April 2008, his office in Lima
Pe13	A leader in APRODEH (the Association for Human Rights)	45-60	M	No religious affiliation	30th April 2008, his office in Lima
Pe14	a leader of an Evangelical seminary in Lima	45-60	M	Evangelical (Free Church of Scotland)	30th April 2008, his office in Lima
Pe15	A leader in the Institute of Communication Studies (an NGO advocating for human rights)	45-60	M	Evangelical (Lutheran)	30th April 2008, Paz y Esperanza office in Lima
Pe16	Lawyer in Cusco	30-44	M	Peruvian Evangelical Church	1st May 2008, a church office in Cusco
Pe17	Professor in Cusco (and former City Councillor)	45-60	M	Peruvian Evangelical Church	2nd May 2008, my hotel in Cusco

Code	Occupation (and name where consent obtained)	Age group (years)	Gen der	Religious affiliation	Date and location of interview
Pe18	Lawyer in Cusco	30-44	F	Peruvian Evangelical Church	2nd May 2008, a church office in Cusco
Pe19	Leader of the Andahuylas synod of the Peruvian Evangelical Church	30-44	M	Peruvian Evangelical Church	5th May 2008, a restaurant in Andahuaylas
Pe20	Evangelical pastor in Andhuaylas	30-44	M	Peruvian Evangelical Church	5th May 2008, my hotel in Andahuaylas
Pe21	Anti-corruption lawyer, Ministry of Justice, Andahuaylas	45-60	M	No religious affiliation	5th May 2008, his office in Andahuaylas
Pe22	Provincial Governor of Andahuaylas	45-60	M	Catholic	5th May 2008, his office in Andahuaylas
Pe23	Commissioner for the Ombudsman for Citizens' Rights, Andahuaylas	45-60	M	Catholic	5th May 2008, his office in Andahuaylas
Pe24	Mayor of Andahuaylas	45-60	M	Catholic	5th May 2008, his office in Andahuaylas
Pe25	A leader of a Christian NGO in Andahuaylas	30-44	M	Evangelical (denomination not recorded)	5th May 2008, his office in Andahuaylas
Pe26	Evangelical pastor (and shop-keeper) in Andahuaylas	30-44	M	Peruvian Evangelical Church	6th May 2008, his shop in Andahuaylas
Pe27	A senior leader of the Presbyterian Church	>60	M	Evangelical (Presbyterian)	7th May 2008, Paz y Esperanza office in Lima
Pe28	An economist working for the Episcopal Commission for Social Action	45-60	M	Catholic	8th May 2008, my hotel in Lima
Pe29	A leader of Proetica (the national office of Transparency International in Peru)	30-44	M	No religious affiliation	8th May 2008, his office in Lima
Pe30	A law lecturer in Lima	30-44	M	Catholic	9th May 2008, his office in Lima
Pe31	General Secretary of the Bible Society, and a former Senator	>60	M	Evangelical (Presbyterian)	9th May 2008, his office in Lima
Pe32	Graham Gordon, responsible for the Advocacy and Communications department of Paz y Esperanza (a Christian NGO)	30-44	M	Evangelical (denomination not recorded)	9th May 2008, his office in Lima
Pe33	A leader of the National Evangelical Council (CONEP)	45-60	M	Evangelical (denomination not recorded)	10th May 2008, his office in Lima

Bibliography

Afronet
    2002: 'Nchekelako: An African reader on corruption in Zambia' Lusaka: Afronet
Bainbridge WS and Stark R
    1980: 'Sectarian Tension' *Review of Religious Research* 22:105-124
Barrett DB, Kurian GT, Johnson TM eds
    2001: *World Christian Encyclopedia* 2nd edn Oxford: Oxford University Press
Barro, Robert
    2000: 'Inequality and Growth in a Panel of Countries' *Journal of Economic Growth*
    5:5-32
Barro RJ and Mccleary RM
    2003: 'Religion and Economic Growth Across Countries' *American Sociological
    Review* 68:760-81
Bebbington, David
    1989: *Evangelicalism in Modern Britain: A history from the 1730s to the 1980s*
    London: Unwin Hyman
Berger, Peter
    1999: *The Desecularization of the World: Resurgent religion and world politics*
    Grand Rapids Michigan: Eerdmans
Best, Lloyd
    1968: 'Outlines of a Model of Pure Plantation Economy' *Social and Economic
    Studies* 17:283-328
Bosch, David
    1991: *Transforming Mission: Paradigm shifts in theology of mission* New York:
    Orbis Books, Mary Knoll
Boyce, James
    1993: *The Philippines: The political economy of growth and impoverishment in the
    Marcos era* London: Macmillan
Burnett, David
    2002: *Clash of Worlds* 2nd edn London: Monarch Books
Caldwell JC and Schindlmayr T
    2002: 'Historical Population Estimates: Unravelling the consensus' *Population and
    Development Review* 28/2:183-204
Cameron MA and Mauceri P
    1997: *The Peruvian Labyrinth: Polity, society, economy* Pennsylvania: Pennsylvania
    State University Press
Chabal P and Daloz J-P
    1999: *Africa Works: Disorder as political instrument* Oxford: James Currey

Chasteen, John
    2001: *Born in Blood and Fire: A concise history of Latin America* London: WW
    Norton
Chikulo, Bornwell
    2000: 'Corruption and Accumulation in Zambia' in Hope and Chikulo 2000:161-82
Chweya L, Tuta JK and Akivaga SK, Edited by Sihanya B
    2005: *Control of Corruption in Kenya: Legal-political dimensions 2001-2004*
    Nairobi: Claripress
Collier, Paul
    2007: *The Bottom Billion: Why the poorest countries are failing and what can be
    done about it* Oxford: Oxford University Press
    2010: *The Plundered Planet: How to reconcile prosperity with nature* London:
    Allen Lane
Corpuz, Onofre
    1997: *An Economic History of the Philippines* Quezon City: University of the
    Philippines Press
Courtenay, Percy
    1980: *Plantation Agriculture* London: Bell and Hyman
Crabtree J and Thomas J
    1998: *Fujimori's Peru: The political economy* London: Institute of Latin American
    Studies
David, Randy
    2001: *Reflections on Sociology and Philippine Society* Quezon City: University of
    the Philippines Press
Diamond, Jared
    1997: *Guns, Germs and Steel* London: Random House
Easterly, William
    2007: 'Inequality Does Cause Underdevelopment: Insights from a new instrument'
    Journal of Development Economics 84/2:755-76
Eckstein, Harry
    1966: 'Case Study and Theory in Political Science' in Gomm, Hammersley and
    Foster 2000:119-64
Eliade, Mercia ed
    1987: *The Encyclopaedia of Religion* New York: Macmillan
Encyclopædia Britannica
    2010: 'The Protestant Heritage' Encyclopædia Britannica Online Library Edition
    Available at http://library.eb.co.uk/eb/article-9109446 Accessed on 21.4.10
Engerman SL and Sokoloff KL
    1997: 'Factor Endowments, Institutions, and Differential Paths of Growth Among
    New World Economies: A view from economic historians in the United States' in
    Haber S 1997:275-304
    2002: 'Factor Endowments, Inequality, and Paths of Development among New
    World Economies' National Bureau for Economic Research Working Paper 9259,
    Cambridge MA

2005: 'Colonialism, Inequality, and Long-Run Paths of Development' National Bureau for Economic Research Working Paper 11057, Cambridge MA

Freston, Paul
2009: *Evangelical Christianity and Democracy in Latin America* Oxford: Oxford University Press

Gavin M and Hausmann R
1998: 'Nature, Development and Distribution in Latin America: Evidence on the role of geography, climate and natural resources' Inter-American Development Bank Research Department Working Paper 378, Washington DC

Gifford, Paul
1998: *African Christianity: Its public role* London: Hurst and Co
2009: *Christianity, Politics and Public Life in Kenya* London: Hurst and Co

Gitari, David
1996: *In Season and Out of Season: Sermons to a nation* Oxford: Regnum

Githiga, Gideon
2001: *The Church as a Bulwark against Authoritarianism: Development of church and state relations in Kenya with particular reference to the years after political independence, 1963-1992* Oxford: Regnum

Githongo, John
2006: 'Inequality, Ethnicity and the Fight against Corruption in Africa: A personal perspective' Lecture given at the Oxford Centre for Mission Studies on 15th August 2006

Gradstein M, Milanovic B and Ying Y
2001: 'Democracy, Ideology and Income Inequality: An empirical analysis' World Bank Policy Research Working Paper No. 2561, Washington DC

Guiso LA, Sapienza P and Zingales LG
2003: 'People's Opium? Religion and economic attitudes' *Journal of Monetary Economics* 50/1: 225-82

Hastings, Adrian
1994: *The Church in Africa, 1450-1950* Oxford: Clarendon Press

Heidenheimer AJ and Johnston M eds
2002: *Political Corruption: Concepts and contexts* 3rd edn London: Transaction Publishers

Hofstede, Geert
1980: *Culture's Consequences: International differences in work-related values* Beverly Hills California: Sage

Hope KR and Chikulo BC eds
2000: *Corruption and Development in Africa: Lessons from country case studies* London: Macmillan

Press Horton, Robin
1971: 'African Conversion' Africa: *Journal of the International African Institute* 41/2:85-108

Huntington, Samuel
    1991: *The Third Wave: Democratization in the late twentieth century* London:
    University of Oklahoma Press
Ikenga-Metuh, Emefie
    1987: 'The Shattered Microcosm: A critical survey of explanations of conversion in
    Africa' in Petersen 1987
Jhingran, Saral
    1989: *Aspects of Hindu Morality* Delhi: Motilal Banarsidass
Johnson, Benton
    1963: 'On Church and Sect' *American Sociological Review* 28:539-549
Johnston, Michael
    2005: *Syndromes of Corruption: Wealth, power and democracy* Cambridge:
    Cambridge University Press
Johnstone P, Mandryk J and Johnstone R
    2001: *Operation World: 21st century edition* Carlisle: Paternoster Publishing
Kang, David
    2002: *Crony Capitalism: Corruption and development in South Korea and the
    Philippines* Cambridge: Cambridge University Press
Karanja, John
    2009: 'Evangelical attitudes towards democracy in Kenya' in Ranger 2009:67-94
Kaufmann D, Kraay A and Mastruzzi M
    2004: 'Governance Matters III: Governance indicators for 1996-2002' *World Bank
    Economic Review* 18/2:253-87
Kaufmann D, Montoriol-Garriga J and Recanatini F
    2008: 'How Does Bribery Affect Public Service Delivery? Micro-evidence from
    service users and public officials in Peru' World Bank Policy Research Working
    Paper 4492, Washington DC
Klaren, Peter
    2000: *Peru: Society and nationhood in the Andes* Oxford: Oxford University Press
Knighton, Ben ed
    2009: *Religion and Politics in Kenya: Essays in honour of a meddlesome priest* New
    York: Palgrave Macmillan
Kuznets, Simon
    1955: 'Economic Growth and Income Inequality' *American Economic Review* 45:1-
    28
Landes, David
    1998: *The Wealth and Poverty of Nations: Why some are so rich and some so poor*
    London: Abacus
Latourette, Kenneth
    1939-47: *A History of the Expansion of Christianity* London: Eyre and Spottiswoode
Lausanne Movement
    1974: 'The Lausanne Covenant' Available at http://www.lausanne.org/covenant
    Accessed on 20.4.10

Laver, Roberto
    2010: '"Good news" in the fight against corruption' *Review of Faith and International Affairs* 8/4:49-57
Leamer EE, Maul H, Rodriguez S and Schott PK
    1999: 'Does Natural Resource Abundance Increase Latin American Income Inequality?' *Journal of Development Economics* 59:3-42
Leff, Nathaniel
    1964: 'Economic Development through Bureaucratic Corruption' *American Behavioral Scientist* 8/3:8-14
Lim, David
    2009: 'Consolidating Democracy: Filipino Evangelicals in between 'People Power' events, 1986-2001' in Lumsdaine 2009:235-84
Lipset SM and Lenz GS
    2000: 'Corruption, Culture and Markets' in Harrison and Huntington 2000: 112-24
Lonsdale, John
    2009: 'Compromised Critics: Religion in Kenya's politics' in Knighton 2009:57-94
López, Dario
    2009: 'Evangelicals and Politics in Fujimori's Peru' in Freston 2009:131-62
Lumsdaine, David ed
    2009: *Evangelical Christianity and Democracy in Asia* Oxford: Oxford University Press
Martin, David
    1990: *Tongues of Fire: The explosion of Protestantism in Latin America* Oxford: Blackwell
    1999: 'The Evangelical Upsurge and Its Political Implications' in Berger 1999:37-49
    2002: *Pentecostalism: The world their parish* Oxford: Blackwell
Maxwell, David
    2000: 'In Defence of African Creativity' *Journal of Religion in Africa* 30/4: 468-81
McCoy, Alfred
    1994: *An Anarchy of Families: State and family in the Philippines* Quezon City: Ateneo De Manila University Press
McEvedy C and Jones R
    1978: *Atlas of World Population History* New York: Penguin
Merton, Robert
    1938: *Science, Technology and Society in Seventeenth Century England* Atlantic Highlands, NJ: Humanities Press
Miller, Darrow
    2001: *Discipling Nations: The power of truth to transform cultures* Seattle: YWAM Publishing
Monk, William ed
    1858: *Dr. Livingstone's Cambridge lectures* Cambridge

Mwangi, Stephen Njihia
  2008: 'Episcopal leadership in the Anglican church of Kenya: A critique' MPhil.
  Thesis, Oxford Centre for Mission Studies/University of Wales
Ndege, Peter
  2000: 'Decline of the Economy, 1973-95' in Ogot and Ochieng 2000:204-228
Neild, Robert
  2002: *Public Corruption: The dark side of social evolution* London: Anthem Press
North DC, Wallis JJ and Weingast BR
  2006: 'A Conceptual Framework for Interpreting Recorded Human History'
  National Bureau for Economic Research Working Paper 12795, Cambridge MA
North DC, Wallis JJ, Webb SB and Weingast BR
  2007: 'Limited Access Orders in the Developing World: A new approach to the
  problems of development' World Bank Policy Research Working Paper No. 4359,
  Washington DC
Ogot BA and Ochieng WR eds
  2000: *Kenya: the Making of a Nation. A hundred years of Kenya's history, 1895-
  1995* Maseno Kenya: Institute of Research and Postgraduate Studies, Maseno
  University
Oliver, Roland
  1991: *The African Experience* London: Weidenfeld & Nicolson
Oxford University Press
  2010: *Oxford English Dictionary Online* Available at
  http://dictionary.oed.com/entrance.dtl Accessed on 18.4.10
Petersen, KH (ed.)
  1987: *Religion, Development, and African Identity* Uppsala: Scandinavian Institute
  of African Studies
Phiri, Isabel
  2009: 'President Fredrick Chiluba and Zambia: Evangelicals and democracy in a
  "Christian Nation"' in Ranger 2009:95-130
Ranger, Terence
  2009: *Evangelical Christianity and Democracy in Africa* Oxford: Oxford University
  Press
Ravallion, Martin
  2005: 'Inequality is Bad for the Poor' World Bank Policy Research Working Paper
  3677, Washington DC
Sanneh, Lamin
  1993: *Encountering the West, Christianity and the Global Cultural Process: The
  African dimension* Maryknoll: Orbis
Stark, Rodney
  1996: *The Rise of Christianity* Princeton: Princeton University Press
Stott, John
  2006: *The Cross of Christ*; 20th anniversary edition Leicester: Inter-Varsity Press

Suico, Joseph
  2003: 'Institutional and Individualistic Dimensions of Transformational
  Development: The case of Pentecostal churches in the Philippines' Ph.D Thesis,
  Oxford Centre for Mission Studies / University of Wales
Tearfund UK
  2008: 'Economic Justice Global Advocacy Programme: An action plan towards
  producing a comprehensive 3-year gap strategy' Tearfund UK, Teddington
Tongoi DO and Kariithi KK
  2005: *Building a Prosperous Kenya: A perspective for the church, God's primary
  agency for social transformation* Nairobi: Christians for a Just Society
Treisman, Daniel
  2000: 'The Causes of Corruption: A cross-national study' *Journal of Public
  Economics* 76/3:399-457
Trimingham, John
  1959: *Islam in West Africa* Oxford: Clarendon Press
Troeltsch, Ernst
  1912: *The Social Teaching of the Christian Churches* Translated by Wyon O 1931
  London: Allen & Unwin
United Nations COMTRADE Database
  2006: Available at http://unstats.un.org/unsd/cr/registry/regcs Accessed on 1.11.06
US State Department
  2009: 'Background Note: Rwanda' Available at
  http://www.state.gov/r/pa/ei/bgn/2861.htm#econ Accessed 7.10.09
Weber, Max
  1930 [1904]: *The Protestant Ethic and the Spirit of Capitalism* tr Talcott Parsons
  London: Allen & Unwin
  1948: *From Max Weber: Essays in sociology* tr and ed Gerth H and Wright Mills C
  London: Routledge & Kegan Paul
  1968: *Economy and Society: An outline of interpretive sociology* tr of the 4th
  German edn eds Roth G and Wittich C New York: Bedminster Press
Wickberg, Edgar
  1964: 'The Chinese Mestizo in Philippine History' *Journal of Southeast Asian
  History* 5/1:62-99
Wilson, Bryan
  1970: *Religious Sects: A sociological study* London: Weidenfeld & Nicolson
  1988: 'The Functions of Religion: a Reappraisal' *Religion* 18:199-216
Woodberry, Robert
  2004: 'The Shadow of Empire: Christian missions, colonial policy, and democracy
  in postcolonial societies' PhD thesis, University of North Carolina at Chapel Hill
World Bank
  2001: *Attacking Poverty: World Development Report 2000/2001* Oxford: Oxford
  University Press
  2005: *Equity and Development: World Development Report 2006* Oxford: Oxford
  University Press

2007a: 'Strengthening Bank Group Engagement on Governance and Anticorruption' Available at http://siteresources.worldbank.org/DEVCOMMINT/Documentation/21046515/DC2 006-0017(E)-Governance.pdf Accessed 24.3.07

2007b: 'Overview of Anticorruption' Available at http://web.worldbank.org/WBSITE/EXTERNAL/TOPICS/EXTPUBLICSECTORA NDGOVERNANCE/EXTANTICORRUPTION/0,,contentMDK:21540659~menuP K:384461~pagePK:148956~piPK:216618~theSitePK:384455,00.html Accessed 17.7.10

2007c: 'World Development Indicators' Available at http://publications.worldbank.org/WDI/ Accessed 20.8.07

World Institute for Development Economics Research
2005: 'World Income Inequality Database version 2a' Available at http://www.wider.unu.edu/research/Database/en_GB/database/ Accessed 3.6.07

World Trade Organisation
2009: 'International Trade Statistics' Available at http://www.wto.org/english/res_e/statis_e/its2009_e/its09_merch_trade_product_e.p df Accessed 23.12.11

Wrong, Michaela
2009: *It's Our Turn to Eat: The story of a Kenyan whistleblower* London: Fourth Estate

Index

Africa
  conversion, 36, 37, 38
  corruption different from Asia, 122, 194
  corruption within churches, 63, 64, 133, 187, 188
  cost of corruption, 199
  data limitations, 17
  economic inequality, 3, 47
  large public sector, 42, 47
  natural resources, 199
  part of the new Christian world, 8
  population density, 26, 39
  potential role of Christians, 199
  role of the state, 114
  traditional beliefs, 38
  values, 102, 105, 122
Agriculture, 13, 14, 15, 39, 69
Algeria, 3
Asia
  conversion, 39
  corruption different from Africa, 122
  hinterlands of conquest, 31, 33, 47
  part of the new Christian world, 8
  population density, 26, 39, 195
Australia, 8, 21, 26, 27, 32, 33
Bangladesh, 3
Bebbington's definition of Evangelicals, 8, 9
Bolivia, 32
Botswana, 32
Brazil, 32
British rule, 95, 114, 129, 144
  and control of corruption, 52, 53, 54
  and missionaries, 101
  and size of government, 42, 46, 195
British South Africa Company, 129
Buddhism
  as a major religion, 8
  attitude to economic inequality, 6
  conversion, 33
  levels of corruption, 25, 44, 187
  resistance to Christianity, 38

statistical association with causes of economic inequality, 22
Canada, 8, 27, 33
Central African Republic, 32
Chile, 32, 155
China
  economic dominance in the Philippines, 39, 40, 69
  economic exploitation of Africa, 199
  economic inequality, 3
  expulsion of missionaries, 179
  limited impact of western colonization, 32
  resistance to conversion, 36
  source of dualistic theology, 86, 193
Church-sect theory, 185, 187, 188, 190
Climate, 25, 31
Colonial Development and Welfare Act 1940, 42
Colonialism
  and Christian mission, 40, 41, 119
  and corruption, 52, 59
  and development, 42
  farm colonies, 31
  in Kenya, 95
  in the Philippines, 69, 192
  in Zambia, 129
  influence of indigenous conditions, 31, 32, 47, 195
  interests of different Western groups, 41
  mining, 65
  model of leadership, 105
  plantation colonies, 31, 65
  resentment, 37
  trading settlements, 32
Conversion, 179
  and better governance, 76, 77, 78, 79, 93, 167, 170, 172, 186, 189, 190
  and cultural pride, 37
  and missionaries, 41

REGNUM EDINBURGH CENTENARY SERIES

David A. Kerr, Kenneth R. Ross (Eds)
Mission Then and Now
2009 / 978-1-870345-73-6 / 343pp (paperback)
2009 / 978-1-870345-76-7 / 343pp (hardback)

No one can hope to fully understand the modern Christian missionary movement without engaging substantially with the World Missionary Conference, held at Edinburgh in 1910. This book is the first to systematically examine the eight Commissions which reported to Edinburgh 1910 and gave the conference much of its substance and enduring value. It will deepen and extend the reflection being stimulated by the upcoming centenary and will kindle the missionary imagination for 2010 and beyond.

Daryl M. Balia, Kirsteen Kim (Eds)
Witnessing to Christ Today
2010 / 978-1-870345-77-4 / 301pp (hardback)

This volume, the second in the Edinburgh 2010 series, includes reports of the nine main study groups working on different themes for the celebration of the centenary of the World Missionary Conference, Edinburgh 1910. Their collaborative work brings together perspectives that are as inclusive as possible of contemporary world Christianity and helps readers to grasp what it means in different contexts to be 'witnessing to Christ today'.

Claudia Währisch-Oblau, Fidon Mwombeki (Eds)
Mission Continues
Global Impulses for the 21st Century
2010 / 978-1-870345-82-8 / 271pp (hardback)

In May 2009, 35 theologians from Asia, Africa and Europe met in Wuppertal, Germany, for a consultation on mission theology organized by the United Evangelical Mission: Communion of 35 Churches in Three Continents. The aim was to participate in the 100th anniversary of the Edinburgh conference through a study process and reflect on the challenges for mission in the 21st century. This book brings together these papers written by experienced practitioners from around the world.

Brian Woolnough and Wonsuk Ma (Eds)
Holistic Mission
God's Plan for God's People
2010 / 978-1-870345-85-9 / 268pp (hardback)

Holistic mission, or integral mission, implies God is concerned with the whole person, the whole community, body, mind and spirit. This book discusses the meaning of the holistic gospel, how it has developed, and implications for the church. It takes a global, eclectic approach, with 19 writers, all of whom have much experience in, and commitment to, holistic mission. It addresses critically and honestly one of the most exciting, and challenging, issues facing the church today. To be part of God's plan for God's people, the church must take holistic mission to the world.

Kirsteen Kim and Andrew Anderson (Eds)
Mission Today and Tomorrow
2010 / 978-1-870345-91-0 / 450pp (hardback)

There are moments in our lives when we come to realise that we are participating in the triune God's mission. If we believe the church to be as sign and symbol of the reign of God in the world, then we are called to witness to Christ today by sharing in God's mission of love through the transforming power of the Holy Spirit. We can all participate in God's transforming and reconciling mission of love to the whole creation.

Tormod Engelsviken, Erling Lundeby and Dagfinn Solheim (Eds)
The Church Going Glocal
Mission and Globalisation
2011 / 978-1-870345-93-4 / 262pp (hardback)

The New Testament church is… universal and local at the same time. The universal, one and holy apostolic church appears in local manifestations. Missiologically speaking… the church can take courage as she faces the increasing impact of globalisation on local communities today. Being universal and concrete, the church is geared for the simultaneous challenges of the glocal and local.

Marina Ngurusangzeli Behera (Ed)
Interfaith Relations after One Hundred Years
Christian Mission among Other Faiths
2011 / 978-1-870345-96-5 / 338pp (hardback)

The essays of this book reflect not only the acceptance and celebration of pluralism within India but also by extension an acceptance as well as a need for unity among Indian Christians of different denominations. The essays were presented and studied at a preparatory consultation on Study Theme II: Christian Mission Among Other Faiths at the United Theological College, India July 2009.

Lalsangkima Pachuau and Knud Jørgensen (Eds)
Witnessing to Christ in a Pluralistic Age
Christian Mission among Other Faiths
2011 / 978-1-870345-95-8 / 277pp (hardback)

In a world where plurality of faiths is increasingly becoming a norm of life, insights on the theology of religious plurality are needed to strengthen our understanding of our own faith and the faith of others. Even though religious diversity is not new, we are seeing an upsurge in interest on the theologies of religion among all Christian confessional traditions. It can be claimed that no other issue in Christian mission is more important and more difficult than the theologies of religions.

Beth Snodderly and A Scott Moreau (Eds)
Evangelical Frontier Mission
Perspectives on the Global Progress of the Gospel
2011 / 978-1-870345-98-9 / 312pp (hardback)

This important volume demonstrates that 100 years after the World Missionary Conference in Edinburgh, Evangelism has become truly global. Twenty-first-century Evangelism continues to focus on frontier mission, but significantly, and in the spirit of Edinburgh 1910, it also has re-engaged social action.

Rolv Olsen (Ed)
Mission and Postmodernities
2011 / 978-1-870345-97-2 / 279pp (hardback)

This volume takes on meaning because its authors honestly struggle with and debate how we should relate to postmodernities. Should our response be accommodation, relativizing or counter-culture? How do we strike a balance between listening and understanding, and at the same time exploring how postmodernities influence the interpretation and application of the Bible as the normative story of God's mission in the world?

Cathy Ross (Ed)
Life-Widening Mission
2012 / 978-1-908355-00-3 / 163pp (hardback)

It is clear from the essays collected here that the experience of the 2010 World Mission Conference in Edinburgh was both affirming and frustrating for those taking part - affirming because of its recognition of how the centre of gravity has moved in global Christianity; frustrating because of the relative slowness of so many global Christian bodies to catch up with this and to embody it in the way they do business and in the way they represent themselves. These reflections will - or should - provide plenty of food for thought in the various councils of the Communion in the coming years.

Beate Fagerli, Knud Jørgensen, Rolv Olsen, Kari Storstein Haug and Knut Tveitereid (Eds)
A Learning Missional Church
Reflections from Young Missiologists
2012 / 978-1-908355-01-1 / 218pp (hardback)

Cross-cultural mission has always been a primary learning experience for the church. It pulls us out of a mono-cultural understanding and helps us discover a legitimate theological pluralism which opens up for new perspectives in the Gospel. Translating the Gospel into new languages and cultures is a human and divine means of making us learn new 'incarnations' of the Good News.

Emma Wild-Wood & Peniel Rajkumar (Eds)
Foundations for Mission
2012 / 978-1-908355-12-6 / 303pp (hardback)

This volume provides an important resource for those wishing to gain an overview of significant issues in contemporary missiology whilst understanding how they are applied in particular contexts

REGNUM STUDIES IN GLOBAL CHRISTIANITY

David Emmanuel Singh (Ed)
Jesus and the Cross
Reflections of Christians from Islamic Contexts
2008 / 978-1-870345-65-1 / 226pp

The Cross reminds us that the sins of the world are not borne through the exercise of power but through Jesus Christ's submission to the will of the Father. The papers in this volume are organised in three parts: scriptural, contextual and theological. The central question being addressed is: how do Christians living in contexts, where Islam is a majority or minority religion, experience, express or think of the Cross?

Sung-wook Hong
Naming God in Korea
The Case of Protestant Christianity
2008 / 978-1-870345-66-8 / 170pp (hardback)

Since Christianity was introduced to Korea more than a century ago, one of the most controversial issues has been the Korean term for the Christian 'God'. This issue is not merely about naming the Christian God in Korean language, but it relates to the question of theological contextualization - the relationship between the gospel and culture - and the question of Korean Christian identity. This book demonstrates the nature of the gospel in relation to cultures, i.e., the universality of the gospel expressed in all human cultures.

Hubert van Beek (Ed)
Revisioning Christian Unity
The Global Christian Forum
2009 / 978-1-870345-74-3 / 288pp (hardback)

This book contains the records of the Global Christian Forum gathering held in Limuru near Nairobi, Kenya, on 6 – 9 November 2007 as well as the papers presented at that historic event. Also included are a summary of the Global Christian Forum process from its inception until the 2007 gathering and the reports of the evaluation of the process that was carried out in 2008.

Young-hoon Lee
The Holy Spirit Movement in Korea
Its Historical and Theological Development
2009 / 978-1-870345-67-5 / 174pp (hardback)
This book traces the historical and theological development of the Holy Spirit
Movement in Korea through six successive periods (from 1900 to the present
time). These periods are characterized by repentance and revival (1900-20),
persecution and suffering under Japanese occupation (1920-40), confusion and
division (1940-60), explosive revival in which the Pentecostal movement
played a major role in the rapid growth of Korean churches (1960-80), the
movement reaching out to all denominations (1980-2000), and the new context
demanding the Holy Spirit movement to open new horizons in its mission
engagement (2000-).

Paul Hang-Sik Cho
Eschatology and Ecology
Experiences of the Korean Church
2010 / 978-1-870345-75-0 / 260pp (hardback)
This book raises the question of why Korean people, and Korean Protestant
Christians in particular, pay so little attention to ecological issues. The author
argues that there is an important connection (or elective affinity) between this
lack of attention and the other-worldly eschatology that is so dominant within
Korean Protestant Christianity.

Dietrich Werner, David Esterline, Namsoon Kang, Joshva Raja (Eds)
The Handbook of Theological Education in World Christianity
Theological Perspectives, Ecumenical Trends, Regional Surveys
2010 / 978-1-870345-80-4 / 800pp
This major reference work is the first ever comprehensive study of
Theological Education in Christianity of its kind. With contributions from over
90 international scholars and church leaders, it aims to be easily accessible
across denominational, cultural, educational, and geographic boundaries. The
Handbook will aid international dialogue and networking among theological
educators, institutions, and agencies.

David Emmanuel Singh & Bernard C Farr (Eds)
Christianity and Education
Shaping of Christian Context in Thinking
2010 / 978-1-870345-81-1 / 374pp
Christianity and Education is a collection of papers published in
Transformation: An International Journal of Holistic Mission Studies over a
period of 15 years. The articles represent a spectrum of Christian thinking
addressing issues of institutional development for theological education,
theological studies in the context of global mission, contextually
aware/informed education, and academies which deliver such education,
methodologies and personal reflections.

J.Andrew Kirk
Civilisations in Conflict?
Islam, the West and Christian Faith
2011 / 978-1-870345-87-3 / 205pp

Samuel Huntington's thesis, which argues that there appear to be aspects of Islam that could be on a collision course with the politics and values of Western societies, has provoked much controversy. The purpose of this study is to offer a particular response to Huntington's thesis by making a comparison between the origins of Islam and Christianity.

David Emmanuel Singh (Ed)
Jesus and the Incarnation
Reflections of Christians from Islamic Contexts
2011 / 978-1-870345-90-3 / 245pp

In the dialogues of Christians with Muslims nothing is more fundamental than the Cross, the Incarnation and the Resurrection of Jesus. Building on the *Jesus and the Cross*, this book contains voices of Christians living in various 'Islamic contexts' and reflecting on the Incarnation of Jesus. The aim and hope of these reflections is that the papers weaved around the notion of 'the Word' will not only promote dialogue among Christians on the roles of the Person and the Book but, also, create a positive environment for their conversations with Muslim neighbours.

Ivan M Satyavrata
God Has Not left Himself Without Witness
2011 / 978-1-870345-79-8 / 260pp

Since its earliest inception the Christian Church has had to address the question of what common ground exits between Christian faiths and other religions. This issue is not merely of academic interest but one with critical existential and socio-political consequences. This study presents a case for the revitalization of the fulfillment tradition based on a recovery and assessment of the fulfillment approaches of Indian Christian converts in the pre-independence period.

Bal Krishna Sharma
From this World to the Next
Christian Identity and Funerary Rites in Nepal
2013 / 978-1-908355-08-9 / 238pp

This book explores and analyses funerary rite struggles in a nation where Christianity is a comparatively recent phenomenon, and many families have multi-faith, who go through traumatic experiences at the death of their family members. The author has used an applied theological approach to explore and analyse the findings in order to address the issue of funerary rites with which the Nepalese church is struggling.

J Kwabena Asamoah-Gyada
Contemporary Pentecostal Christianity
Interpretations from an African Context
2013 / 978-1-908355-07-2 / 238pp

Pentecostalism is the fastest growing stream of Christianity in the world. The real evidence for the significance of Pentecostalism lies in the actual churches they have built and the numbers they attract. This work interprets key theological and missiological themes in African Pentecostalism by using material from the live experiences of the movement itself.

REGNUM STUDIES IN MISSION

Kwame Bediako
Theology and Identity
The Impact of Culture upon Christian Thought in the Second Century and in Modern Africa
1992 / 978-1870345-10-1 / 507pp
The author examines the question of Christian identity in the context of the Graeco–Roman culture of the early Roman Empire. He then addresses the modern African predicament of quests for identity and integration.

Christopher Sugden
Seeking the Asian Face of Jesus
The Practice and Theology of Christian Social Witness in Indonesia and India 1974–1996
1997 / 1-870345-26-6 / 496pp
This study focuses on contemporary holistic mission with the poor in India and Indonesia combined with the call to transformation of all life in Christ with micro-credit enterprise schemes. 'The literature on contextual theology now has a new standard to rise to' – Lamin Sanneh (Yale University, USA).

Hwa Yung
Mangoes or Bananas?
The Quest for an Authentic Asian Christian Theology
1997 / 1-870345-25-5 / 274pp
Asian Christian thought remains largely captive to Greek dualism and Enlightenment rationalism because of the overwhelming dominance of Western culture. Authentic contextual Christian theologies will emerge within Asian Christianity with a dual recovery of confidence in culture and the gospel.

Keith E. Eitel
Paradigm Wars
The Southern Baptist International Mission Board Faces the Third Millennium
1999 / 1-870345-12-6 / 140pp
The International Mission Board of the Southern Baptist Convention is the
largest denominational mission agency in North America. This volume
chronicles the historic and contemporary forces that led to the IMB's recent
extensive reorganization, providing the most comprehensive case study to date
of a historic mission agency restructuring to continue its mission purpose into
the twenty-first century more effectively.

Samuel Jayakumar
Dalit Consciousness and Christian Conversion
Historical Resources for a Contemporary Debate
1999 / 81-7214-497-0 / 434pp
(Published jointly with ISPCK)
The main focus of this historical study is social change and transformation
among the Dalit Christian communities in India. Historiography tests the
evidence in the light of the conclusions of the modern Dalit liberation
theologians.

Vinay Samuel and Christopher Sugden (Eds)
Mission as Transformation
A Theology of the Whole Gospel
1999 / 978-18703455-13-2 / 522pp
This book brings together in one volume twenty five years of biblical
reflection on mission practice with the poor from around the world. This
volume helps anyone understand how evangelicals, struggling to unite
evangelism and social action, found their way in the last twenty five years to
the biblical view of mission in which God calls all human beings to love God
and their neighbour; never creating a separation between the two.

Christopher Sugden
Gospel, Culture and Transformation
2000 / 1-870345-32-0 / 152pp
A Reprint, with a New Introduction,
of Part Two of Seeking the Asian Face of Jesus
Gospel, Culture and Transformation explores the practice of mission
especially in relation to transforming cultures and communities. -
'Transformation is to enable God's vision of society to be actualised in all
relationships: social, economic and spiritual, so that God's will may be
reflected in human society and his love experienced by all communities,
especially the poor.'

Bernhard Ott
Beyond Fragmentation: Integrating Mission and Theological Education
A Critical Assessment of some Recent Developments
in Evangelical Theological Education
2001 / 1-870345-14-2 / 382pp

Beyond Fragmentation is an enquiry into the development of Mission Studies in evangelical theological education in Germany and German-speaking Switzerland between 1960 and 1995. The author undertakes a detailed examination of the paradigm shifts which have taken place in recent years in both the theology of mission and the understanding of theological education.

Gideon Githiga
The Church as the Bulwark against Authoritarianism
Development of Church and State Relations in Kenya, with Particular
Reference to the Years after Political Independence 1963-1992
2002 / 1-870345-38-x / 218pp

'All who care for love, peace and unity in Kenyan society will want to read this careful history by Bishop Githiga of how Kenyan Christians, drawing on the Bible, have sought to share the love of God, bring his peace and build up the unity of the nation, often in the face of great difficulties and opposition.' Canon Dr Chris Sugden, Oxford Centre for Mission Studies.

Myung Sung-Hoon, Hong Young-Gi (eds.)
Charis and Charisma
David Yonggi Cho and the Growth of Yoido Full Gospel Church
2003 / 978-1870345-45-3 / 218pp

This book discusses the factors responsible for the growth of the world's largest church. It expounds the role of the Holy Spirit, the leadership, prayer, preaching, cell groups and creativity in promoting church growth. It focuses on God's grace (charis) and inspiring leadership (charisma) as the two essential factors and the book's purpose is to present a model for church growth worldwide.

Samuel Jayakumar
Mission Reader
Historical Models for Wholistic Mission in the Indian Context
2003 / 1-870345-42-8 / 250pp
(Published jointly with ISPCK)

This book is written from an evangelical point of view revalidating and reaffirming the Christian commitment to wholistic mission. The roots of the 'wholistic mission' combining 'evangelism and social concerns' are to be located in the history and tradition of Christian evangelism in the past; and the civilizing purpose of evangelism is compatible with modernity as an instrument in nation building.

Bob Robinson
Christians Meeting Hindus
An Analysis and Theological Critique of the Hindu-Christian Encounter in India
2004 / 987-1870345-39-2 / 392pp

This book focuses on the Hindu-Christian encounter, especially the intentional meeting called dialogue, mainly during the last four decades of the twentieth century, and specifically in India itself.

Gene Early
Leadership Expectations
How Executive Expectations are Created and Used in a Non-Profit Setting
2005 / 1-870345-30-4 / 276pp

The author creates an Expectation Enactment Analysis to study the role of the Chancellor of the University of the Nations-Kona, Hawaii. This study is grounded in the field of managerial work, jobs, and behaviour and draws on symbolic interactionism, role theory, role identity theory and enactment theory. The result is a conceptual framework for developing an understanding of managerial roles.

Tharcisse Gatwa
The Churches and Ethnic Ideology in the Rwandan Crises 1900-1994
2005 / 978-1870345-24-8 / 300pp
(Reprinted 2011)

Since the early years of the twentieth century Christianity has become a new factor in Rwandan society. This book investigates the role Christian churches played in the formulation and development of the racial ideology that culminated in the 1994 genocide.

Julie Ma
Mission Possible
Biblical Strategies for Reaching the Lost
2005 / 978-1870345-37-1 / 142pp

This is a missiology book for the church which liberates missiology from the specialists for the benefit of every believer. It also serves as a textbook that is simple and friendly, and yet solid in biblical interpretation. This book links the biblical teaching to the actual and contemporary missiological settings with examples, making the Bible come alive to the reader.

Allan Anderson, Edmond Tang (Eds)
Asian and Pentecostal
The Charismatic Face of Christianity in Asia
2005 / 978-1870345-94-1 / 500pp
(Published jointly with APTS Press)

This book provides a thematic discussion and pioneering case studies on the history and development of Pentecostal and Charismatic churches in the countries of South Asia, South East Asia and East Asia.

I. Mark Beaumont
Christology in Dialogue with Muslims
A Critical Analysis of Christian Presentations of Christ for Muslims
from the Ninth and Twentieth Centuries
2005 / 978-1870345-46-0 / 227pp

This book analyses Christian presentations of Christ for Muslims in the most creative periods of Christian-Muslim dialogue, the first half of the ninth century and the second half of the twentieth century. In these two periods, Christians made serious attempts to present their faith in Christ in terms that take into account Muslim perceptions of him, with a view to bridging the gap between Muslim and Christian convictions.

Thomas Czövek,
Three Seasons of Charismatic Leadership
A Literary-Critical and Theological Interpretation of the Narrative of
Saul, David and Solomon
2006 / 978-1870345-48-4 / 272pp

This book investigates the charismatic leadership of Saul, David and Solomon. It suggests that charismatic leaders emerge in crisis situations in order to resolve the crisis by the charisma granted by God. Czovek argues that Saul proved himself as a charismatic leader as long as he acted resolutely and independently from his mentor Samuel. In the author's eyes, Saul's failure to establish himself as a charismatic leader is caused by his inability to step out from Samuel's shadow.

Richard Burgess
Nigeria's Christian Revolution
The Civil War Revival and Its Pentecostal Progeny (1967-2006)
2008 / 978-1-870345-63-7 / 347pp

This book describes the revival that occurred among the Igbo people of Eastern Nigeria and the new Pentecostal churches it generated, and documents the changes that have occurred as the movement has responded to global flows and local demands. As such, it explores the nature of revivalist and Pentecostal experience, but does so against the backdrop of local socio-political and economic developments, such as decolonisation and civil war, as well as broader processes, such as modernisation and globalisation.

David Emmanuel Singh & Bernard C Farr (Eds)
Christianity and Cultures
Shaping Christian Thinking in Context
2008 / 978-1-870345-69-9 / 271pp

This volume marks an important milestone, the 25th anniversary of the Oxford Centre for Mission Studies (OCMS). The papers here have been exclusively sourced from Transformation, a quarterly journal of OCMS, and seek to provide a tripartite view of Christianity's engagement with cultures by focusing on the question: how is Christian thinking being formed or reformed through its interaction with the varied contexts it encounters? The subject matters include different strands of theological-missiological thinking, socio-political engagements and forms of family relationships in interaction with the host cultures.

Tormod Engelsviken, Ernst Harbakk, Rolv Olsen, Thor Strandenæs (Eds)
Mission to the World
Communicating the Gospel in the 21st Century:
Essays in Honour of Knud Jørgensen
2008 / 978-1-870345-64-4 / 472pp (hardback)

Knud Jørgensen is Director of Areopagos and Associate Professor of Missiology at MF Norwegian School of Theology. This book reflects on the main areas of Jørgensen's commitment to mission. At the same time it focuses on the main frontier of mission, the world, the content of mission, the Gospel, the fact that the Gospel has to be communicated, and the context of contemporary mission in the 21st century.

Al Tizon
Transformation after Lausanne
Radical Evangelical Mission in Global-Local Perspective
2008 / 978-1-870345-68-2 / 281pp

After Lausanne '74, a worldwide network of radical evangelical mission theologians and practitioners use the notion of "Mission as Transformation" to integrate evangelism and social concern together, thus lifting theological voices from the Two Thirds World to places of prominence. This book documents the definitive gatherings, theological tensions, and social forces within and without evangelicalism that led up to Mission as Transformation. And it does so through a global-local grid that points the way toward greater holistic mission in the 21st century.

Bambang Budijanto
Values and Participation
Development in Rural Indonesia
2009 / 978-1-870345-70-4 / 237pp

Socio-religious values and socio-economic development are inter-dependant, inter-related and are constantly changing in the context of macro political structures, economic policy, religious organizations and globalization; and micro influences such as local affinities, identity, politics, leadership and beliefs. The book argues that the comprehensive approach in understanding the socio-religious values of each of the three local Lopait communities in Central Java is essential to accurately describing their respective identity.

Alan R. Johnson
Leadership in a Slum
A Bangkok Case Study
2009 / 978-1-870345-71-2 / 238pp

This book looks at leadership in the social context of a slum in Bangkok from a different perspective than traditional studies which measure well educated Thais on leadership scales derived in the West. Using both systematic data collection and participant observation, it develops a culturally preferred model as well as a set of models based in Thai concepts that reflect on-the-ground realities. It concludes by looking at the implications of the anthropological approach for those who are involved in leadership training in Thai settings and beyond.

Titre Ande
Leadership and Authority
Bula Matari and Life - Community Ecclesiology in Congo
2010 / 978-1-870345-72-9 / 189pp

Christian theology in Africa can make significant development if a critical understanding of the socio-political context in contemporary Africa is taken seriously, particularly as Africa's post-colonial Christian leadership based its understanding and use of authority on the Bula Matari model. This has caused many problems and Titre proposes a Life-Community ecclesiology for liberating authority, here leadership is a function, not a status, and 'apostolic succession' belongs to all people of God.

Frank Kwesi Adams
Odwira and the Gospel
A Study of the Asante Odwira Festival and its Significance for Christianity in Ghana
2010 /978-1-870345-59-0 / 232pp

The study of the Odwira festival is the key to the understanding of Asante religious and political life in Ghana. The book explores the nature of the Odwira festival longitudinally - in pre-colonial, colonial and post-independence Ghana - and examines the Odwira ideology and its implications for understanding the Asante self-identity. Also discussed is how some elements of faith portrayed in the Odwira festival can provide a framework for Christianity to engage with Asante culture at a greater depth.

Bruce Carlton
Strategy Coordinator
Changing the Course of Southern Baptist Missions
2010 / 978-1-870345-78-1 / 268pp

This is an outstanding, one-of-a-kind work addressing the influence of the non-residential missionary/strategy coordinator's role in Southern Baptist missions. This scholarly text examines the twentieth century global missiological currents that influenced the leadership of the International

Mission Board, resulting in a new paradigm to assist in taking the gospel to the nations.

Julie Ma & Wonsuk Ma
Mission in the Spirit:
Towards a Pentecostal/Charismatic Missiology
2010 / 978-1-870345-84-2 / 312pp

The book explores the unique contribution of Pentecostal/Charismatic mission from the beginning of the twentieth century. The first part considers the theological basis of Pentecostal/Charismatic mission thinking and practice. Special attention is paid to the Old Testament, which has been regularly overlooked by the modern Pentecostal/Charismatic movements. The second part discusses major mission topics with contributions and challenges unique to Pentecostal/Charismatic mission. The book concludes with a reflection on the future of this powerful missionary movement. As the authors served as Korean missionaries in Asia, often their missionary experiences in Asia are reflected in their discussions.

S. Hun Kim & Wonsuk Ma (eds.)
Korean Diaspora and Christian Mission
2011-978-1-870345-91-0 / 301pp (hardback)

As a 'divine conspiracy' for Missio Dei, the global phenomenon of people on the move has shown itself to be invaluable. In 2004 two significant documents concerning Diaspora were introduced, one by the Filipino International Network and the other by the Lausanne Committee for World Evangelization. These have created awareness of the importance of people on the move for Christian mission. Since then, Korean Diaspora has conducted similar research among Korean missions, resulting in this book

Jin Huat Tan
Planting an Indigenous Church
The Case of the Borneo Evangelical Mission
2011 / 978-1-870345-99-6 / 363pp

Dr Jin Huat Tan has written a pioneering study of the origins and development of Malaysia's most significant indigenous church. This is an amazing story of revival, renewal and transformation of the entire region chronicling the powerful effect of it evident to date! What can we learn from this extensive and careful study of the Borneo Revival, so the global Christianity will become ever more dynamic?

Bill Prevette
Child, Church and Compassion
Towards Child Theology in Romania
2012 / 978-1-908355-03-4 / 377pp

Bill Prevett comments that "children are like 'canaries in a mine shaft'; they provide a focal point for discovery and encounter of perilous aspects of our world that are often ignored." True, but miners also carried a lamp to see into the subterranean darkness. This book is such a lamp. It lights up the subterranean world of children and youth in danger of exploitation, and as it does so travels deep into their lives and also into the activities of those who seek to help them.

Samuel Cyuma
Picking up the Pieces
The Church and Conflict Resolution in South Africa and Rwanda
2012 / 978-1-908355-02-7 / 373pp

In the last ten years of the 20th century, the world was twice confronted with unbelievable news from Africa. First, there was the end of Apartheid in South Africa, without bloodshed, due to responsible political and Church leaders. The second was the mass killings in Rwanda, which soon escalated into real genocide. Political and Church leaders had been unable to prevents this crime against humanity. In this book, the question is raised: can we compare the situation in South Africa with that in Rwanda? Can Rwandan leaders draw lessons from the peace process in South Africa?

Peter Rowan
Proclaiming the Peacemaker
The Malaysian Church as an Agent of Reconciliation in a Multicultural Society
2012 / 978-1-908355-05-8 / 268pp

With a history of racial violence and in recent years, low-level ethnic tensions, the themes of peaceful coexistence and social harmony are recurring ones in the discourse of Malaysian society. In such a context, this book looks at the role of the church as a reconciling agent, arguing that a reconciling presence within a divided society necessitates an ethos of peacemaking.

Edward Ontita
Resources and Opportunity
The Architecture of Livelihoods in Rural Kenya
2012 / 978-1-908355-04-1 / 328pp

Poor people in most rural areas of developing countries often improvise resources in unique ways to enable them make a living. Resources and Opportunity takes the view that resources are dynamic and fluid, arguing that villagers co-produce them through redefinition and renaming in everyday practice and use them in diverse ways. The book focuses on ordinary social activities to bring out people's creativity in locating, redesigning and embracing livelihood opportunities in processes.

Kathryn Kraft
Searching for Heaven in the Real World
A Sociological Discussion of Conversion in the Arab World
2012 / 978-1-908355-15-7 / 1428pp

Kathryn Kraft explores the breadth of psychological and social issues faced by Arab Muslims after making a decision to adopt a faith in Christ or

Christianity, investigating some of the most surprising and significant challenges new believers face.

Wessley Lukose
Contextual Missiology of the Spirit
Pentecostalism in Rajasthan, India
2013 / 978-1-908355-09-6 / 256pp

This book explores the identity, context and features of Pentecostalism in Rajasthan, India as well as the internal and external issues facing Pentecostals. It aims to suggest 'a contextual missiology of the Spirit,' as a new model of contextual missiology from a Pentecostal perspective. It is presented as a glocal, ecumenical, transformational, and public missiology.

REGNUM RESOURCES FOR MISSION

Knud Jørgensen
Equipping for Service
Christian Leadership in Church and Society
2012 / 978-1-908355-06-5 / 168pp

This book is written out of decades of experience of leading churches and missions in Ethiopia, Geneva, Norway and Hong Kong. Combining the teaching of Scripture with the insights of contemporary management philosophy, Jørgensen writes in a way which is practical and applicable to anyone in Christian service. "The intention has been to challenge towards a leadership relevant for work in church and mission, and in public and civil society, with special attention to leadership in Church and organisation."

For the up-to-date listing of the Regnum books see www.ocms.ac.uk/regnum

regnum

Regnum Books International

Regnum is an Imprint of The Oxford Centre for Mission Studies
St. Philip and St. James Church, Woodstock Road, Oxford, OX2 6HR
Web: www.ocms.ac.uk/regnum

REGNUM EDINBURGH CENTENARY SERIES

David A. Kerr, Kenneth R. Ross (Eds)
Mission Then and Now
2009 / 978-1-870345-73-6 / 343pp (paperback)
2009 / 978-1-870345-76-7 / 343pp (hardback)

No one can hope to fully understand the modern Christian missionary movement without engaging substantially with the World Missionary Conference, held at Edinburgh in 1910. This book is the first to systematically examine the eight Commissions which reported to Edinburgh 1910 and gave the conference much of its substance and enduring value. It will deepen and extend the reflection being stimulated by the upcoming centenary and will kindle the missionary imagination for 2010 and beyond.

Daryl M. Balia, Kirsteen Kim (Eds)
Witnessing to Christ Today
2010 / 978-1-870345-77-4 / 301pp (hardback)

This volume, the second in the Edinburgh 2010 series, includes reports of the nine main study groups working on different themes for the celebration of the centenary of the World Missionary Conference, Edinburgh 1910. Their collaborative work brings together perspectives that are as inclusive as possible of contemporary world Christianity and helps readers to grasp what it means in different contexts to be 'witnessing to Christ today'.

Claudia Währisch-Oblau, Fidon Mwombeki (Eds)
Mission Continues
Global Impulses for the 21st Century
2010 / 978-1-870345-82-8 / 271pp (hardback)

In May 2009, 35 theologians from Asia, Africa and Europe met in Wuppertal, Germany, for a consultation on mission theology organized by the United Evangelical Mission: Communion of 35 Churches in Three Continents. The aim was to participate in the 100th anniversary of the Edinburgh conference through a study process and reflect on the challenges for mission in the 21st century. This book brings together these papers written by experienced practitioners from around the world.

Brian Woolnough and Wonsuk Ma (Eds)
Holistic Mission
God's Plan for God's People
2010 / 978-1-870345-85-9 / 268pp (hardback)

Holistic mission, or integral mission, implies God is concerned with the whole person, the whole community, body, mind and spirit. This book discusses the meaning of the holistic gospel, how it has developed, and implications for the church. It takes a global, eclectic approach, with 19 writers, all of whom have much experience in, and commitment to, holistic mission. It addresses critically and honestly one of the most exciting, and challenging, issues facing the church today. To be part of God's plan for God's people, the church must take holistic mission to the world.

Kirsteen Kim and Andrew Anderson (Eds)
Mission Today and Tomorrow
2010 / 978-1-870345-91-0 / 450pp (hardback)

There are moments in our lives when we come to realise that we are participating in the triune God's mission. If we believe the church to be as sign and symbol of the reign of God in the world, then we are called to witness to Christ today by sharing in God's mission of love through the transforming power of the Holy Spirit. We can all participate in God's transforming and reconciling mission of love to the whole creation.

Tormod Engelsviken, Erling Lundeby and Dagfinn Solheim (Eds)
The Church Going Glocal
Mission and Globalisation
2011 / 978-1-870345-93-4 / 262pp (hardback)

The New Testament church is… universal and local at the same time. The universal, one and holy apostolic church appears in local manifestations. Missiologically speaking… the church can take courage as she faces the increasing impact of globalisation on local communities today. Being universal and concrete, the church is geared for the simultaneous challenges of the glocal and local.

Marina Ngurusangzeli Behera (Ed)
Interfaith Relations after One Hundred Years
Christian Mission among Other Faiths
2011 / 978-1-870345-96-5 / 338pp (hardback)

The essays of this book reflect not only the acceptance and celebration of pluralism within India but also by extension an acceptance as well as a need for unity among Indian Christians of different denominations. The essays were presented and studied at a preparatory consultation on Study Theme II: Christian Mission Among Other Faiths at the United Theological College, India July 2009.

Lalsangkima Pachuau and Knud Jørgensen (Eds)
Witnessing to Christ in a Pluralistic Age
Christian Mission among Other Faiths
2011 / 978-1-870345-95-8 / 277pp (hardback)

In a world where plurality of faiths is increasingly becoming a norm of life, insights on the theology of religious plurality are needed to strengthen our understanding of our own faith and the faith of others. Even though religious diversity is not new, we are seeing an upsurge in interest on the theologies of religion among all Christian confessional traditions. It can be claimed that no other issue in Christian mission is more important and more difficult than the theologies of religions.

Beth Snodderly and A Scott Moreau (Eds)
Evangelical Frontier Mission
Perspectives on the Global Progress of the Gospel
2011 / 978-1-870345-98-9 / 312pp (hardback)

This important volume demonstrates that 100 years after the World Missionary Conference in Edinburgh, Evangelism has become truly global. Twenty-first-century Evangelism continues to focus on frontier mission, but significantly, and in the spirit of Edinburgh 1910, it also has re-engaged social action.

Rolv Olsen (Ed)
Mission and Postmodernities
2011 / 978-1-870345-97-2 / 279pp (hardback)

This volume takes on meaning because its authors honestly struggle with and debate how we should relate to postmodernities. Should our response be accommodation, relativizing or counter-culture? How do we strike a balance between listening and understanding, and at the same time exploring how postmodernities influence the interpretation and application of the Bible as the normative story of God's mission in the world?

Cathy Ross (Ed)
Life-Widening Mission
2012 / 978-1-908355-00-3 / 163pp (hardback)
It is clear from the essays collected here that the experience of the 2010 World Mission Conference in Edinburgh was both affirming and frustrating for those taking part - affirming because of its recognition of how the centre of gravity has moved in global Christianity; frustrating because of the relative slowness of so many global Christian bodies to catch up with this and to embody it in the way they do business and in the way they represent themselves. These reflections will - or should - provide plenty of food for thought in the various councils of the Communion in the coming years.

Beate Fagerli, Knud Jørgensen, Rolv Olsen, Kari Storstein Haug and
Knut Tveitereid (Eds)
A Learning Missional Church
Reflections from Young Missiologists
2012 / 978-1-908355-01-1 / 218pp (hardback)
Cross-cultural mission has always been a primary learning experience for the church. It pulls us out of a mono-cultural understanding and helps us discover a legitimate theological pluralism which opens up for new perspectives in the Gospel. Translating the Gospel into new languages and cultures is a human and divine means of making us learn new 'incarnations' of the Good News.

Emma Wild-Wood & Peniel Rajkumar (Eds)
Foundations for Mission
2012 / 978-1-908355-12-6 / 303pp (hardback)
This volume provides an important resource for those wishing to gain an overview of significant issues in contemporary missiology whilst understanding how they are applied in particular contexts.

Wonsuk Ma & Kenneth R Ross (Eds)
Mission Spirituality and Authentic Discipleship
2013 / 978-1-908355-24-9 / 248pp (hardback)
This book argues for the primacy of spirituality in the practice of mission. Since God is the primary agent of mission and God works through the power of the Holy Spirit, it is through openness to the Spirit that mission finds its true character and has its authentic impact.

REGNUM STUDIES IN GLOBAL CHRISTIANITY

David Emmanuel Singh (Ed)
Jesus and the Cross
Reflections of Christians from Islamic Contexts
2008 / 978-1-870345-65-1 / 226pp
The Cross reminds us that the sins of the world are not borne through the exercise of power but through Jesus Christ's submission to the will of the Father. The papers in this volume are organised in three parts: scriptural, contextual and theological. The central question

being addressed is: how do Christians living in contexts, where Islam is a majority or minority religion, experience, express or think of the Cross?

Sung-wook Hong
Naming God in Korea
The Case of Protestant Christianity
2008 / 978-1-870345-66-8 / 170pp (hardback)

Since Christianity was introduced to Korea more than a century ago, one of the most controversial issues has been the Korean term for the Christian 'God'. This issue is not merely about naming the Christian God in Korean language, but it relates to the question of theological contextualization - the relationship between the gospel and culture - and the question of Korean Christian identity. This book demonstrates the nature of the gospel in relation to cultures, i.e., the universality of the gospel expressed in all human cultures.

Hubert van Beek (Ed)
Revisioning Christian Unity
The Global Christian Forum
2009 / 978-1-870345-74-3 / 288pp (hardback)

This book contains the records of the Global Christian Forum gathering held in Limuru near Nairobi, Kenya, on 6 – 9 November 2007 as well as the papers presented at that historic event. Also included are a summary of the Global Christian Forum process from its inception until the 2007 gathering and the reports of the evaluation of the process that was carried out in 2008.

Young-hoon Lee
The Holy Spirit Movement in Korea
Its Historical and Theological Development
2009 / 978-1-870345-67-5 / 174pp (hardback)

This book traces the historical and theological development of the Holy Spirit Movement in Korea through six successive periods (from 1900 to the present time). These periods are characterized by repentance and revival (1900-20), persecution and suffering under Japanese occupation (1920-40), confusion and division (1940-60), explosive revival in which the Pentecostal movement played a major role in the rapid growth of Korean churches (1960-80), the movement reaching out to all denominations (1980-2000), and the new context demanding the Holy Spirit movement to open new horizons in its mission engagement (2000-).

Paul Hang-Sik Cho
Eschatology and Ecology
Experiences of the Korean Church
2010 / 978-1-870345-75-0 / 260pp (hardback)

This book raises the question of why Korean people, and Korean Protestant Christians in particular, pay so little attention to ecological issues. The author argues that there is an important connection (or elective affinity) between this lack of attention and the other-worldly eschatology that is so dominant within Korean Protestant Christianity.

Dietrich Werner, David Esterline, Namsoon Kang, Joshva Raja (Eds)
The Handbook of Theological Education in World Christianity
Theological Perspectives, Ecumenical Trends, Regional Surveys
2010 / 978-1-870345-80-4 / 800pp

This major reference work is the first ever comprehensive study of Theological Education in Christianity of its kind. With contributions from over 90 international scholars and church leaders, it aims to be easily accessible across denominational, cultural, educational, and geographic boundaries. The Handbook will aid international dialogue and networking among theological educators, institutions, and agencies.

David Emmanuel Singh & Bernard C Farr (Eds)
Christianity and Education
Shaping of Christian Context in Thinking
2010 / 978-1-870345-81-1 / 374pp

Christianity and Education is a collection of papers published in *Transformation: An International Journal of Holistic Mission Studies* over a period of 15 years. The articles represent a spectrum of Christian thinking addressing issues of institutional development for theological education, theological studies in the context of global mission, contextually aware/informed education, and academies which deliver such education, methodologies and personal reflections.

J.Andrew Kirk
Civilisations in Conflict?
Islam, the West and Christian Faith
2011 / 978-1-870345-87-3 / 205pp

Samuel Huntington's thesis, which argues that there appear to be aspects of Islam that could be on a collision course with the politics and values of Western societies, has provoked much controversy. The purpose of this study is to offer a particular response to Huntington's thesis by making a comparison between the origins of Islam and Christianity.

David Emmanuel Singh (Ed)
Jesus and the Incarnation
Reflections of Christians from Islamic Contexts
2011 / 978-1-870345-90-3 / 245pp

In the dialogues of Christians with Muslims nothing is more fundamental than the Cross, the Incarnation and the Resurrection of Jesus. Building on the *Jesus and the Cross*, this book contains voices of Christians living in various 'Islamic contexts' and reflecting on the Incarnation of Jesus. The aim and hope of these reflections is that the papers weaved around the notion of 'the Word' will not only promote dialogue among Christians on the roles of the Person and the Book but, also, create a positive environment for their conversations with Muslim neighbours.

Ivan M Satyavrata
God Has Not left Himself Without Witness
2011 / 978-1-870345-79-8 / 260pp

Since its earliest inception the Christian Church has had to address the question of what common ground exits between Christian faiths and other religions. This issue is not merely of academic interest but one with critical existential and socio-political consequences. This study presents a case for the revitalization of the fulfillment tradition based on a recovery and assessment of the fulfillment approaches of Indian Christian converts in the pre-independence period.

Bal Krishna Sharma
From this World to the Next
Christian Identity and Funerary Rites in Nepal
2013 / 978-1-908355-08-9 / 238pp

This book explores and analyses funerary rite struggles in a nation where Christianity is a comparatively recent phenomenon, and many families have multi-faith, who go through traumatic experiences at the death of their family members. The author has used an applied theological approach to explore and analyse the findings in order to address the issue of funerary rites with which the Nepalese church is struggling.

J Kwabena Asamoah-Gyada
Contemporary Pentecostal Christianity
Interpretations from an African Context
2013 / 978-1-908355-07-2 / 238pp

Pentecostalism is the fastest growing stream of Christianity in the world. The real evidence for the significance of Pentecostalism lies in the actual churches they have built and the numbers they attract. This work interprets key theological and missiological themes in African Pentecostalism by using material from the live experiences of the movement itself.

Isabel Apawo Phiri & Dietrich Werner (Eds)
Handbook of Theological Education in Africa
2013 / 978-1-908355-19-5 / 1110pp (hardback)
The *Handbook of Theological Education in Africa* is a wake-up call for African churches to give proper prominence to theological education institutions and their programmes which serve them. It is unique, comprehensive and ambitious in its aim and scope.

Hope Antone, Wati Longchar, Hyunju Bae, Huang Po Ho, Dietrich Werner (Eds)
Asian Handbook for Theological Education and Ecumenism
2013 / 978-1-908355-300 / 675pp (hardback)
This impressive and comprehensive book focuses on key resources for teaching Christian unity and common witness in Asian contexts. It is a collection of articles that reflects the ongoing 'double wrestle' with the texts of biblical tradition as well as with contemporary contexts. It signals an investment towards the future of the ecumenical movement in Asia.

REGNUM STUDIES IN MISSION

Kwame Bediako
Theology and Identity
The Impact of Culture upon Christian Thought in the Second Century and in Modern Africa
1992 / 978-1870345-10-1 / 507pp
The author examines the question of Christian identity in the context of the Graeco–Roman culture of the early Roman Empire. He then addresses the modern African predicament of quests for identity and integration.

Christopher Sugden
Seeking the Asian Face of Jesus
The Practice and Theology of Christian Social Witness
in Indonesia and India 1974–1996
1997 / 1-870345-26-6 / 496pp
This study focuses on contemporary holistic mission with the poor in India and Indonesia combined with the call to transformation of all life in Christ with micro-credit enterprise schemes. 'The literature on contextual theology now has a new standard to rise to' – Lamin Sanneh (Yale University, USA).

Hwa Yung
Mangoes or Bananas?
The Quest for an Authentic Asian Christian Theology
1997 / 1-870345-25-5 / 274pp

Asian Christian thought remains largely captive to Greek dualism and Enlightenment rationalism because of the overwhelming dominance of Western culture. Authentic contextual Christian theologies will emerge within Asian Christianity with a dual recovery of confidence in culture and the gospel.

Keith E. Eitel
Paradigm Wars
The Southern Baptist International Mission Board Faces the Third Millennium
1999 / 1-870345-12-6 / 140pp

The International Mission Board of the Southern Baptist Convention is the largest denominational mission agency in North America. This volume chronicles the historic and contemporary forces that led to the IMB's recent extensive reorganization, providing the most comprehensive case study to date of a historic mission agency restructuring to continue its mission purpose into the twenty-first century more effectively.

Samuel Jayakumar
Dalit Consciousness and Christian Conversion
Historical Resources for a Contemporary Debate
1999 / 81-7214-497-0 / 434pp
(Published jointly with ISPCK)

The main focus of this historical study is social change and transformation among the Dalit Christian communities in India. Historiography tests the evidence in the light of the conclusions of the modern Dalit liberation theologians.

Vinay Samuel and Christopher Sugden (Eds)
Mission as Transformation
A Theology of the Whole Gospel
1999 / 978-18703455-13-2 / 522pp

This book brings together in one volume twenty five years of biblical reflection on mission practice with the poor from around the world. This volume helps anyone understand how evangelicals, struggling to unite evangelism and social action, found their way in the last twenty five years to the biblical view of mission in which God calls all human beings to love God and their neighbour; never creating a separation between the two.

Christopher Sugden
Gospel, Culture and Transformation
2000 / 1-870345-32-0 / 152pp
A Reprint, with a New Introduction,
of Part Two of Seeking the Asian Face of Jesus

Gospel, Culture and Transformation explores the practice of mission especially in relation to transforming cultures and communities. - 'Transformation is to enable God's vision of society to be actualised in all relationships: social, economic and spiritual, so that God's will may be reflected in human society and his love experienced by all communities, especially the poor.'

Bernhard Ott
Beyond Fragmentation: Integrating Mission and Theological Education
A Critical Assessment of some Recent Developments
in Evangelical Theological Education
2001 / 1-870345-14-2 / 382pp

Beyond Fragmentation is an enquiry into the development of Mission Studies in evangelical theological education in Germany and German-speaking Switzerland between 1960 and 1995. The author undertakes a detailed examination of the paradigm shifts which have taken place in recent years in both the theology of mission and the understanding of theological education.

Gideon Githiga
The Church as the Bulwark against Authoritarianism
Development of Church and State Relations in Kenya, with Particular Reference to the
Years after Political Independence 1963-1992
2002 / 1-870345-38-x / 218pp

'All who care for love, peace and unity in Kenyan society will want to read this careful history by Bishop Githiga of how Kenyan Christians, drawing on the Bible, have sought to share the love of God, bring his peace and build up the unity of the nation, often in the face of great difficulties and opposition.' Canon Dr Chris Sugden, Oxford Centre for Mission Studies.

Myung Sung-Hoon, Hong Young-Gi (eds.)
Charis and Charisma
David Yonggi Cho and the Growth of Yoido Full Gospel Church
2003 / 978-1870345-45-3 / 218pp

This book discusses the factors responsible for the growth of the world's largest church. It expounds the role of the Holy Spirit, the leadership, prayer, preaching, cell groups and creativity in promoting church growth. It focuses on God's grace (charis) and inspiring leadership (charisma) as the two essential factors and the book's purpose is to present a model for church growth worldwide.

Samuel Jayakumar
Mission Reader
Historical Models for Wholistic Mission in the Indian Context
2003 / 1-870345-42-8 / 250pp
(Published jointly with ISPCK)

This book is written from an evangelical point of view revalidating and reaffirming the Christian commitment to wholistic mission. The roots of the 'wholistic mission' combining 'evangelism and social concerns' are to be located in the history and tradition of Christian evangelism in the past; and the civilizing purpose of evangelism is compatible with modernity as an instrument in nation building.

Bob Robinson
Christians Meeting Hindus
An Analysis and Theological Critique of the Hindu-Christian Encounter in India
2004 / 987-1870345-39-2 / 392pp

This book focuses on the Hindu-Christian encounter, especially the intentional meeting called dialogue, mainly during the last four decades of the twentieth century, and specifically in India itself.

Gene Early
Leadership Expectations
How Executive Expectations are Created and Used in a Non-Profit Setting
2005 / 1-870345-30-4 / 276pp

The author creates an Expectation Enactment Analysis to study the role of the Chancellor of the University of the Nations-Kona, Hawaii. This study is grounded in the field of managerial work, jobs, and behaviour and draws on symbolic interactionism, role theory, role identity theory and enactment theory. The result is a conceptual framework for developing an understanding of managerial roles.

Tharcisse Gatwa
The Churches and Ethnic Ideology in the Rwandan Crises 1900-1994
2005 / 978-1870345-24-8 / 300pp
(Reprinted 2011)

Since the early years of the twentieth century Christianity has become a new factor in Rwandan society. This book investigates the role Christian churches played in the formulation and development of the racial ideology that culminated in the 1994 genocide.

Julie Ma
Mission Possible
Biblical Strategies for Reaching the Lost
2005 / 978-1870345-37-1 / 142pp

This is a missiology book for the church which liberates missiology from the specialists for the benefit of every believer. It also serves as a textbook that is simple and friendly, and yet solid in biblical interpretation. This book links the biblical teaching to the actual and contemporary missiological settings with examples, making the Bible come alive to the reader.

I. Mark Beaumont
Christology in Dialogue with Muslims
A Critical Analysis of Christian Presentations of Christ for Muslims
from the Ninth and Twentieth Centuries
2005 / 978-1870345-46-0 / 227pp

This book analyses Christian presentations of Christ for Muslims in the most creative periods of Christian-Muslim dialogue, the first half of the ninth century and the second half of the twentieth century. In these two periods, Christians made serious attempts to present their faith in Christ in terms that take into account Muslim perceptions of him, with a view to bridging the gap between Muslim and Christian convictions.

Thomas Czövek,
Three Seasons of Charismatic Leadership
A Literary-Critical and Theological Interpretation of the Narrative of
Saul, David and Solomon
2006 / 978-1870345-48-4 / 272pp

This book investigates the charismatic leadership of Saul, David and Solomon. It suggests that charismatic leaders emerge in crisis situations in order to resolve the crisis by the charisma granted by God. Czovek argues that Saul proved himself as a charismatic leader as long as he acted resolutely and independently from his mentor Samuel. In the author's eyes, Saul's failure to establish himself as a charismatic leader is caused by his inability to step out from Samuel's shadow.

Richard Burgess
Nigeria's Christian Revolution
The Civil War Revival and Its Pentecostal Progeny (1967-2006)
2008 / 978-1-870345-63-7 / 347pp

This book describes the revival that occurred among the Igbo people of Eastern Nigeria and the new Pentecostal churches it generated, and documents the changes that have occurred as the movement has responded to global flows and local demands. As such, it explores the nature of revivalist and Pentecostal experience, but does so against the backdrop of local socio-political and economic developments, such as decolonisation and civil war, as well as broader processes, such as modernisation and globalisation.

David Emmanuel Singh & Bernard C Farr (Eds)
Christianity and Cultures
Shaping Christian Thinking in Context
2008 / 978-1-870345-69-9 / 271pp

This volume marks an important milestone, the 25th anniversary of the Oxford Centre for Mission Studies (OCMS). The papers here have been exclusively sourced from Transformation, a quarterly journal of OCMS, and seek to provide a tripartite view of Christianity's engagement with cultures by focusing on the question: how is Christian thinking being formed or reformed through its interaction with the varied contexts it encounters? The subject matters include different strands of theological-missiological thinking, socio-political engagements and forms of family relationships in interaction with the host cultures.

Tormod Engelsviken, Ernst Harbakk, Rolv Olsen, Thor Strandenæs (Eds)
Mission to the World
Communicating the Gospel in the 21st Century:
Essays in Honour of Knud Jørgensen
2008 / 978-1-870345-64-4 / 472pp (hardback)

Knud Jørgensen is Director of Areopagos and Associate Professor of Missiology at MF Norwegian School of Theology. This book reflects on the main areas of Jørgensen's commitment to mission. At the same time it focuses on the main frontier of mission, the world, the content of mission, the Gospel, the fact that the Gospel has to be communicated, and the context of contemporary mission in the 21st century.

Al Tizon
Transformation after Lausanne
Radical Evangelical Mission in Global-Local Perspective
2008 / 978-1-870345-68-2 / 281pp

After Lausanne '74, a worldwide network of radical evangelical mission theologians and practitioners use the notion of "Mission as Transformation" to integrate evangelism and social concern together, thus lifting theological voices from the Two Thirds World to places of prominence. This book documents the definitive gatherings, theological tensions, and social forces within and without evangelicalism that led up to Mission as Transformation. And it does so through a global-local grid that points the way toward greater holistic mission in the 21st century.

Bambang Budijanto
Values and Participation
Development in Rural Indonesia
2009 / 978-1-870345-70-4 / 237pp

Socio-religious values and socio-economic development are inter-dependant, inter-related and are constantly changing in the context of macro political structures, economic policy, religious organizations and globalization; and micro influences such as local affinities, identity, politics, leadership and beliefs. The book argues that the comprehensive approach in understanding the socio-religious values of each of the three local Lopait communities in Central Java is essential to accurately describing their respective identity.

Alan R. Johnson
Leadership in a Slum
A Bangkok Case Study
2009 / 978-1-870345-71-2 / 238pp

This book looks at leadership in the social context of a slum in Bangkok from a different perspective than traditional studies which measure well educated Thais on leadership scales derived in the West. Using both systematic data collection and participant observation, it develops a culturally preferred model as well as a set of models based in Thai concepts that reflect on-the-ground realities. It concludes by looking at the implications of the anthropological approach for those who are involved in leadership training in Thai settings and beyond.

Titre Ande
Leadership and Authority
Bula Matari and Life - Community Ecclesiology in Congo
2010 / 978-1-870345-72-9 / 189pp

Christian theology in Africa can make significant development if a critical understanding of the socio-political context in contemporary Africa is taken seriously, particularly as Africa's post-colonial Christian leadership based its understanding and use of authority on the Bula Matari model. This has caused many problems and Titre proposes a Life-Community ecclesiology for liberating authority, here leadership is a function, not a status, and 'apostolic succession' belongs to all people of God.

Frank Kwesi Adams
Odwira and the Gospel
A Study of the Asante Odwira Festival and its Significance for Christianity in Ghana
2010 /978-1-870345-59-0 / 232pp

The study of the Odwira festival is the key to the understanding of Asante religious and political life in Ghana. The book explores the nature of the Odwira festival longitudinally - in pre-colonial, colonial and post-independence Ghana - and examines the Odwira ideology and its implications for understanding the Asante self-identity. Also discussed is how some elements of faith portrayed in the Odwira festival can provide a framework for Christianity to engage with Asante culture at a greater depth.

Bruce Carlton
Strategy Coordinator
Changing the Course of Southern Baptist Missions
2010 / 978-1-870345-78-1 / 268pp

This is an outstanding, one-of-a-kind work addressing the influence of the non-residential missionary/strategy coordinator's role in Southern Baptist missions. This scholarly text examines the twentieth century global missiological currents that influenced the leadership of the International Mission Board, resulting in a new paradigm to assist in taking the gospel to the nations.

Julie Ma & Wonsuk Ma
Mission in the Spirit:
Towards a Pentecostal/Charismatic Missiology
2010 / 978-1-870345-84-2 / 312pp

The book explores the unique contribution of Pentecostal/Charismatic mission from the beginning of the twentieth century. The first part considers the theological basis of Pentecostal/Charismatic mission thinking and practice. Special attention is paid to the Old Testament, which has been regularly overlooked by the modern Pentecostal/Charismatic movements. The second part discusses major mission topics with contributions and challenges unique to Pentecostal/Charismatic mission. The book concludes with a reflection on the future of this powerful missionary movement. As the authors served as Korean missionaries in Asia, often their missionary experiences in Asia are reflected in their discussions.

Allan Anderson, Edmond Tang (Eds)
Asian and Pentecostal
The Charismatic Face of Christianity in Asia
2011 / 978-1870345-94-1 / 500pp
(Revised Edition)

This book provides a thematic discussion and pioneering case studies on the history and development of Pentecostal and Charismatic churches in the countries of South Asia, South East Asia and East Asia.

S. Hun Kim & Wonsuk Ma (eds.)
Korean Diaspora and Christian Mission
2011 / 978-1-870345-91-0 / 301pp (hardback)

As a 'divine conspiracy' for Missio Dei, the global phenomenon of people on the move has shown itself to be invaluable. In 2004 two significant documents concerning Diaspora were introduced, one by the Filipino International Network and the other by the Lausanne Committee for World Evangelization. These have created awareness of the importance of people on the move for Christian mission. Since then, Korean Diaspora has conducted similar research among Korean missions, resulting in this book

Jin Huat Tan
Planting an Indigenous Church
The Case of the Borneo Evangelical Mission
2011 / 978-1-870345-99-6 / 363pp

Dr Jin Huat Tan has written a pioneering study of the origins and development of Malaysia's most significant indigenous church. This is an amazing story of revival, renewal and transformation of the entire region chronicling the powerful effect of it evident to date! What can we learn from this extensive and careful study of the Borneo Revival, so the global Christianity will become ever more dynamic?

Bill Prevette
Child, Church and Compassion
Towards Child Theology in Romania
2012 / 978-1-908355-03-4 / 377pp

Bill Prevett comments that "children are like 'canaries in a mine shaft'; they provide a focal point for discovery and encounter of perilous aspects of our world that are often ignored." True, but miners also carried a lamp to see into the subterranean darkness. This book is such a lamp. It lights up the subterranean world of children and youth in danger of exploitation, and as it does so travels deep into their lives and also into the activities of those who seek to help them.

Samuel Cyuma
Picking up the Pieces
The Church and Conflict Resolution in South Africa and Rwanda
2012 / 978-1-908355-02-7 / 373pp

In the last ten years of the 20th century, the world was twice confronted with unbelievable news from Africa. First, there was the end of Apartheid in South Africa, without bloodshed, due to responsible political and Church leaders. The second was the mass killings in Rwanda, which soon escalated into real genocide. Political and Church leaders had been unable to prevents this crime against humanity. In this book, the question is raised: can we compare the situation in South Africa with that in Rwanda? Can Rwandan leaders draw lessons from the peace process in South Africa?

Peter Rowan
Proclaiming the Peacemaker
The Malaysian Church as an Agent of Reconciliation in a Multicultural Society
2012 / 978-1-908355-05-8 / 268pp

With a history of racial violence and in recent years, low-level ethnic tensions, the themes of peaceful coexistence and social harmony are recurring ones in the discourse of Malaysian society. In such a context, this book looks at the role of the church as a reconciling agent, arguing that a reconciling presence within a divided society necessitates an ethos of peacemaking.

Edward Ontita
Resources and Opportunity
The Architecture of Livelihoods in Rural Kenya
2012 / 978-1-908355-04-1 / 328pp

Poor people in most rural areas of developing countries often improvise resources in unique ways to enable them make a living. Resources and Opportunity takes the view that resources are dynamic and fluid, arguing that villagers co-produce them through redefinition and renaming in everyday practice and use them in diverse ways. The book focuses on ordinary social activities to bring out people's creativity in locating, redesigning and embracing livelihood opportunities in processes.

Kathryn Kraft
Searching for Heaven in the Real World
A Sociological Discussion of Conversion in the Arab World
2012 / 978-1-908355-15-7 / 1428pp

Kathryn Kraft explores the breadth of psychological and social issues faced by Arab Muslims after making a decision to adopt a faith in Christ or Christianity, investigating some of the most surprising and significant challenges new believers face.

Wessley Lukose
Contextual Missiology of the Spirit
Pentecostalism in Rajasthan, India
2013 / 978-1-908355-09-6 / 256pp

This book explores the identity, context and features of Pentecostalism in Rajasthan, India as well as the internal and external issues facing Pentecostals. It aims to suggest 'a contextual missiology of the Spirit,' as a new model of contextual missiology from a Pentecostal perspective. It is presented as a glocal, ecumenical, transformational, and public missiology.

Paul M Miller
Evangelical Mission in Co-operation with Catholics:
Pentecostalism in Rajasthan, India
2013 / 978-1-908355-17-1 / 256pp

This book brings the first thorough examination of the discussions going on within Evangelicalism about the viability of a good conscience dialogue with Roman Catholics. Those who are interested in evangelical world missions and Roman Catholic views of world missions will find this informative.

REGNUM RESOURCES FOR MISSION

Knud Jørgensen
Equipping for Service
Christian Leadership in Church and Society
2012 / 978-1-908355-06-5 / 168pp

This book is written out of decades of experience of leading churches and missions in Ethiopia, Geneva, Norway and Hong Kong. Combining the teaching of Scripture with the insights of contemporary management philosophy, Jørgensen writes in a way which is practical and applicable to anyone in Christian service. "The intention has been to challenge towards a leadership relevant for work in church and mission, and in public and civil society, with special attention to leadership in Church and organisation."

GENERAL REGNUM TITLES

Vinay Samuel, Chris Sugden (eds.)
The Church in Response to Human Need
1987 / 1870345045 / xii+268pp

Philip Sampson, Vinay Samuel, Chris Sugden (eds.)
Faith and Modernity
Essays in modernity and post-modernity
1994 / 1870345177 / 352pp

Klaus Fiedler
The Story of Faith Missions
1994 / 0745926878 / 428pp

Douglas Peterson
Not by Might nor by Power
A Pentecostal Theology of Social Concern in Latin America
1996 / 1870345207 / xvi+260pp

David Gitari
In Season and Out of Season
Sermons to a Nation
1996 / 1870345118 / 155pp

David. W. Virtue
A Vision of Hope
The Story of Samuel Habib
1996 / 1870345169 / xiv+137pp

Everett A Wilson
Strategy of the Spirit
J.Philip Hogan and the Growth of the Assemblies of God Worldwide, 1960 - 1990
1997 /1870345231/214

Murray Dempster, Byron Klaus, Douglas Petersen (Eds)
The Globalization of Pentecostalism
A Religion Made to Travel
1999 / 1870345290 / xvii+406pp

Peter Johnson, Chris Sugden (eds.)
Markets, Fair Trade and the Kingdom of God
Essays to Celebrate Traidcraft's 21st Birthday
2001 / 1870345193 / xii+155pp

Robert Hillman, Coral Chamberlain, Linda Harding
Healing & Wholeness
Reflections on the Healing Ministry
2002 / 978-1- 870345-35- 4 / xvii+283pp

David Bussau, Russell Mask
Christian Microenterprise Development
An Introduction
2003 / 1870345282 / xiii+142pp

David Singh
Sainthood and Revelatory Discourse
An Examination of the Basis for the Authority of Bayan in Mahdawi Islam
2003 / 8172147285 / xxiv+485pp

For the up-to-date listing of the Regnum books visit www.ocms.ac.uk/regnum

regnum

Regnum Books International

Regnum is an Imprint of The Oxford Centre for Mission Studies
St. Philip and St. James Church
Woodstock Road
Oxford, OX2 6HR
Web: www.ocms.ac.uk/regnum